Learning the Wonders

An introduction to creating great server applications with Project Wonder

by

Markus Ruggiero

Learning the Wonders

Copyright © 2013 by Markus Ruggiero

rucotec

Published by rucotec GmbH, Switzerland
ISBN 978-3-9524233-0-1

Table of Contents

Table of Contents

About this book

WebObjects is a very mature technology. Unfortunately WebObjects being a product of Apple Inc. has not seen much support from Apple for the last couple years. Due to political reasons Apple has set WebObjects' status to deprecated. Nevertheless there is a vivid community developing tools and frameworks to work with and enhance WebObjects. The toolset is known as WOLips, an Eclipse plugin. Project Wonder is an extensive collection of frameworks on top of and often replacing WebObjects. Both WOLips and Project Wonder are open source.

Several very good books about WebObjects have come out during the high time of WebObjects. Unfortunately with Apple pulling back the commercial side of creating new books and updating existing ones appeared not so interesting to large publishing houses. The last official commercial publication came out around 2005 with one book having an update in 2008. Since then the tools and the frameworks have made huge steps forward. Today the only documentation for all the new and enhanced features is available from *wiki.wocommunity.org* and some scattered private homepages. This is a vast collection of information written by programmers for programmers. However there was, and still is, nothing geared towards the beginner. WebObjects and Project Wonder have quite a steep learning curve; getting started just from the available documentation is difficult at best. All the old books are still valid resources for concepts but they are all based on the old toolset and thus confusing for the beginner.

Everyone in the community agrees that new programmers should be brought aboard. During WOWODC 2012, the World Wide Wonder Developer Conference, I decided that a modern book was needed. What you have in front of you is the result of that decision. I have written the book in my spare time, it is currently kind of a hobby project. However I do already have ideas for a successor.

Who should read this book?

This book is intended for any programmer who wants to start creating powerful server applications with WebObjects and Project Wonder. You should be fluent with Java and the Eclipse IDE, albeit no need to be a guru. You should have a good basic understanding of object-oriented concepts. It also helps if you have basic knowledge of html and css, as well as know how to handle a relational database. The ability of being able to at least read some SQL helps. The book will extensively cover many conceptual details, but it is not meant as a guide to starting programming at all.

The primary focus for this book was to make things clear. Each and every example has been played through and everything has been documented with a screenshot. You should be able to follow every step and redo them on your own. The screenshots will show you how things are supposed to look. While the book tells you what to do, it also details the *why* and so enables you to do things differently if you want to.

About the Author

Markus Ruggiero has been programming professionally since the mid 1980's. He started to use WebObjects in 2000. Around the same time Markus Ruggiero wrote his first course book. Since then he has written many more. All are widely being used in formal teaching of young application development professionals in Switzerland's dual-track system of vocational and professional education and training

Today Markus Ruggiero is part-time teaching all sorts of programming topics ranging from structured to object oriented programming, web technologies, and relational database design. When he is not teaching he works for his own company doing primarily project work for large international customers – of course all the big projects are Wonder based!

Markus Ruggiero has a master of science in applied physics and a degree in pedagogics.

You can reach him through the official web page for this book:

http://learningthewonders.com

About the Book Cover

Some twenty years ago I rescued a bunch of old Olivetti boards on hinges. I can't remember exactly why I did this, because they were just useless junk. But they somehow looked like a book in need for a cover and that made me take the boards home. I stowed them away in the basement, thinking, that once I have enough time I am going to complete **The Book**.

In 2011 the German computer and technology magazine c't called for a contest under the motto *"Mach Flott den Schrott"* (create something out of old computer hardware parts). Around the same time, I was introduced to a friend of a friend, who, I learned later, was a professional bookbinder. She was immediately fascinated when I told her about the old computer boards in need of a cover. She helped me create a beautiful book, looking some 200+ years old. The book won second price in the aesthetics category and was nominated third and fifth in two more categories.

Markus Ruggiero, Summer 2013

Preface

By Charles (Chuck) Hill

Earlier this year, I needed to introduce a person that I recently hired to Wonder and WebObjects. Having no other resources, I grabbed some blank paper and a pen and sat John (his real name!) down. An hour or so later, John looked dazed, confused, and pretty much done for the day. There have been a few books on WebObjects published over the years. Sacha Mallais and I brought Practical WebObjects to the market in 2004 in an attempt to share some hard won knowlege. It was our hope to follow this up with an introductory book. Alas, that was never to happen. When Markus Ruggiero said he was going to write one, I thought he was crazy. I knew first hand how much work it was. What I did not know well enough was Markus! Not only did he write the missing introductory book, he also managed to cover Project Wonder which is a vital part of any modern WebObjects-based application. The Wonder community is fortunate to have this book written by someone with Markus' deep technical knowlege and pedagogical background.

The early days of WebObjects were characterized by fragmented add-ons, mostly closed source commerical products. NetStruxr's release of the original Projects Wonder frameworks as Open Source became a rallying point for new functionality. Wonder continues to be the cutting edge of new technology based on the WebObjects framework. It demonstrates the elegance with which technologies like REST and Ajax can be integrated with the original technology of a decade before. Wonder leverages the power of WebObjects and makes application development even more effective.

This book may change the way you think about software. Using this technology for the last 15 years has certainly changed mine. The core WebObjects technology started in the late 1990s It is old; that can't be denied. The origin was eons ago in technology terms. Beware: that does not make it outdated, this is not COBOL. It is still used today by those who know its secrets, its strengths, and its power. The engineers who designed and built the WebObjects foundation upon which Wonder was created were remarkable in their understanding of Object Orientation and how to design for extensibility and long-term maintainability. They were visionaries. Many went on to found today's popular technologies. We have much to learn from them.

What can Wonder and WebObjects teach you? It is a treasure trove of design patterns and well thought out design that has withstood the tests of time and highly varied environments. WebObjects was model driven years before Model Driven Architecture became a common term. It had one of the first commercially successful Object-Relational Mappers and inspired and influenced many who followed, incuding the CoreDate framework used by iOS. The component based, stateful UI layer provided an entirely different paradigm for writing web applications. The rule-based DirectToWeb (D2W) technology remains revolutionary to this day. Your software development palette will be much richer from exposure to these ideas, goals, and technologies.

Whether you are a student of software design, or looking to build a maintainable, scalable server application, this book will provide an excellent education. WebObjects/Wonder is the best choice for a server-based service for iOS applications. As I hire and train new people in WebObjects and Wonder, Learning the Wonders is going to be extremely valuable for me. Look deeply here; there is much of value to be learned. John will be pleased, but not as much as my next hire who won't have to suffer through my introduction!

Acknowledgments

There are so many great people who helped create this book, most unknowingly. When I started to learn WebObjects and later Wonder the folks from the webobjects-dev mailing list have been and still are the ones that helped me the most. People like Chuck Hill, Ramsey Gurley, the various Davids (Avendasora, Holt, LeBer), Kieran Kelleher, Mike Schrag, Pascal Robert, and many many others (sorry, it's just impossible to mention every name here) answered mine and other's questions with great knowledge. In addition the various books about WebObjects and particularly the famous Practical WebObjects by Charles Hill and Sacha Mallais were an invaluable source of wisdom. Meeting you all at WOWODC (WebObjects and Wonder Developer Conference) was a great experience in its own. I do hope I can give something back to the community with his book.

Thank you!

Markus Ruggiero, Summer 2013

Overview

The book is divided into five parts.

Part 1 will introduce you to WebObjects and Project Wonder and give you a bit of history. Main focus will then be setting up the development environment. You will learn what is needed and how to install all the necessary tools. It gives hands-on tips for directory layout and configuration options.

In **Part 2** we will cover all the basics of WebObjects and Project Wonder. You will learn how a wonder application works, how the tools work. We will extensively cover important concepts and see how to take advantage.

Part C is dedicated to one of the most important issues: how to properly and elegantly access a relational database from a pure object-oriented application. You will learn about modeling your business objects and how to map objects, attributes, and relationships to a relational database.

Part D is kind of a grab bag for various things. You will learn about cookies, some very sophisticated framework classes and mechanisms, and we will have a deeper look into debugging.

After successfully creating your application, you probably want to deploy it to a server. Deployment is the big topic in **Part E**. We are going to see how you build your application for deployment, how to set up a deployment environment, and of course how to run your application inside the deployment environment.

Conventions used in this book

We use *italics* for any filename, URL, name for an executable program or script, and names for our own classes and code elements.

Names for standard framework objects like class names are printed in a `mono-spaced` font. The same font is used for all `code fragments` and `method names` inside the flow of text. Method names like `takeValuesFromRequest()` always have opening and closing parentheses. Method parameters are usually not shown, unless they are important in the current context.

All user interface elements like buttons, menu items, or text field labels are shown in SMALL CAPS

Important new definitions, concepts, or terms are emphasized with **_bold/italics_**

```
Code listings are in mono-spaced font and boxed
```

The dollar sign $ in code sections denotes the command line prompt. If the distinction between Unix commands and DOS commands is important, DOS> may be used as a prompt for DOS command lines.

Sometimes it is important that a command is written all on one line, but the printed line breaks. In such a case, the return arrow ↵ denotes that the command should not break.

Part A - The Environment

1   Introduction

You are about to learn a lot. Yes, really. And it won't come easy. But the reward will be tremendous!

Let me give you an overview of what's to come:

We are going to learn how to use Project Wonder to create really great applications for the web. At the beginning we will play with rather simple HTML user interfaces but you will see that the Web 2.0 lies just ahead. Project Wonder is very sophisticated and mature but it needs some getting into. We will go there together.

No application can live without data, and in most cases data lives in a relational database. So we need a way to access relational databases and work with that data. You will learn how to bridge the gap between a modern Web 2.0 application that is programmed in pure object-oriented fashion and the relational world.

Oh, did I mention that Project Wonder is pure Java? The big vast Java world is out there just waiting to be called into your application.

For a start here is a bit of history.

1.1   A bit of history

In the 1990's a company called **NeXT** was trying to come to market with great new hardware and an even greater operating system called **NeXTSTEP**. NeXT was founded by Steve Jobs, the man who created Apple Computer. One of the main goals of the NeXT operating system was to provide a clean object oriented interface to the programmer. For this NeXT used a programming language called **Objective-C**. In 1996 Apple bought NeXT and made NeXTSTEP the foundation of the modern Mac OS X as well as later iOS, the operating system for iPhone and iPad. Still today a modern descendant of Objective-C is the implementation language for Mac and iOS programs.

In the NeXT era NeXT built a framework that allowed object oriented access to relational databases. This framework was called EOF Enterprise Objects Framework. When in the mid 1990's "The Web" started to become more wide-spread NeXT created another set of frameworks called **WebObjects** to generate applications with an html user interface so that the applications could be used from everywhere where there was an internet connection and a browser available. WebObjects and EOF were marketed together under the name of WebObjects.

The merger with NeXT brought WebObjects into Apple's hands. Around the year 2001/2002 Apple rewrote WebObjects (including EOF) in the Java language, thus making it more interesting to the "outside" world. At the same time, Apple lowered the price from $50,000 to $699.

Apple themselves used and still uses WebObjects heavily for their internal projects. This is continuing today with WebObjects being an important tool for Apple. Look at some of the URLs when you surf the Apple homepage. You will often see the string "WebObjects" embedded. No Apple Store, no iTunes Music Store, no Apple Developer Connection, and many more would have been possible to create in such a short time frame without WebObjects.

Apple had their own development tools for Objective-C and Java. However the non-Apple Java world started to use cross-platform tools, most often Eclipse, for developing Java applications. WebObjects was Java but Eclipse could not be used to develop WebObjects applications because there were no WebObjects specific tools available for Eclipse. All the Apple / NeXT tools were written in Objective-C and over the years it become more and more difficult to keep them running as modern Mac OS X evolved. A group of open source developers started to create the necessary tools as plug-ins for Eclipse for developing WebObjects applications, resulting in the WOLips toolset. At the same time other groups using WebObjects started to build and provide to the community their own WebObjects extensions frameworks. These frameworks eventually were collected under the name Project Wonder.

Today **Project Wonder** is an immense set of frameworks providing all sorts of functionality from simple generation of html output, sending emails, creating RSS feeds, creating PDF and Excel files, working with WebServices, to full Web 2.0 Ajax applications. In addition, Project Wonder has implementations of augmented versions of many standard WebObjects classes fixing bugs and teaching them new tricks. WebObjects is still part of Project Wonder, but more and more of WebObjects has been superseded by Project Wonder classes.

1.2   Where do we stand today?

Project Wonder is a very mature set of frameworks for building the most sophisticated web applications. WebObjects is at the core of Project Wonder. Today we are not programming with WebObjects any more (well, sort of, this is not really true) but we create Project Wonder applications.

In the last couple years Apple has shifted focus from being a computer company to creating more consumer lifestyle products like iPod, iPhone, and more. WebObjects is clearly not a consumer thing and thus Apple, seeing a lively and grown up community to take over, decided to not provide support for WebObjects anymore. When you go to Apple's web site and search for WebObjects, you will not find much - and what you find is marked deprecated. This is unfortunate, but pure company politics. However do not despair: you have Project Wonder! Project Wonder is today's WebObjects. Project Wonder is open source and supported by a great community.

Now let's really start with this book and dive into the wonders of Project Wonder!

1.3   What do you need to create great Project Wonder applications?

First of all you need a computer. Not just any computer but it ought to be an Apple Mac running a modern version of Mac OS X. Apple licensing states that all WebObjects development must be done on Apple hardware platform. Deployment is allowed wherever you have a modern Java runtime environment (Mac OS X, Microsoft Windows, Linux, any Unix, and whatever else you might have and want to use). This license limitation is for the WebObjects frameworks only. Project Wonder has no such limitation!

As WebObjects is pure java there is no technical limitation for development on any platform as long as there is Eclipse available. People have Project Wonder/WebObjects development environments running on Windows and Linux. Think of a Windows installation running on an Apple Mac with Boot Camp. This is clearly a scenario where the development tools run on Apple hardware platform. Throughout this book we will run our development environment on Mac OS X but we will show you how to set it up on Windows, too! Where there are differences, we will point them out.

What else do you need besides a computer? You need the Project Wonder frameworks, WebObjects and the WOLips Eclipse plugins. And our course you need Eclipse. Oh, and not to forget you probably want some kind of relational database.

We will set up our development environment together a bit later on. Let's first get some overview of things.

1.4 Hi-level overview of the frameworks

Some of you may not be really clear what we mean when talking about frameworks. So let's first set things straight and then have a look at what frameworks we have available.

1.4.1 What is a Framework?

Unlike a class library that is just a collection of classes, using a framework is a lot more. A **framework** not only contains classes but also resources like images, templates, other types of files, and even embedded other frameworks. The purpose of the classes in a framework is to provide a more or less defined set of functionality. Often you can use single classes from a framework for your purpose, but normally you use the functionality of the framework as a whole. Classes in the framework play together to do what they are supposed to do. In most cases, the control of what is happening lies with the framework and not with your application. Your application just provides classes and objects to the framework. The framework objects do the job with the help of your application objects and classes.

The framework being in control is very different to classic programming, where your application code controls everything and you just make use of objects and classes from a library. This is known as **inversion of control** or **Hollywood principle** (as the agent tells the actor: "Don't call us, we'll call you").

In a typical Project Wonder application your public static void main(String[] args) - method contains one line of code where it immediately hands over control to the Project Wonder frameworks

Here is a first look at some of the frameworks available.

1.4.2 WebObjects Frameworks

WebObjects is a set of many frameworks; many of them have been superseded by Project Wonder frameworks. For the sake of compatibility, the Project Wonder frameworks kept the names and packages the same. So even if things are still called WebObjects-something, many classes are not "WebObjects" any more. Anyway here is a list of some of the most important WebObjects frameworks:

Framework	Purpose
JavaFoundation	Contains the basic classes used throughout WebObjects and Wonder
JavaWOExtensions	As its name says provides more classes and basic functionality
JavaWebObjects	Well, as its name implies, this is the framework for the "WebObjects" functionality (generation of html)

Framework	Purpose
JavaWOWebServicesClient, JavaWOWebServicesGeneration, JavaWOWebServicesSupport	A set of several frameworks that make it possible to provide and consume web services (JEE integration)
JavaJDBCAdaptor	Provides connectivity via JDBC to relational databases
JavaEOAccess, JavaEOControl, JavaEOGeneration and many more	An extensive set of frameworks that implement the whole object-relational mapping. These frameworks are probably the most sophisticated ones in the whole Project Wonder/WebObjects universe.
JavaDirectToWeb, JavaDTWGeneration	Direct to Web is a technology that allows you to create a database web application without any line of code.

There are many more.

1.4.3 Project Wonder Frameworks

Here is a list of some of the frameworks making up Project Wonder:

Framework	Purpose
ERExtensions	A core framework. It provides all the basic Project Wonder functionality
ERDirectToWeb	Basic enhancements to WebObjects Direct To Web technology
ERPrototypes	Allows database vendor independent specification of data types
ERJavaMail	Uses standard java mail for working with emails
ExcelGenerator, ERExcelLook	Create real Microsoft Excel files from your data
ERPDFGeneration	Create PDF files
Ajax, AjaxLook, ERJQuery and many more	Use those to create great Web 2.0 rich interface applications

And many more. If you have a particular problem you need to solve, Project Wonder probably has a framework for you. Need Captchas? Use ERCaptcha. You want to support *OpenID* for login into your application? There is EROpenID. And so on.

2   Setting up your development environment

Let's assume we start with a more or less virgin installation of our development computer.

2.1   What do you need?

Let's look at the hardware as well as software requirements.

2.1.1   Hardware suitable for Project Wonder development

To be able to create great Project Wonder applications you need a decent computer. Any computer that can run at least Apple Mac OS X 10.6 (Snow Leopard) or Microsoft Windows Vista, and is equipped with at least 4GB of RAM, should be sufficient.

On the Apple platform any recent Mac Mini, Mac Pro, iMac, Mac Book Air, or Mac Book (Pro) would be a good system for development.

2.1.2   Software needed for Project Wonder development

If your operating system is at least Mac OS X Leopard or Windows Vista, you are fine. Development on Linux is possible as well, but as this is not so common, we will not cover it here. There is information available online.

You need a couple of frameworks and some tools, namely Eclipse and the WOLips plugin.

You can download installers for the tools and the frameworks. Open up your browser and surf to the following address *http://wocommunity.org/documents/tools/*

Download *WOInstaller.jar* and *Golipse.app_latest.zip*. You might want to bookmark this page and come back later to download more interesting things. For the moment *WOInstaller* and *Golipse* is what we need.

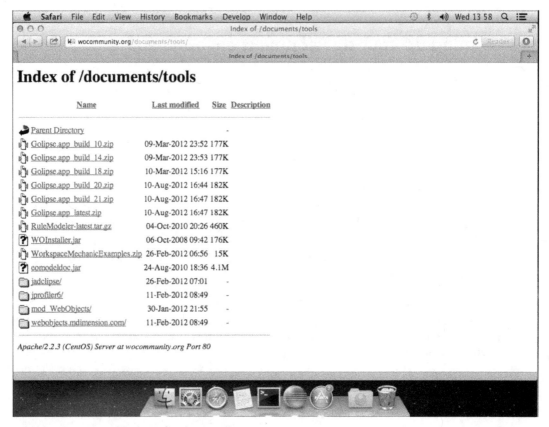

Picture 2-1   Download site for the installers

Of course you need a relational database server. This can be any of the standard products like MySQL, Postgres, Oracle, and others. As long as you can get a JDBC driver for the database server, you should be all set. Install the database server on your development machine or on any other system; just make sure you have network access from your development system to the database. Throughout this book we will work with a locally installed MySQL database server. However where needed, we will give you tips for other products as well.

2.2   Where goes what?

On a Mac there are two main locations where frameworks are stored. */System/Library* is reserved for all Apple system software. The original WebObjects installation put all the frameworks into that location. This is not a good idea today. Leave */System* alone! Some tools and additional things got installed into */Library*. This is ok but we want full control over our installation (and the modern Project Wonder tools support this). So we are going to install into a completely different location. The following is our suggestion. You can choose whatever other location suits your style.

We create a Development-folder on the root level of our hard drive. Call it *Development*. On Windows this would normally be on the C:\ drive. You may need admin privileges to create the folder. Change the access rights of the *Development* folder so that it belongs to you.

Caution

Please avoid spaces or international characters in file and path names. Some tools and frameworks might get upset otherwise and things might not work properly.

Create another folder named *Libraries* inside the *Development* folder and inside this yet another one called *WOnder*. This will be the location where all the frameworks are going to end up.

Here is a screen shot from a Mac showing */Development/Libraries/WOnder*:

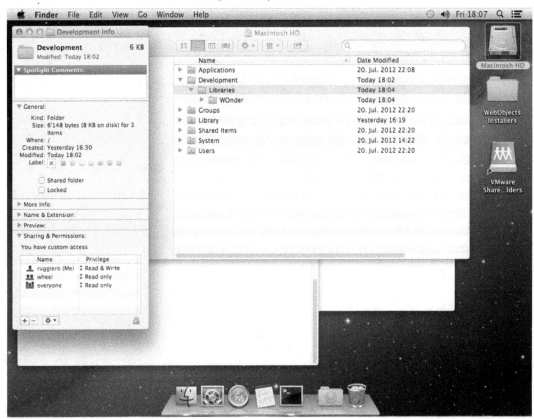

Picture 2-2   The Development folder with its substructure

On a Windows system you would have *C:\Development\Libraries\WOnder* (do you really need a screen shot from a Windows system, too?)

The basic idea is that everything goes inside this */Development* folder. At the end the */Development* folder will contain at least four subfolders:

/Development/Libraries
    This folder will contain all the compiled frameworks

/Development/WonderSource
    This folder will contain the source code to the frameworks.

/Development/Tools
    This is the location where all the tools will reside (e.g. Eclipse)

/Development/workspace
>   This is your Eclipse workspace.

Of course you are free to choose another layout. However throughout this book we will work with this folder structure.

2.3   Installing the tools

You need Eclipse and the WOLips plugins. *Golipse* is a Mac application that downloads Eclipse and WOLips and configures everything for optimal Project Wonder development. If you are installing the development environment on Windows you, cannot use *Golipse*. Instead you must download and install Eclipse und WOLips manually.

Manual installation would also be what you want if you already have Eclipse on your system and just need the WOLips plugin. We'll cover manual installation a bit further down.

2.3.1 Automatic installation of Eclipse and WOLips

Automatic installation will only work on Mac OS X.

Unpack *Golipse.app_latest.zip* if not yet done and start *Golipse* by double clicking its icon.

From the popup select where to put Eclipse. You can select any location. Create a *Tools* folder inside your */Development* folder and select this new folder for the install location of *Golipse*.

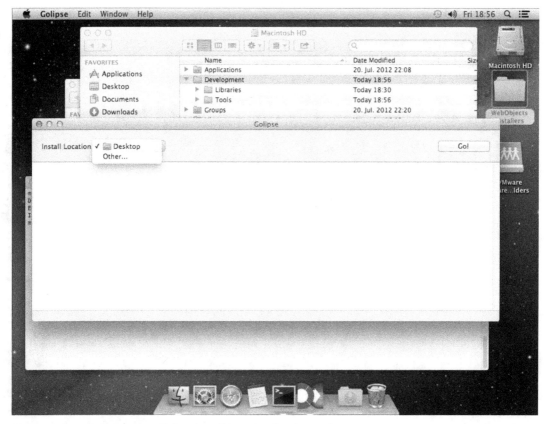

Picture 2-3   Golipse.app - Select install location for the tools

Press the *Go!* button and have some coffee while Eclipse and WOLips are being downloaded and installed.

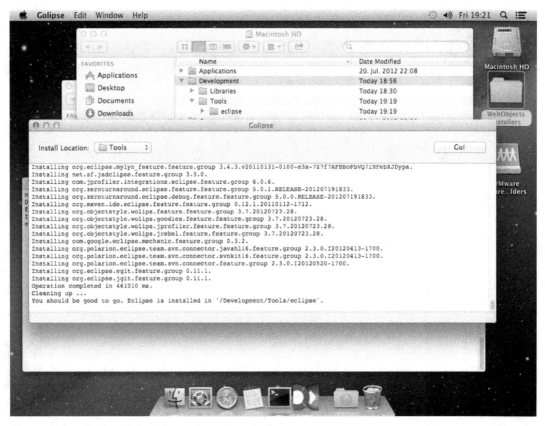

Picture 2-4   Golipse.app - The tools are installed

As you can see from the summary lines at the bottom of the log output, the download and installation took quite some time, but all is well now.

2.3.2   Manual installation of Eclipse and WOLips

This is needed on Windows or if you already have an Eclipse IDE that you want to use. Go to *http://www.eclipse.org* and download Eclipse. As of the writing of this book Eclipse 3.7 was the latest stable version. Eclipse 4.2 was available but the WOLips tools were not yet ready. This might be different when you read this book. Important thing is that Eclipse and WOLips go together. So for Eclipse 3.7 you need WOLips 3.7, Eclipse 4.2 would then require WOLips 4.2.

Open your copy of Eclipse and go to *HELP -> INSTALL NEW SOFTWARE*. When you start Eclipse it might ask which workspace to use. Go with the default or pick any empty directory. In our case we will create a workspace-folder inside */Development*.

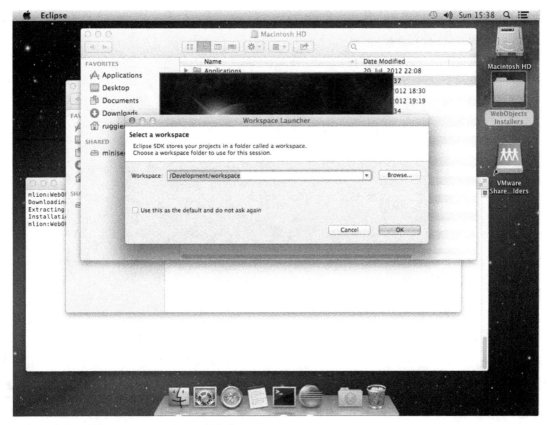

Picture 2-5   Eclipse creating a new Workspace

When Eclipse is up and running, open the *HELP* Menu and select *INSTALL NEW SOFTWARE*. Add a new site and name it. You can name it anyway you like, but it makes a lot of sense naming things according to their meaning. Thus we name it *WOLips*.

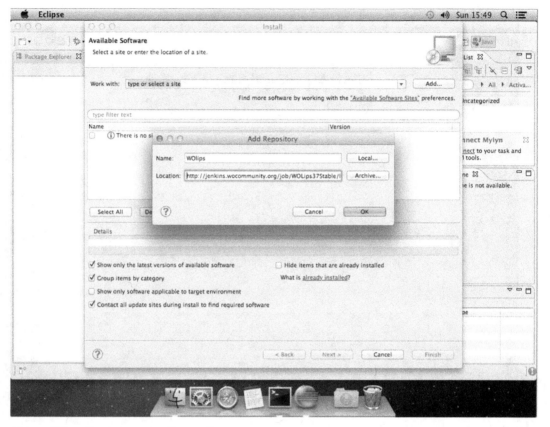

Picture 2-6   Create a new software site

Put the following URL into the location field:

http://jenkins.wocommunity.org/job/WOLips37Stable/lastSuccessfulBuild/artifact/temp/dist

Then press *OK*.

After a moment you will be presented with the following screen. If instead you get an error message you have probably mistyped the location URL.

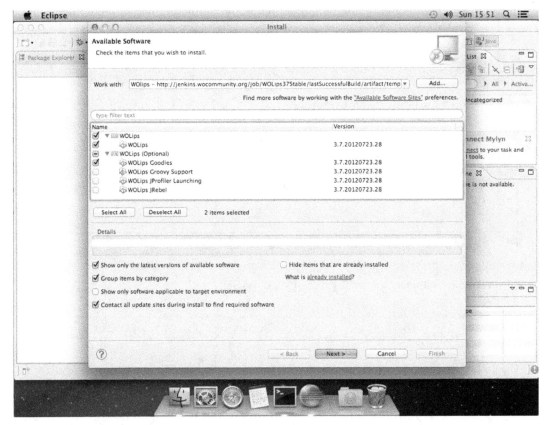

Picture 2-7   Select the parts of WOLips to install

For the moment check *WOLIPS* and *WOLIPS (OPTIONAL)* -> *WOLIPS GOODIES*. Then press *NEXT>*. Confirm the installation, accept the license, and after some moments Eclipse is ready for restart.

2.4   Installing the frameworks

There are several frameworks to install for WebObjects and Project Wonder. WebObjects must be downloaded from Apple's site, Project Wonder is available from the community site. We can make use of an installer or install things manually. If things don't work the way you expect, it is sometimes necessary to manually fix the installation.

The Project Wonder frameworks are distributed in binary form as well as in source code for your own compilation. We will look into both ways to install Project Wonder.

2.4.1   Installing WebObjects

For the installation of WebObjects you need *WOInstaller.jar* which you hopefully already downloaded from *http://wocommunity.org/documents/tools/*.

Open a Terminal window and cd to your preferred download location. When you run *WOInstaller.jar* from the command line without any options, you will get the following output:

```
$ java -jar WOInstaller.jar
usage: java -jar WOInstaller.jar [5.3.3|5.4.3] [destinationFolder]

Example:
WO 5.3.3 on Windows
        java -jar WOInstaller.jar 5.3.3 C:\Apple

WO 5.3.3 on OS X (in alternate folder)
        java -jar WOInstaller.jar 5.3.3 /opt
$
```

Enter the following command (substitute your folder path). Note that we are going to download WebObject Version 5.4.3. This is the latest official set of frameworks. On a Macintosh the command looks like this:

```
$ java -jar WOInstaller.jar 5.4.3 /Development/Libraries/WOnder/
```

On a Windows system substitute the proper Windows path:

```
DOS> java -jar WOInstaller.jar 5.4.3 C:\Development\Libraries\WOnder\
```

The program will tell you what it's doing, and there will be some progress output. Be patient, as this will take a couple minutes.

Here are the results:

Picture 2-8   WebObjects is installed

The installation has created sub-folders underneath */Development/Libraries/WOnder*. Feel free to explore the newly installed stuff.

Next comes the installation of Project Wonder.

2.4.2 Installing Project Wonder

Project Wonder is open source and you can install the frameworks either as a binary download or build them from source. Both ways are ok. Just pick what you feel better with. However we strongly recommend a source installation. Having the source and being able to debug right into it is an invaluable thing for learning.

Installing from source code

The source code for the Project Wonder frameworks is maintained in a public repository on *github*[1]. There are several command line and GUI tools available to access *git* repositories. An out-of-the-box Mac OS X system does not have a git command. You could download the developer tools from Apple's site, you could use *MacPorts* or any other package manager to get *git* or you can search for a

---

[1] Github is a large public repository for open source projects. It is based on the git version control system.

GUI-tool. There is also the possibility to simply download the complete source packaged as a *.zip*-file. In this tutorial for simplicity we use the downloadable *.zip* distribution.

Open your browser and enter the following address (note the *https* protocol):

https://github.com/projectwonder/wonder

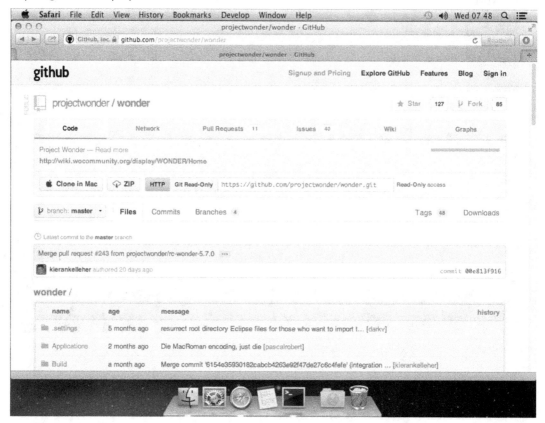

Picture 2-9   *Project Wonder on github*

Download the zipped source by clicking on the *ZIP* button. Unpack the file. Create another directory inside our */Development* folder and call it *WOnderSource*. Put the contents of the unzipped folder into this new directory.

Picture 2-10   Project Wonder source downloaded and unpacked

The wolips.properties file

There is one important file we need to create. This file specifies the correct locations for the built frameworks. You remember? We have created */Development/Libraries/WOnder*. That's where we want all the stuff to be installed. Now we need to tell WOLips where things are. To make life easy for us WOLips creates a default configuration file when you create your first application in WOLips. We are going to use WOLips to create such a default file and will then build upon that.

Follow the next steps. We are not particularly concerned with things. Later on we are going to look at what this all means. For now, just follow on.

Start Eclipse again, pointing it to the correct workspace when asked. Then open the menu *WINDOW -> OPEN PERSPECTIVE -> WOLIPS*.

Setting up your development environment

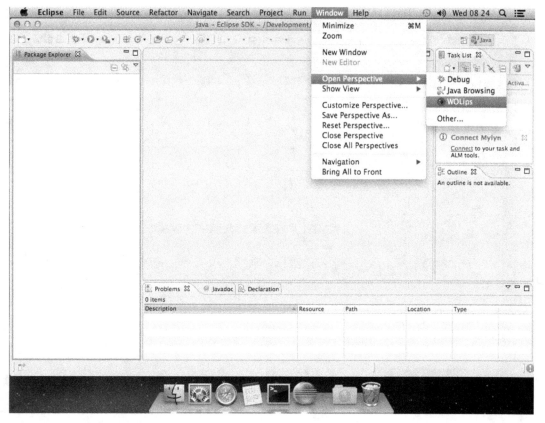

Picture 2-11   Open WOLips perspective

This will open the WOLips perspective, which will look something like this:

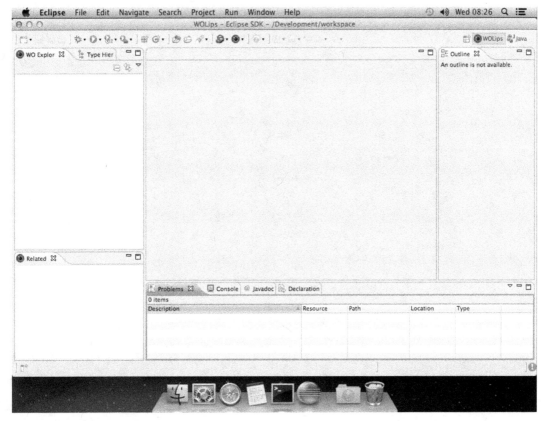

Picture 2-12   The WOLips perspective in Eclipse

Create a new Project Wonder application by going to menu *FILE -> NEW -> WONDER APPLICATION.*

Picture 2-13   Create new Wonder application

In the following dialog give that new application a name like *"BasicConcepts"* and click finish. This will create a project and (more importantly here) the default configuration file for WOLips.

At the moment, we are not interested in the project but will come back to it a bit later. *BasicConcepts* will serve as the project to explain all the basic concepts of a Project Wonder application (hence the name for this project). And as the problem report view in Eclipse tells you, the application cannot build anyway due to a handful of errors. We ignore the errors for the moment and terminate Eclipse.

When we created that first Project Wonder application WOLips created the default *wolips.properties* file. You will find this file in the following location (those directories might be hidden by your operating system's file browser, Finder or Explorer, you know how to make them visible, don't you?)

Mac OS X   */Users/ruggiero/Library/Application Support/WOLips*

Windows 7   *C:\Users\ruggiero\AppData\Roaming\WOLips*

These are locations inside your home folder. Substitute your user name accordingly instead of *ruggiero*.

Here is the content of the default **wolips.properties** on a Mac OS X system

File: *wolips.properties* on Mac OS X

```
wo.api.root=/Developer/Documentation/DocSets/↵
com.apple.ADC_Reference_Library.WebObjectsReference.docset/Contents/Resources/↵
Documents/documentation/InternetWeb/Reference/WO542Reference
wo.apps.root=/Library/WebObjects/Applications
wo.bootstrapjar=/System/Library/WebObjects/JavaApplications/wotaskd.woa/↵
WOBootstrap.jar
wo.extensions=/Library/WebObjects/Extensions
wo.local.frameworks=/Library/Frameworks
wo.local.root=/
wo.network.frameworks=/Network/Library/Frameworks
wo.network.root=/Network
wo.system.frameworks=/System/Library/Frameworks
wo.system.root=/System
wo.user.frameworks=/Users/ruggiero/Library/Frameworks
wo.user.root=/Users/ruggiero
```

Note that all lines start with wo. Some lines are rather long and break over several print lines. Don't let this confuse you! The same remark applies to the *wolips.properties* on Windows:

File: *wolips.properties* on Windows

```
wo.api.root=/Developer/ADC%20Reference%20Library/documentation/WebObjects/↵
Reference/API
wo.apps.root=C:\\Apple\\Library\\WebObjects\\Applications
wo.bootstrapjar=C:\\Apple\\Library\\WebObjects\\JavaApplications\\wotaskd.woa\↵
\WOBootstrap.jar
wo.dir.local.library.frameworks=C:\\Apple\\Local\\Library\\Frameworks
wo.dir.user.home.library.frameworks=C:\\Users\\ruggiero\\Library\\Frameworks
wo.extensions=C:\\Apple\\Local\\Library\\WebObjects\\Extensions
wo.local.frameworks=C:\\Apple\\Local\\Library\\Frameworks
wo.local.root=C:\\Apple\\Library\\Local
wo.network.frameworks=C:\\Network\\Library\\Frameworks
wo.network.root=C:\\Network
wo.system.frameworks=C:\\Apple\\Library\\Frameworks
wo.system.root=C:\\Apple\\Library
wo.user.frameworks=C:\\Users\\ruggiero\\Library\\Frameworks
wo.user.root=C:\\Users\\ruggiero
wolips.properties=wolips.properties
```

There is actually only one real difference between the Mac version and the Windows version. As on Windows the backslash and the colon are used in path names they must be properly escaped because the properties parser would not work. The escape character is the \.

Editing wolips.properties

As you can easily see, there are various file system paths noted in *wolips.properties*. We have to adapt those to our environment. Simply open *wolips.properties* with a text editor and make the following changes:

Change all paths starting with either */Library* or */System/Library* so that they read */Development/Libraries/WOnder/Library* and */Development/Libraries/WOnder/System/Library* (basically replace the initial "/" by "/Development/Libraries/WOnder/")

For a Windows *wolips.properties* replace "C:\\Apple\\" by "C:\\Development\\".

Setting up your development environment

Of course this assumes you laid out your directory structure like we did. Adapt the paths to your structure if needed.

Note

Not all paths in wolips.properties are really needed. E.g. wo.api.root looks weird and particularly on Windows makes no sense at all. We will come back later and fix things.

This is how your *wolips.properties* looks like when you followed our suggested folder layout (Mac version shown):

File: fixed *wolips.properties* on Mac OS X

```
wo.api.root=/Developer/Documentation/DocSets/↵
com.apple.ADC_Reference_Library.WebObjectsReference.docset/Contents/Resources/↵
Documents/documentation/InternetWeb/Reference/WO542Reference
wo.apps.root=/Development/Libraries/WOnder/Library/WebObjects/Applications
wo.bootstrapjar=/Development/Libraries/WOnder/System/Library/WebObjects/↵
JavaApplications/wotaskd.woa/WOBootstrap.jar
wo.extensions=/Development/Libraries/WOnder/Library/WebObjects/Extensions
wo.local.frameworks=/Development/Libraries/WOnder/Library/Frameworks
wo.local.root=/Development/Libraries/WOnder/
wo.network.frameworks=/Network/Library/Frameworks
wo.network.root=/Network
wo.system.frameworks=/Development/Libraries/WOnder/System/Library/Frameworks
wo.system.root=/Development/Libraries/WOnder/System
wo.user.frameworks=/Users/ruggiero/Library/Frameworks
wo.user.root=/Users/ruggiero
```

Compiling the frameworks

Now we want to compile the Project Wonder frameworks. Where should the compiled frameworks go? Of course they should be put in a location where WOLips can find them - and this information is in your *wolips.properties* file. So make a copy of your *wolips.properties* file and put it into the folder where the Project Wonder source is. Rename the copied file to *build.properties*. The build-process will read this file and know where to put things.

Picture 2-14   build.properties in your WOnderSource directory

Let's build the frameworks. For this we need to make use of the **ant** tool. If ant is not yet installed on your computer you can go to *http://ant.apache.org* and download it from there. For details consult the online installation instructions at *http://ant.apache.org/manual/index.html*.

Open a terminal window (or a DOS box) and cd to the Project Wonder source directory. Issue the following command:

```
$ ant frameworks
```

The compilation process can take a minute or two. You will see messages fly by, some may be warnings but there should not be any errors. At the end, there should be a success message and the total time used.

When something does not work, ant will display an error message. A typical problem is that the compile process cannot find certain needed classes. Check the paths in your *build.properties* file. Most probably something is not correct there.

If you get a message telling you that ant cannot be found or is an unknown command or something else is wrong with ant itself, check if you have properly installed ant and the command is in your *PATH*.

Setting up your development environment

On windows you may see messages flying by telling you something about un-mapable characters. This happens because some Java files contain comments in Japanese. You can safely ignore these warnings, the code compiles fine anyway.

The frameworks are now compiled, but they are not yet installed in the correct location. Issue the following command:

```
$ sudo ant frameworks.install
```

The install command must be run as super user. It needs the elevated privileges for a proper installation. On Windows run it from an admin account or open a console with admin privileges. No need for sudo there.

Hopefully you will be greeted by a *BUILD SUCCESSFUL* message.

Installing the binary frameworks

There is an archive available of all the Project Wonder frameworks ready built. Download it from *http://jenkins.wocommunity.org/job/Wonder/lastSuccessfulBuild/artifact/Root/Roots/Wonder-Frameworks.tar.gz*.

Use any available tool to unpack the archive. On Mac OS X double clicking the downloaded file in the Finder should be sufficient, on Windows you can use e.g. *WinZip* or *WinRar*. Of course the file can also be expanded from the command line in a terminal window with the following command:

```
$ tar -xzvf Wonder-Frameworks.tar.gz
```

You get a folder named *Wonder-Framework* that contains all the frameworks. Move the frameworks (not the folder itself) to */Development/Libraries/WOnder/Library/Frameworks* (or on Windows *C:\Development\Libraries\WOnder\Library\Frameworks*). Here is a screen shot that shows where things should be:

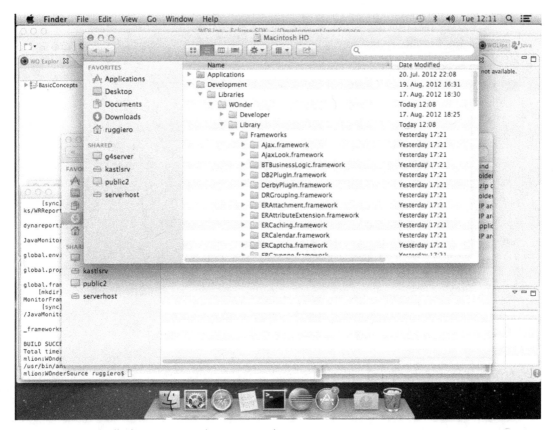

Picture 2-15   Installed Project Wonder Frameworks

That's it; you are done!

2.4.3 Final test if everything is installed properly

Open Eclipse again. You should still have that project *BasicConcepts*. This project did have a couple of build errors. These should now be gone.

You can run the application by selecting from the context menu *RUN AS -> WOAPPLICATION*

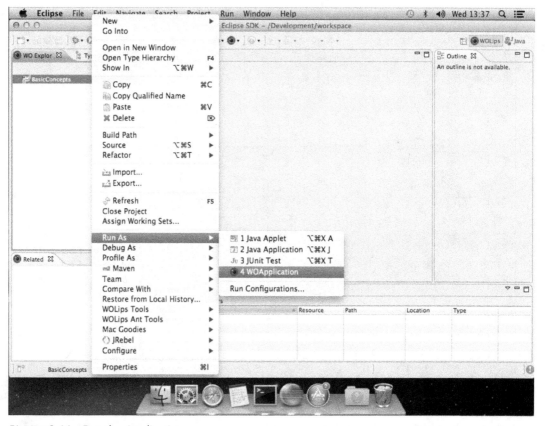

Picture 2-16   Run the Application

Eclipse will search for classes containing main() methods. Pick Application from package your.app and hit *OK*.

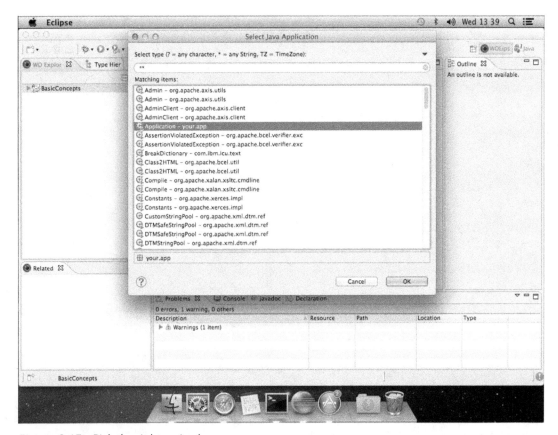

Picture 2-17   Pick the right main class

After a moment your default browser should open and display the famous greeting to the world. If you do this on a Windows system, you must open the browser manually. Look in the Console window in Eclipse. At the very end of the startup messages you should see a line telling you what the URL of your application is. Copy this to your browser, hit enter, and the greeting should appear.

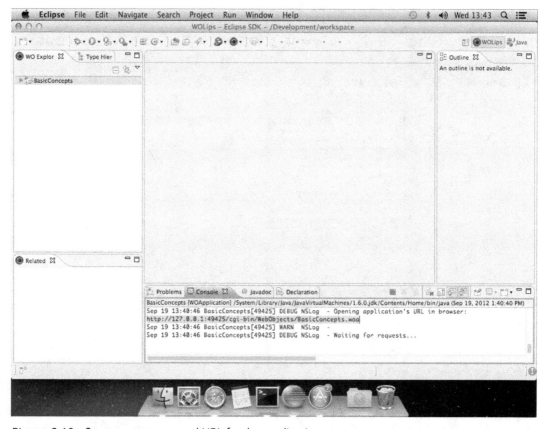

Picture 2-18   Startup messages and URL for the application

What if you get an error message instead of a nice running application? There is one typical problem that can show up:

You get an error message telling you that the main method cannot be found because the class *Application* in package your.app is not known.

That is easy to fix! Remember, you created the *BasicConcepts* project without a proper *wolips.properties* file. So WOLips configured your project with default paths for the frameworks. Now we have the frameworks and the *wolips.properties* file has the correct paths, but your project is still wrong. Go into PROJECT menu and CLEAN... the project. This should rebuild everything based on the correct properties.

3 Where to get help

Sometimes things do not work as expected, sometimes you need some hand holding (yes, even seasoned programmers need hand holding from time to time), oftentimes you want to know more about a class, or how to do certain things, or how to use a framework.

Here are the most important resources:

The Wonder Wiki

http://wiki.wocommunity.org/dashboard.action

This is your starting point for everything Wonder related. Wonder has a very lively community and the wiki provides all the information you need.

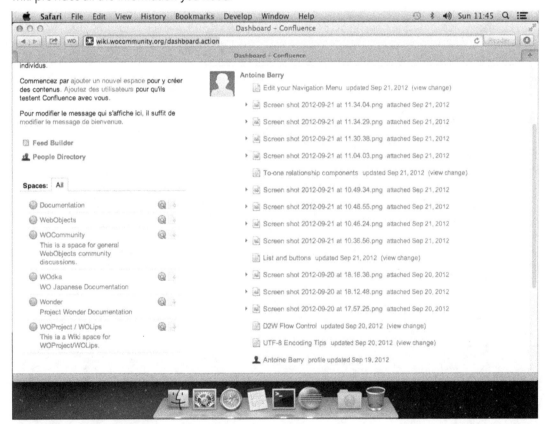

Picture 3-1 The wiki entry point for everything Wonder related

WebObjects classes and API documentation

http://api.webobjects.me/wo542/

The documentation has not changed significantly from version 5.4.2 to the current one 5.4.3, so it was not updated.

Where to get help

Wonder frameworks, classes and API documentation

http://jenkins.wocommunity.org/job/Wonder/lastSuccessfulBuild/javadoc/?

Mailing list

There are several mailing lists available related to Wonder and WebObjects. Apple hosts the most important one. You can find it here: *https://lists.apple.com/mailman/listinfo/webobjects-dev* .

Ask questions, post tips, and maybe even give answers! All the Wonder "gurus" and all the ordinary folks hang out there. Do not be afraid of asking "stupid" questions. Never forget

The most stupid question is the one you have and dare not ask!

All the members on this list are more than happy to help you. We want you! And we can only get you on board by helping you!

Wonderbar

This is an extension for Apple's Safari and Google Chrome from Ken Ishimoto. Go to *http://www.ksroom.com/App/WebObjects/Kisa.woa/wa/safariExtensions* and download **Wonderbar**. It installs right into your browser and gives you direct access to most all online resources. Here is *Wonderbar* in action:

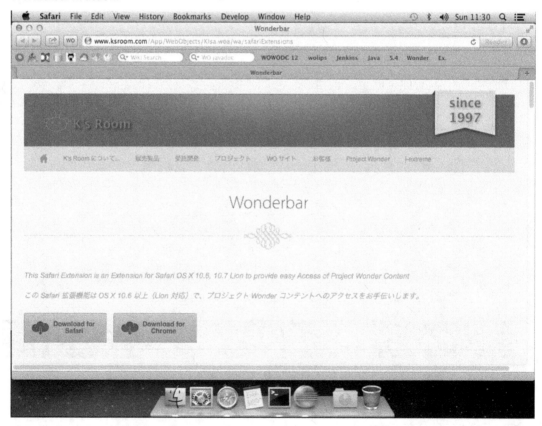

Picture 3-2   Wonderbar installed in Safari

You will probably use the following resources the most:

- Java API Documentation

- WebObjects Classes and API Documentation

- Wonder Classes and API Documentation

Part B - Basic Concepts and Classes

4   Our first application

In this chapter we will have a first look at a Wonder application. We will see how Wonder ties into the request-response-loop for a web application. In subsequent chapters you will then learn all the details. Also in this chapter you will learn a lot about the tools and how to work with Eclipse/WOLips.

4.1   Overview of the request-response-loop

The following graphic shows what happens when the user enters a URL for a Wonder application in his or her browser.

Picture 4-1   Overview of Request-Response-Loop

A URL in the browser is actually a request to a server to return some form of resource. Thus the browser sends this request to a web server. The web server analyzes the URL and figures that it cannot handle this request on its own. From the URL part *.../Apps/WebObjects/...* it knows that this request must be forwarded to the *WOAdaptor*. The **WOAdaptor** is a piece of software that connects the web server to the Wonder application. The Wonder application then analyzes the rest of the URL and generates whatever was requested. The results of this are sent back from the Wonder application to the *WOAdaptor* and from there to the web server for the ultimate delivery to the browser for display. The *WOAdaptor* is the middleman between the web and the Wonder application. It translates http protocol to and from something that an object oriented Wonder application can understand.

4.2   Direct connect during development

The Wonder frameworks implement their own simple web server. This allows any Wonder application to work without a "real" web server and there is no need for the *WOAdaptor*. This makes things simple for development but is usually not recommended for deployment. And sometimes, direct connect hides problems that only arise when using a web server and the *WOAdaptor*. Some developers frown upon using direct connect at all even during development. In this book we will work with direct connect throughout, as we want to focus on developing Wonder applications. There are good articles on the wiki about setting up development through a web server.

You can easily distinguish a direct connect URL from one that addresses the application through a web server:

A typical direct connect URL has a port number after the hostname:

http://localhost:34725/cgi-bin/WebObjects/BasicConcepts...

You do not have to set up anything, direct connect is the default for development.

4.3   Layout of the *BasicConcepts* Project

Let's have a closer look at what we get when creating a Wonder application in Eclipse. When you followed the installation instructions from the previous chapters, you already have a project called *BasicConcepts*. If not, switch to WOLips perspective and create an out-of-the-box Wonder application. Call it *BasicConcepts*. You do not have to change anything, just enter the name and hit create.

Here is the WOLips layout of the project:

Picture 4-2   The layout of the BasicConcepts project

The WO Explorer view on the left shows the general layout of the project.

The following folders are created:

The *Sources* folder contains your Java source code. WOLips automatically generates two default packages (your.app and your.app.components).

The *Components* folder contains all your page templates. Basically every result page, that your application generates, is created from a template in the *Components* folder and some piece of Java code from the your.app.components package. The components template consists of several files.

These are kind of hidden inside the component icon. We'll get into the details in a moment. For now just note that you get a default component called *Main WO* and an associated Java class file *Main.java*.

Referenced Libraries is a folder you use to put any ready-made jar files into. Very often you put a JDBC driver here.

A Wonder application needs access to several resources when running. Such resources go into the *Resources* folder. We will see examples later on when we start to work with databases.

Static web resources like images and style files go into *WebServerResources*.

Depending on you filter settings in Eclipse you may see other folders as well.

Inside the package your.app you'll find the default Java class files for *Application*, *Session*, and *DirectAction*. For now you can ignore *DirectAction.java*. We'll get to this class in a later chapter.

The *Application* class is extremely simple. It contains a default constructor and a one line main() method. This is because *Application* extends ERXApplication. ERXApplication is the Wonder framework class that represents the application you are creating. The main() method is just the required Java entry point for your application. It immediately hands over control to the Wonder frameworks.

The *Session* class is there because every web application needs some kind of session handling (more on sessions later). So it makes sense to be able to have access to the session. The frameworks expect you to have a *Session* class that extends the framework class ERXSession.

Let's run the *BasicConcepts* application. Context click on *Application.java* and from the popup menu select *RUN AS -> WO APPLICATION*. After a moment you will see the startup messages in the console view and your default browser should open.

Look at the last couple lines in the console view.

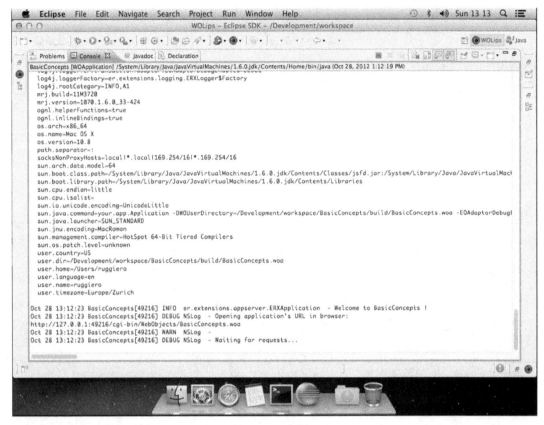

Picture 4-3   Console output of a running Wonder application

Look at the last couple lines. You see the greeting message of your application. Then you are told that it tries to open the application URL in the browser, and finally, that the application is ready and waiting for your requests.

The application's URL in our case is *http://127.0.0.1:49216/cgi-bin/WebObjects/BasicConcepts.woa*

Unfortunately, when on Windows, your browser will not automatically open. So simply copy this line from the console view into your favorite browser.

This is the so-called front door URL of your application. You can clearly see that it is a direct connect URL because there is a port number after the host name.

4.4   Editing and working with Components

Without going too much into details of what a component is, you will learn how to edit components and even create a very simple navigation from one page to a second page. All the details (and more) will be covered in subsequent chapters.

Your running application displays a very simple web page in the browser, greeting the world.

Leave the browser window open but switch back to Eclipse. Do not stop the application, just leave it running.

Double click on *Main WO* in the *Components* folder. You should get the following picture:

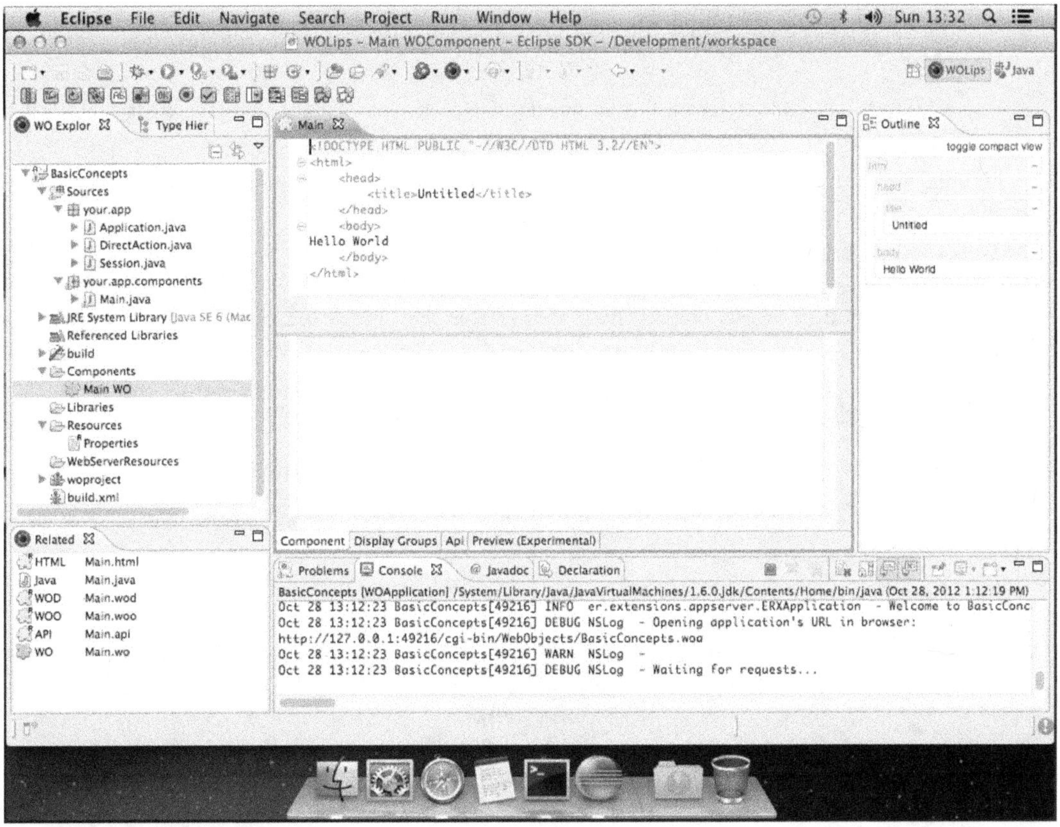

Picture 4-4   Editing Main WO

In the center part of Eclipse you get a split editor. There is some html stuff in the upper part with the lower part just blank.

The Related View at the lower left shows you quite a couple things. Let's see what these are:

HTML – *Main.html*

> The html template. Its content is displayed and ready for editing in the upper part of the editor view

Java – *Main.java*

> This is your Java class file. Double clicking will open it for editing

WOD – *Main.wod*

> This file is shown in the lower part of the editor view. It is a plain text file that at the moment has no content.

WOO – *Main.woo*

> This file is also a plain text file. It is currently empty and not of relevance at the moment.

Our first application

API – *Main.api*

This file is also currently empty and not relevant right now.

WO – *Main.wo*

This is the container for all the component related files (except the Java class file). In the file system, this is actually a real folder.

Click into the html editor window. The outline view at the right shows you the structure of your html code.

First thing you probably notice is, that the html code is still version 3.2. This is extremely outdated. Today the frameworks can generate proper xhtml and html5 code. This version 3.2 is a leftover from the stone ages and obviously nobody has changed it in the default template for a new project. Never mind it is only this initial *Main* component that has old declarations. We are going to fix it right away.

Close the editor tab and delete *Main.java* and *Main WO* as well as *Main.api* from the project. Don't worry that *DirectAction.java* flags an error (it misses *Main.java*).

Context-click or right-click on the empty *Components* folder and select *NEW -> WOCOMPONENT*

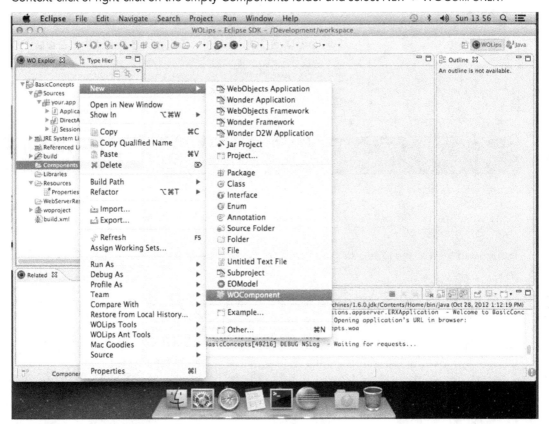

Picture 4-5   Create a new Component

In the following dialog name the component Main and make sure these options are selected:

- GENERATE HTML CONTENTS must be checked.

- Select *XHTML 1.1* from the popup

- Make sure that the encoding is *NSUTF8STRINGENCODING*.

- Put the java class into the proper package (in our example your.app.components)

- Have the java class extend *er.extensions.components.ERXComponent*

Compare with the following screenshot:

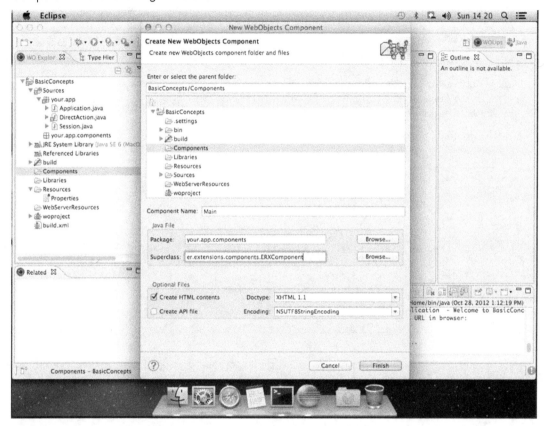

Picture 4-6   Setting properties for a new component

The editor will open automatically after you click Finish.

That looks better now! Enter the greeting to the world in between <body>...</body> tags. Here is how you HTML contents should look:

```
<?xml version="1.0" encoding="UTF-8"?>
<!DOCTYPE html PUBLIC "-//W3C//DTD XHTML 1.1//EN"
    "http://www.w3.org/TR/xhtml11/DTD/xhtml11.dtd">

<html xmlns="http://www.w3.org/1999/xhtml" xml:lang="en">
<head>
    <meta http-equiv="Content-Type" content="text/html; charset=utf-8"/>
    <title>untitled</title>
</head>
```

```
<body>
<p>Hello World</p>
</body>
</html>
```

Go to your browser and reload the page. There should be no difference.

Now let's edit the page a bit. Change the page title from *untitled* to something more interesting like "My Greeting To The World". Also edit the text and maybe change the <p> Tags to <h1>. Reload the page in the browser.

Let's now create a second page just for the fun of it.

Again right click on *Components* and select NEW -> WOCOMPONENT. Make sure everything is properly set (look at the screenshot for the *Main* page, use the very same options). Name the component *Welcome*.

Edit the contents of the HTML part so that it says *Hi*:

```
<?xml version="1.0" encoding="UTF-8"?>
<!DOCTYPE html PUBLIC "-//W3C//DTD XHTML 1.1//EN"
    "http://www.w3.org/TR/xhtml11/DTD/xhtml11.dtd">

<html xmlns="http://www.w3.org/1999/xhtml" xml:lang="en">
<head>
    <meta http-equiv="Content-Type" content="text/html; charset=utf-8"/>
    <title>untitled</title>
</head>
<body>
<p>Hi</p>
</body>
</html>
```

Now comes the big trick. We want to have a hyperlink on our main page that, when clicked, brings us to this new *Welcome* page.

Edit the HTML part of *Main.wo*. Put the following line after the <h1> tags:

```
<webobject name = "hi" >Say Hi</webobject>
```

There is that strange tag <webobject>. The framework parses the HTML template for such <webobject> tags. A <webobject> tag tells the framework to create a snippet of HTML dynamically when the page is requested. The big question is: what should the framework put there? What is the HTML that should be generated?

This question is answered in the lower part of the editor. For this to work, the <webobject> tag needs a name. In our case we name it "hi". You can pick any sensible name you like.

In the lower (still empty) part of the split editor window type "hi : WO" and hit control-space. WOLips will try to find all known classes that start with WO in their name and are suitable in this context. Select WOHyperlink from the popup list.

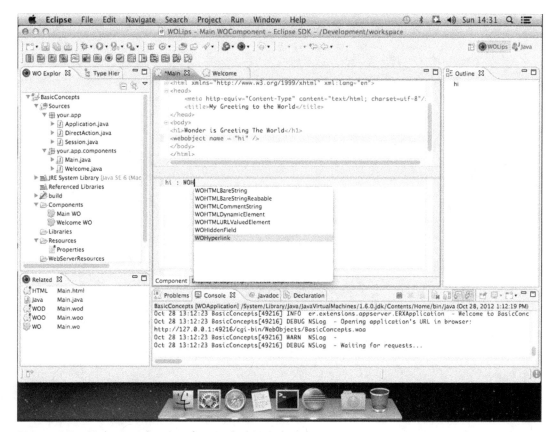

Picture 4-7   Selecting the class for a webobject element

With this we tell the framework, that the template element called "hi" should be an object of class WOHyperklink. WOHyperklink is a framework class; its objects know how to properly generate the HTML code for a hyperlink.

But what should this hyperlink link to? The WOHyperlink object needs some more info. Accepting the selection of WOHyperlink adds opening and closing curly braces. Position the cursor into the area between the braces and hit control-space again. You'll be presented with a list of things to pick from. Pick the one called *action*.

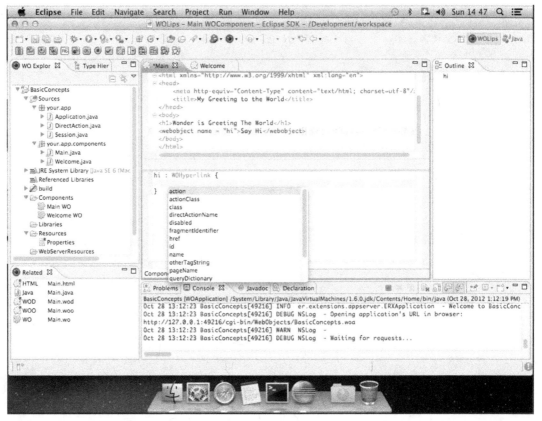

Picture 4-8   Possible bindings of a WOHyperlink.

The list shows you all known **bindings** for a WOHyperlink. Bindings are like the prongs of a connector. You can (and sometimes must) provide information to the object by connecting the proper binding. Not all bindings must be connected at all times. Some bindings are mandatory, some bindings are mutually exclusive, some bindings may be optional. For a WOHyperlink you must connect something to the *action* binding.

Complete your code so that it reads like this:

```
hi : WOHyperlink {
    action = sayHi;
}
```

But what is "sayHi"? That is a method in your Java code. Yes, I know, this method does not yet exist (and WOLips knows this, too; it complains bitterly). So we need to create it.

Open *Main.java*. As we have our hyperlink in *Main.wo* the method we bind to *action* must reside in *Main.java*.

Add the following method sayHi() to your *Main* class:

```
package your.app.components;

import com.webobjects.appserver.WOContext;
import er.extensions.components.ERXComponent;

public class Main extends ERXComponent {
    public Main(WOContext context) {
        super(context);
    }

    public Welcome sayHi() {
        Welcome nextPage = pageWithName(Welcome.class);
        return nextPage;
    }
}
```

What does this method do? We'll go into more details later but here is the short version: it creates an object of type *Welcome*. You remember, *Welcome* is the class that goes along our *Welcome* component. It then returns this object.

We told the framework, that the action for the hyperlink is sayHi. The framework searches for a method with name sayHi that returns a component. It finds this method and calls it. The method creates a component object and returns it to the calling framework.

We have now modified the code for the *Main* object, so we have to stop the still running application and restart it.

Hopefully the main page will now display a hyperlink with the text "say hi". Click it and you should be brought to that very simple welcome page that says hi.

If you get a crash or some kind of error message make sure that you do not have any typos neither in your HTML nor in the binding nor in your Java code.

5 Design patterns

Wonder and WebObjects make extensive use of various design patterns. In this chapter we will look into the two most important ones, Model-View-Controller (MVC) and Key-Value-Coding.

5.1 Model View Controller

Let's first have a refresher on the idea of **Model-View-Controller**. Most applications with some sort of user interface can be divided into tree distinct parts:

- The model covers all the business logic

- The view encompasses the user interface

- The controller mediates between model and view

All the data and the business logic in an application are actually independent of any way data is presented to the user. Business logic dictates what kind of data must be stored (e.g. in a database) and how different data items relate to each other. For instance a sales order may consist of customer data and sales positions. Each sales position must have a reference to an article and of course must know how many items the customer ordered. These are the rules, no matter what. The complete sale can then be presented on a screen for direct viewing, or it is printed on a slip of paper as a receipt, or even massaged into some XML data structure and exported to third party software.

How the data is presented does not change the business rules. Changing business rules may have impact on the presentation (but not necessarily so). The same data can be presented in completely different ways.

Somehow the data from the model must be brought into a form that the view part can display. As soon as the view part becomes interactive with the user entering information and activating actions, there must be "something" that translates the user input into proper data and application functionality that is governed by the business rules. This is the job of the controller, sitting in between the model and the view.

Having such a strict distinction between the data and its presentation allows for easy changes in the presentation as well as changing the internal data without forcing the user to learn a new user interface. As the control part is primarily for getting user input and commands a change in the user interface will often need some adaptation in the controller part.

The following drawing illustrates this.

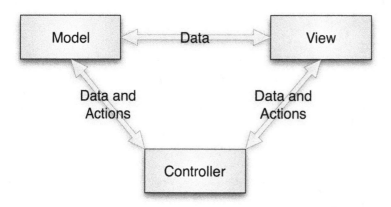

Picture 5-1   Model-View-Controller

The view pulls data for display from the model. Data entered by the user in some type of form is sent from the view to the controller. Sometimes the view can directly talk to the model and update data there. In any case all actions from the view, like buttons clicked by the user, go to the controller. It decides what to do with data and action. The controller translates the button click to calls into the business logic. The model will usually tell the views and the controller that some data has changed, so that the view can update the presentation.

Wonder makes heavy use of this Model-View-Controller pattern.

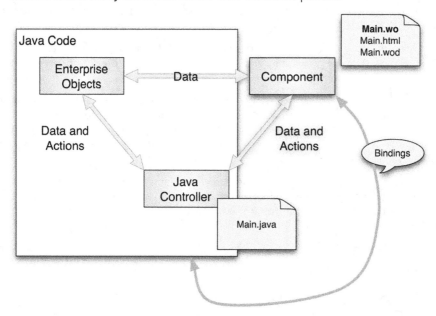

Picture 5-2   MVC in Wonder

In the previous chapter you had a first glimpse at WO component. We saw that there are several files belonging to a component. A WO component is the perfect showcase for MVC:

Model -> Enterprise Objects

This is your business data. We will cover this later in this book when we look at how Wonder works with a database.

View -> Component

The html template file is your view. It defines how things are presented on-screen. It contains static html code and placeholders for dynamic data and action elements.

Controller -> Java Class

The java class file is your primary controller. It prepares data for the dynamic elements and it is responsible to initiate actions when a user clicks a form submit button or a hyperlink. In your Java class you gather data that the user inputs and hand it over to the model. Your Java code coordinates the flow of data and action between the application and the model and the display in the browser.

The bindings file (with extension *.wod*) simply defines the placeholders for dynamic things in the html template and connects them to the java code.

Albeit we have been solely talking about html user interfaces and the template file has an extension of *.html*, this strict split into model-view-controller allows generating not only html, but also xml, or Adobe PDF, or Microsoft Excel files, or anything else for direct download. Wonder has ready-made components for such things and in the very same way you create an html user interface you can layout a PDF file.

Here is a simple rule for making optimal use of MVC:

"Do not put business logic into you Java controller class". Keep it simple.

5.2   Key Value Coding

The second important pattern used throughout all the frameworks is **Key-Value-Coding KVC**. This pattern is heavily used and without it probably nothing would work.

Simple thing: the "key" is the name of something. This "something" can be some data but can also be a reference to an action to take. Key-Value-Coding hides the complexity of figuring out how to get from key to value.

Here is an example. Go back to your *BasicConcepts* project and open *Main.wo* by double clicking.

Design patterns

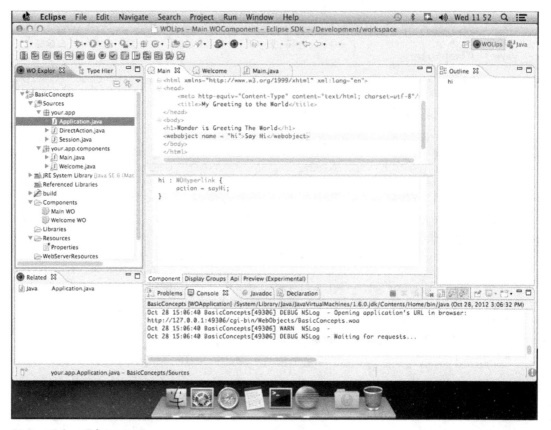

Picture 5-3   Editing Main.wo

You remember: we have inserted a dynamic element into our html template with the webobject-tag. In the lower pane (that is, in the .wod-file), we have a definition for this element and given it an action binding. This is key-value-coding! We do not call a Java method when the user clicks the hyperlink. We only tell the framework to look for a method with the name "sayHi". We specify a key (the string *sayHi*), which is then used during runtime to find a suitable method to call as a reaction on the user activating the hyperlink.

5.2.1 Let's play a bit with key-value-coding

Put the following line into the html template right after the <h1>...</h1> line, just before the hyperlink dynamic element:

```
<p>The name of this application is: <webobject name = "appName" /></p>
```

This means we put a second dynamic element into our page. Of course we need to tell the framework what this element is supposed to be. Edit the .wod in the lower part and add the following definition:

```
appName : WOString {
```

```
    value = application.name;
}
```

This tells the framework to use an object of type WOString to generate the contents. As its name implies it puts a string into the resulting html. Where does it get the string value from? Which string should be displayed? WOString has a value binding. Look at what we bind to value: application.name.

This is key-value-coding at its best. But first just run the program and see what the output is.

Picture 5-4   The application knows its name

Let's follow exactly what is happening here:

application.name is a so called key path because it actually is a path to something. In key-value-coding the path separator is the period character. Thus this path is made up of two parts. Wonder will split the path into the key *application* and the key *name* and try to resolve them one by one.

The controller for the main component is an object of class Main. So the first step is to figure what *application* is. The framework will ask the Main-object for "something" named *application*. The framework does not know what this is nor does it know how Main can resolve it. As Main is ultimately an extension of class WOComponent it inherits a mechanism that allows it to return a reference to the application object because WOComponent implements key-value-coding!

Now that the framework has resolved the first key, it needs to resolve *name*. The framework has received a reference to an object (in this case the application) and now asks this object to provide something called *name*. As the class *Application* inherits from ERXApplication and ultimately from WOApplication it knows how to provide an answer to "return something called name".

Well, that's the application's name. Run the program and see what happens:

To demonstrate that we not just call a method when binding to a key edit the binding and deliberately put a spelling error in like using a k instead of a c in the word application. Eclipse will of course flag this as an error as soon as you save your modification but ignore it for the moment.

Again run the application (you can simply reload the page in the browser) and you should get a screen full of error messages in your browser:

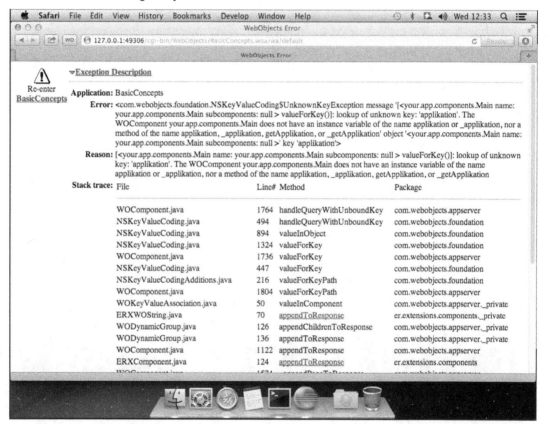

Picture 5-5   Key-value-coding error message

Read the message carefully. Here is the text again:

```
<com.webobjects.foundation.NSKeyValueCoding$UnknownKeyException message
'[<your.app.components.Main name: your.app.components.Main subcomponents: null >
valueForKey()]: lookup of unknown key: 'applikation'. The WOComponent
your.app.components.Main does not have an instance variable of the name applikation
or _applikation, nor a method of the name applikation, _applikation, getApplikation,
```

```
or _getApplikation' object '<your.app.components.Main name: your.app.components.Main
subcomponents: null >' key 'applikation'>
```

The message tells you that key value coding was asked to resolve a key that is not known. Known to whom? KVC goes to the controller object, which is of class Main and asks for something called *applikation*. The controller tries hard to resolve this but ultimately fails. It first checks if there is a (public) instance variable called *applikation* or *_applikation*[2] (which we know there is not because there is this typo in the word *applikation*). KVC then tries various variations of methods to resolve that key. Only when everything fails an exception is thrown.

Let's play a bit more with this and instead of fixing the spelling mistake we implement a method with that k in its name. Add the following lines to your Main.java:

```
public WOApplication getApplikation() {
    return application();
}
```

We create a method getApplikation that should return a reference to the application object. This method uses the application()-Method that the component inherits. To test this method, you need to stop and restart the application. There should not be an error anymore and the application should properly display its name. Eclipse will also not flag an error anymore.

5.2.2 For the Curious: The NSKeyValueCoding Interface

For those who want to know a bit more:

Almost everything in Wonder works with KVC by implementing the ***NSKeyValueCoding*** interface. This interface has two important methods.

```
void takeValueForKey(Object value, String key)
```

Sets the value for the property identified by *key* to *value*.

```
Object valueForKey(String key)
```

Retrieves the value of the property named by *key*.

You can read more about this interface in the WebObjects online documentation.

---

[2] In the old days, when the frameworks were still written in Objective-C, it was customary to denote instance variables using an underscore in front oft the actual name. Thus the check for such a name.

6 Request Response Loop

When a request from a browser is sent to the web server, it will be forwarded to our application. During this, two important objects (and lots of other equally important ones) are involved. For our understanding, we need to look at these two objects and the classes they are instances of.

But at first here is the big picture:

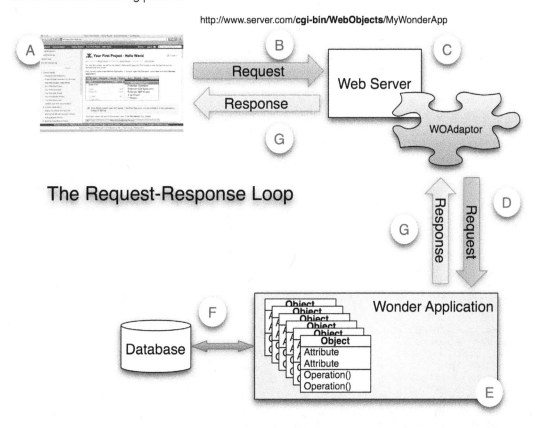

Picture 6-1   The Request-Response-Loop

Let's see what this is all about:

A – A users sits at his or her computer and enters a typical URL for a Wonder application into the browser's address field.

B – The browser sends the request to the Web Server.

C – We have already seen in the introductory section that the URL for our application has the string cgi-bin/WebObjects in it. This is for the Web Server the signal to forward the request to our application. For this to happen, the Web Server has a small piece of code linked into it: the *WOAdaptor*.

D – The *WOAdaptor* knows how to forward the request to our Wonder application.

E – Our Wonder application then processes the request. It makes use of all the framework classes and objects, as well as our own classes and objects, to generate the page the user has requested.

F – Most applications need access to a database. We will see later in this book how a Wonder application works with relational databases.

G – The application generates the response which is then sent back the same way as the request came in. The response is given to the *WOAdaptor*, which in turn passes the answer to the Web Server. The Web Server finally sends the answer back to the user's browser for rendering and display.

6.1 The *WOAdaptor*

The lingua franca of the Web is http. Http is a simple but clever text based protocol that web browser and web server use to talk to each other. On the other hand a Wonder application is a complex thing that consists of objects and classes. An object-oriented application is a completely different world. The *WOAdaptor* is responsible for translating between these different worlds.

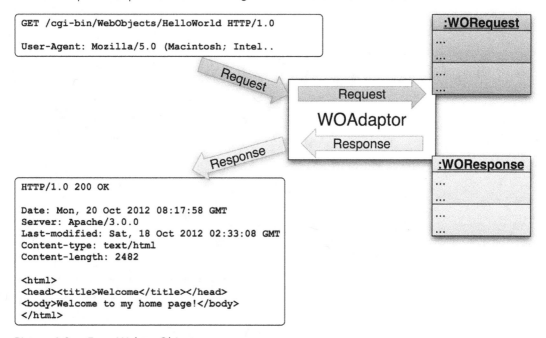

Picture 6-2   From Web to Objects

The typical request to a webserver consists of the GET (or POST) command followed by the URL for the resource. After the GET command the web browser adds some additional information. This information is called request headers. One such info-item is the user-agent string. This tells the web server what kind of browser is making the request. Additional header lines can inform the web server about special capabilities of the browser.

The web server answers in a similar fashion. First it sends some header lines that tell the browser about the web server and what kind of data the answer contains. Only then the actual response data is sent.

Everything between web browser and webserver is plain ASCII text. The *WOAdaptor* takes this incoming text and creates a WORequest object. It packages the request and its accompanying information (the URL and all the header information) into a nice object that can then be sent to the Wonder application.

When the Wonder application is done with composing a response it sends a WOResponse object back to the *WOAdaptor*. The *WOAdaptor* unpacks the information from the object and generates all the headers and text to be sent back to the user's browser as the response.

In short: a Wonder application is pure object-oriented whereas the http protocol is text based. The job of the *WOAdaptor* is to package the http request into an object and forward it to the application and to receive a response object from the Wonder application and translate it back into http plain text.

Let's have a closer look at the two classes WORequest and WOResponse. Both classes are the original WebObjects classes. The Wonder frameworks have extended those classes and added additional functionality and fixed some bugs. These are ERXRequest and ERXResponse. Both are subclasses of the respective WO-classes. The Wonder frameworks usually work with the ERX-variants.

6.2   The classes WORequest and ERXRequest

ERXRequest is the Wonder extension of the original WebObjects WORequest. You normally do not create any WORequest or ERXRequest object[3]. The *WOAdaptor* creates these. However you as a programmer have access to the current request. There are some methods that give you access to the underlying http protocol and particularly the request headers.

Here is a list of some interesting methods

Method	Description
browserLanguages()	returns a list of the languages the browser accepts
headerForKey()	returns the value of a particular header
headers()	returns a list of all header names
cookies()	returns an NSArray of all cookies in the request
cookieValueForKey()	returns the value for a given cookie name

There are many more, which you can find in the documentation. Cookies are part of the http headers, but we will have a dedicated chapter about cookies later in this book.

We are going to play a bit with the request. Put some code into the constructor of *Main.java*.

---

[3] This is not completely true. For an advanced user of Wonder it can make sense in certain circumstances to manually create objects of these classes. This is however beyond the scope of this book.

```
public Main(WOContext context) {
    super(context);
    for (String aKey : context.request().headerKeys()) {
        System.out.println(aKey);
    }
}
```

From the context object passed into the constructor of Main we can get a reference to the request object. We ask the request object for all the header keys and dump them into the console (of course in real life you would do something more sensible with this information).

Stop your *BasicConcepts* project and restart it. In your Eclipse console you should see something like the following list:

```
accept
accept-encoding
accept-language
connection
dnt
host
user-agent
```

We'll dump some of these. Modify your Main()-constructor again and add some more output lines:

```
public Main(WOContext context) {
    super(context);
    for (String aKey : context.request().headerKeys()) {
        System.out.println(aKey);
    }
    System.out.println("accept-language = " +
        context.request().headerForKey("accept-languae"));
    System.out.println("user-agent = " +
        context.request().headerForKey("user-agent"));
    System.out.println("host = " +
        context.request().headerForKey("host"));
}
```

Here is what you get:

```
accept-language = null
user-agent = Mozilla/5.0 (Macintosh; Intel Mac OS X 10_8) AppleWebKit/536.25 (KHTML,
like Gecko) Version/6.0 Safari/536.25
host = 127.0.0.1:49649
```

Accessing the request is mostly of interest when we need access to the request headers. Part of those headers are cookies, which we will cover in a separate chapter towards the end of this book.

6.3   The classes WOResponse and ERXResponse

ERXResponse is the Wonder extension of the original WebObjects WOResponse. A response sent back to the browser actually consists of two parts a) the actual html content and b) some header information for the http protocol. Normally you have nothing much to do with generating the response. The framework will handle everything. However there are cases where it makes a lot of sense to manipulate the generation of the response directly. We will see a bit later how a response is generated, but for a start we can already have a look at some methods of WOResponse.

You can set the http status code with a call to setStatus(int aStatus) or get it back with status(). There is a method to completely set the contents of the response setContent(NSData someData). A call to appendContentData(NSData someData) and a hand full of similarly named methods for appending strings or html fragments allows you to append data to an already populated response object. You can also set an input stream as the source for the response. This allows for streaming downloads.

There are methods for setting (and getting) response headers and setting other http properties like content encoding or caching instructions for the browser. The framework handles all of this automatically for you.

So, when would you need to handle the response yourself? One typical case is the download of some binary file like a picture or PDF file. This is particularly important in cases where the file does not exist but is generated upon a request from the user. You may have to generate a graphic in response to a query or you want to create a nice looking PDF invoice that is then automatically downloaded to the user.

6.4   The classes WOContext and ERXWOContext

During a full request response loop cycle several objects take part in processing. First there are the ERXRequest and the ERXResponse objects but there are other objects involved as well. Whenever a request is made to a Wonder application the application creates an ERXWOContext object. This context serves as a kind of grab bag that holds all things together for one request response cycle. The framework passes this context object around during processing. Most classes provide a context()-Method to return the current context object. When you look up the documentation for the class WOContext you'll find that there are well over a dozen methods. For our purpose the two most important ones are response() and request(). Those return the respective response and request objects. Again, like above, ERXWOContext is a Wonder extension of the original WebObjects class WOContext.

7 Application, Session, and Component Classes

In the previous chapter we have seen how a Wonder application is connected to the world and what classes and objects help in communication between application and the outside. In this chapter we will learn what classes and objects make up a Wonder application.

7.1 The Application class ERXApplication

Every Wonder application is itself an instance of ERXApplication. ERXApplication is an extension to WOApplication. ERXApplication provides the application-wide infrastructure for a running Wonder application.

The primary task for the application object is the handling of the complete request response cycle. The application coordinates the processing of the request and the generation of the response. There are many other tasks that the application is responsible for. ERXApplication provides mechanisms for global error handling, it manages sessions, it has hooks for debugging support, and a ton of other useful things.

When you create a new Wonder application project you automatically get an Application.java file that contains a class *Application*. This class extends ERXApplication. Let's have a look at it:

```java
package your.app;

import er.extensions.appserver.ERXApplication;

public class Application extends ERXApplication {

    public static void main(String[] argv) {
        ERXApplication.main(argv, Application.class);
    }

    public Application() {
        ERXApplication.log.info("Welcome to " + name() + " !");
        /* ** put your initialization code in here ** */
        setAllowsConcurrentRequestHandling(true);
    }
}
```

There is actually not much to see. We have the most minimalistic main()-method a java application needs. This main()-method immediately calls the static main()-method of ERXApplication, thus handing over control to the framework. Eventually inside the framework the application object will be created. At that moment the java runtime environment will call the default constructor Application(). Basically the only thing this constructor does is telling the world that the application is now up.

It is very common to have your own specific initialization code and very often you also need some instance variables and helper methods for your application. You also often want to override or augment request response loop methods or other infrastructure methods the frameworks provide. Therefore each new project receives a ready-made *Application* class for you to customize. This goes so far that the frameworks expect there to be a class called *Application*. You can of course use a different name for your application class but then you would have to tell the framework about it. Sticking with the given default is by far the most common option.

Throughout your application you can get access to the application object via the static method application().

Typical code would then look something like this:

```
Application application = (Application)Application.application();
```

The static method returns an object of type ERXApplication. You must typecast this to *Application* to get access to your instance variables and methods.

7.1.1 Playing with the application class

Go back to your *BasicConcepts* project and open the file *Application.java*. We are going to put a counter into it that counts, how many times the main page is being accessed during the lifetime of the application.

Put an instance variable called *mainPageCounter* with data type int into your *Application* class. Make it private and provide a standard public get-method. We do not need a setter but we provide a simple method to increment the counter. Initialize the counter variable in the application constructor.

Your *Application* class should now look something like this (the code additions are marked in bold):

```
package your.app;

import er.extensions.appserver.ERXApplication;

public class Application extends ERXApplication {

    private int mainPageCounter;

    public static void main(String[] argv) {
        ERXApplication.main(argv, Application.class);
    }

    public Application() {
        ERXApplication.log.info("Welcome to " + name() + " !");
        /* ** put your initialization code in here ** */
        setAllowsConcurrentRequestHandling(true);

        mainPageCounter = 0;
    }

    public int mainPageCounter() {
        return mainPageCounter;
    }

    public void incrementMainPageCounter() {
        mainPageCounter++;
    }
}
```

Edit your *Main.java* file, so that the constructor increments the *mainPageCounter* variable in the application object. You can leave the existing code we used to test key value coding and the request headers in, or you can clean up things a bit. That's what I have done. Here is my *Main.java* (new things marked in bold):

```
package your.app.components;

import your.app.Application;
import com.webobjects.appserver.WOContext;
import er.extensions.components.ERXComponent;

public class Main extends ERXComponent {

    public Main(WOContext context) {
        super(context);
        Application application =
            (Application)Application.application();
        application.incrementMainPageCounter();
    }

    public Welcome sayHi() {
        Welcome nextPage = pageWithName(Welcome.class);
        return nextPage;
    }
}
```

It would be really nice to display the current count. Let's clean up the Main component and add a WOString to display that value.

The file *Main.html*

```
<?xml version="1.0" encoding="UTF-8"?>
<!DOCTYPE html PUBLIC "-//W3C//DTD XHTML 1.1//EN"
    "http://www.w3.org/TR/xhtml11/DTD/xhtml11.dtd">

<html xmlns="http://www.w3.org/1999/xhtml" xml:lang="en">
<head>
    <meta http-equiv="Content-Type" content="text/html; charset=utf-8"/>
    <title>My Greeting to the World</title>
</head>
<body>
    <h1>Wonder is Greeting The World</h1>
    <p>The main page has been created
        <webobject name = "maincount" /> times</p>
    <webobject name = "hi">Say Hi</webobject>
</body>
</html>
```

And the bindings in *Main.wod*

```
hi : WOHyperlink {
    action = sayHi;
}
```

```
maincount : WOString {
    value = application.mainPageCounter;
}
```

That's it.

Run the application and play around with it. Notice that the count is incremented only when a new main page is created, not when you navigate to the welcome page and then return to the main page with the browser's back button. Do the following:

- Open a new window or tab and copy/paste the application's URL into the address bar.

- Close all browser windows but don't stop the application!

- Open a browser window and again paste the URL.

The application maintains the count and displays it properly on the main page.

7.2   The Session class ERXSession

One of the big issues for any web application is preserving state. The http protocol is stateless. Every request from a browser to a server is (technically) completely independent of all other requests before. Thus a webserver has no idea that one request might be related to a response sent back due to an earlier request. For a functioning application however, it is a must that requests and responses can be related. This is where so-called sessions come into play.

When a user sends the first request to a web application, the application must somehow try to remember the response it sends back and must be able to recognize a later request and relate it to those earlier requests and answers. For such a scheme to work, there need to be two things a) local storage in the application where some context is being kept, and b) some sort of data going to the requester that comes back to the server with the next request. This logical chaining of request, response, next request, next response, etc. is called **establishing a session**.

Oftentimes applications store the whole session context data inside a cookie that is sent back with the response. Usually that cookie will be included with the next request. Receiving such a cookie allows the application to relate requests and responses, thus establishing the session. Cookies have limitations in what and how much data they can support. The required amount of session storage may exceed the amount of data a cookie can transport. Additionally, a user can reject cookies, and thus session information gets lost. Also cookies are simple texts; they can be manipulated easily.

All of these issues are taken care of by Wonder. Wonder applications support arbitrary sessions out-of-the-box. You, the programmer, have nothing to do to make sessions work. However there are some points to consider.

Not every application needs a session in any case. Imagine a request from a user to list some articles from a database. The application compiles the list and sends it back. Finito, done, nothing more required. No need to have a session here.

Imagine on the other hand a rather complex application with lots of interaction and inter-related requests. Here sessions are absolutely mandatory. Wonder provides for both types of application the proper mechanism. Session-less applications can be done with so-called direct actions. There is a full chapter dedicated to direct actions starting on page 223.

As the session is such an important concept and you often need to work with it, each Wonder project contains a ready-made *Session* class. Session extends ERXSession which in turn extends WOSession. Here is the default code for the *Session* class:

```
package your.app;

import er.extensions.appserver.ERXSession;

public class Session extends ERXSession {
    private static final long serialVersionUID = 1L;

    public Session() {
    }
}
```

There is nothing in there, just an empty default constructor.

When you need access to your session object, you can use the following method call:

```
Session session = (Session)session();
```

All your controller classes inherit the session() method from ERXComponent. This method returns an ERXSession object that you need to cast to your *Session* class.

7.2.1 Session mechanics in Wonder

Let's explore how sessions work. We'll start with the standard case. Look at our *BasicConcepts* application by running it. One of the last lines in the console in Eclipse shows the front-door URL. It is called **front-door** *URL*, because this is the URL you use to get started using the application. When you use this URL, you have not yet been interacting with the application and thus there is no session available for you. Here is a typical front-door URL you get when you run the application right from Eclipse *http://127.0.0.1:49816/cgi-bin/WebObjects/BasicConcepts.woa*

The application will create a new *Session* object and generate a unique id that allows it to identify each session. This id is called the **session id**.

What can a user do from this point on in the application to stay inside the session? There are actually only two things. A user can click a hyperlink to navigate to a different page or submit some data he has entered into a form. Both cases must happen in the context of a session.

Look at the page the application sent back to the browser in response to the user knocking at the front door. In the lower part of the screen shot you see the raw html code.

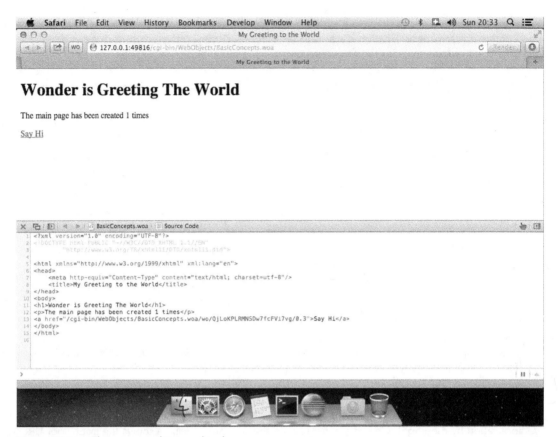

Picture 7-1   The page and its raw html source

See that weird looking href URL that has been generated for the hyperlink?

/cgi-bin/WebObjects/BasicConcepts.woa/wo/QjLoKPLRMNSDw7fcFVi7vg/0.3

The left part up to *woa* is the same as the front door URL. Then, on the right side, follows the generated session id QjLoKPLRMNSDw7fcFVi7vg. This session id is a standard part of any URL in a Wonder application. Whenever the user clicks the hyperlink, the session id will be sent to the application. The request object and the application object together will find the session object with this session id and restore it from an internal session store.

This is the default mechanism in Wonder: Session id is part of the generated URLs in the response.

7.2.2 Session id with cookies

You can change the default so that the session id will be stored in a cookie. This makes the URLs cleaner looking (some people prefer it that way).

Let's test this right away.

Edit your default session constructor by adding two lines of code.

```
package your.app;
```

```
import er.extensions.appserver.ERXSession;

public class Session extends ERXSession {
    private static final long serialVersionUID = 1L;

    public Session() {
        super();

        setStoresIDsInCookies(true);
        setStoresIDsInURLs(false);
    }
}
```

Stop the application, save the edited *Session.java*, and restart the application. From the outside there should be no difference. The hyperlink works as before. But look at the generated raw html:

Picture 7-2   No session id in generated URL

The generated URL for the hyperlink has no session id anymore. Check the cookies and you'll find one cookie with name ***wosid*** (short for Wonder session id) that contains the session id.

We can look at the cookies that our browser has received. Yup, there it is!

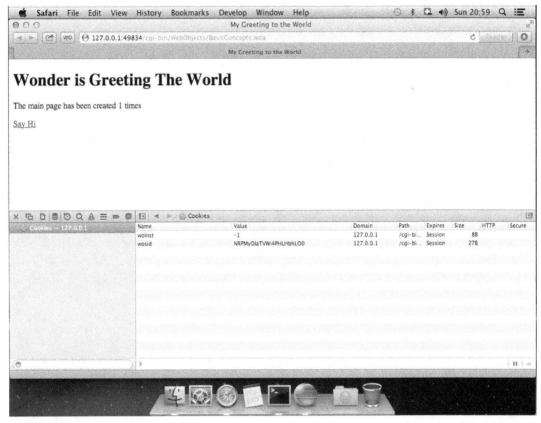

Picture 7-3   Session id in cookie

7.2.3 Lifetime of a session

A session is created every time the front door URL is requested. You can imagine that a busy application with many users might have to deal with many sessions at a time. This can put quite a load on the application. Each session object can contain a lot of data and therefore require a lot of storage and processing. Another problem with any web application is that the application per default does not get any notification when a user closes a browser window or simply just walks away from his computer. So all the sessions hang around unused and block resources. Wonder framework limits the lifetime of an idle session. The default is 60 minutes. Whenever a session has not been touched for this many minutes, the session is considered dead, and will be removed. You can set this **session timeout** application wide for all sessions, and you can adjust the timeout value for each session individually.

Setting the default session timeout is best done in the *Application* constructor. When that constructor executes you can be sure that no session exists.

Put the following line in the constructor of *Application*:

```
setSessionTimeOut(5 * 60);
```

The method setSessionTimeOut() needs the timeout period in seconds. The given example will therefore ensure that any session can be idle for 5 minutes max. After that the session object will be removed. We can test this by setting the timeout to 1 minute. Edit the call to setSessionTimeOut() in the *Application* constructor accordingly. Restart your *BasicConcepts* application and immediately click the hyperlink. Everything is as it should be. Use the browser's back button to go back to the main page. Now wait for a bit over a minute and only then click the hyperlink again. During this one minute the session has been idle. As the session timeout is set to 1 minute we expect the session to be cleared from the application. What happens when you now click the hyperlink?

Picture 7-4   Session timeout

You can terminate a session at any time. This is useful when you want to provide some kind of logout to a user. Here is how this works.

ERXSession has a terminate() method that is called to terminate a session. When a session timeout occurs, the framework will call this method. We can also call terminate(). It is often a good idea to override terminate() in your *Session* class. This allows for cleanup when a session is about to terminate.

Edit your Session.java file and add the following method:

```
@Override
public void terminate() {
```

```
    System.out.println("Session terminating...");
    super.terminate();
}
```

While still having a relatively short session timeout, stop and restart the application, and observe what happens when the session timeout occurs. The terminate() method is automatically called and the message "Session terminating..." is shown in your Eclipse console.

For the next test we remove the code that shortens the session lifetime to one minute (you remember, we have done this in the application constructor) and add a WOHyperlink to the *Main* page.

Main.html

```
<?xml version="1.0" encoding="UTF-8"?>
<!DOCTYPE html PUBLIC "-//W3C//DTD XHTML 1.1//EN"
    "http://www.w3.org/TR/xhtml11/DTD/xhtml11.dtd">

<html xmlns="http://www.w3.org/1999/xhtml" xml:lang="en">
<head>
    <meta http-equiv="Content-Type" content="text/html; charset=utf-8"/>
    <title>My Greeting to the World</title>
</head>
<body>
    <h1>Wonder is Greeting The World</h1>
    <p>The main page has been created <webobject name = "maincount" /> times</p>
    <webobject name = "hi">Say Hi</webobject><br />
    <webobject name = "logout">logout</webobject>
</body>
</html>
```

Main.wod

```
hi : WOHyperlink {
    action = sayHi;
}

logout : WOHyperlink {
    action = logout;
}

maincount : WOString {
    value = application.mainPageCounter;
}
```

We also need to add a logout() method to the *Main* class. Add the following method:

```
public Main logout() {
    session().terminate();
    Main nextPage = pageWithName(Main.class);
    return nextPage;
}
```

Run the application (stop it if it is still running). You see your logout hyperlink on the *Main* page. Click it and observe in the Eclipse console that your session terminates. Now click "Sys Hi". You immediately get the session timeout error message.

Note

The session will not terminate immediately when you call terminate(). *It will finish the current request/response loop and terminate after being put to* sleep().

7.3   The view/controller combo WOComponent **and the controller class** ERXComponent

Objects of type ERXComponent are responsible for generating the user interface. We have been using classes derived from ERXComponent so far without really caring about details.

7.3.1 What is a (WO)component?

The word WOComponent is used for different things. WOComponent is a java class, but we developers sometimes speak of a WebObjects component, or WOComponent, or just component, when we actually mean the whole package consisting of an object, the template, and bindings. A component is an object that can generate a complete html response or just some part of it. Components can be nested in a tree-like structure. This means a component may have child components. A component consists of several parts, which we will see in the following sections.

7.3.2 Layout of a component

Look at the project layout in Eclipse and compare that with the file system view:

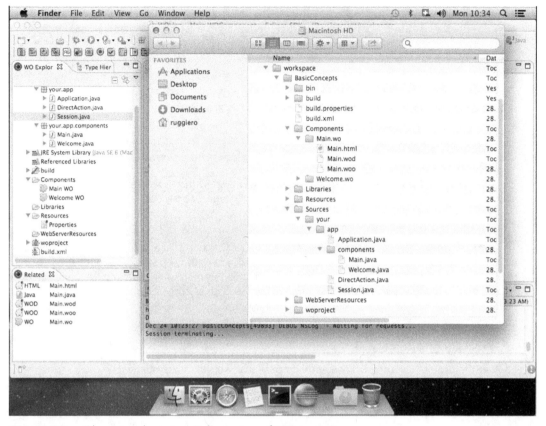

Picture 7-5   File system layout vs. Eclipse view of WOComponent

In Eclipse, under Components, you have the two components Main WO and Welcome WO. In the file system, you see that these are actually folders called Main.wo and Welcome.wo with three files each inside. In Main.wo you see Main.html, Main.wod, and Main.woo. Welcome.wo contains an analogous set of files. Companion to the component folder is a java source file with the same name. For Main WO component folder this is Main.java.

In Model-View-Controller lingo, Main.wo with its contents corresponds to the view part and Main.java implements the controller part. We simply call this a *component* or *WebObjects Component* or short WOComponent.

A WOComponent is responsible to generate the user interface. The controller class is ERXComponent extending the WebObjects class WOComponent.

You do not instantiate ERXComponent objects directly. You need to create a subclass of ERXComponent. WOLips does this for you when you chose *Create new* WOComponent either from the File menu or from the context menu in your project.

There are a couple of important methods a component controller has. The single most important one is pageWithName(). This method is used to create new component objects. Simply calling new to create a new object is not enough. As a WOComponent consists of several files and is deeply embedded into the infrastructure of the frameworks, a much more complex initialization is needed than a simple call to the constructor. The method pageWithName() accomplishes this. We have already used this method when we created the Welcome page upon acting on the "Say Hi" hyperlink.

7.3.3 Creating a new component object

The following code shows you the typical sequence when you need to create a new page (WOComponent).

```
public Welcome sayHi() {
    // create the new page component
    Welcome nextPage = pageWithName(Welcome.class);

    // maybe set some values by calling appropriate setter methods
    nextPage.setGreeting("Hello");

    // return the component so that the framework takes over control.
    // The framework will then ask the Welcome object to do its job
    return nextPage;
}
```

First you create a new component object by calling pageWithName(). There are two variants of this method. One takes the name of a component, a string, as parameter. This method returns a WOComponent that must then be cast to your type. ERXComponent provides a newer variant that takes a Class object as parameter. This method returns an object you do not have to cast anymore. You will find both variants used in the literature as well as in sample code and even in the source code for the Wonder frameworks. Oftentimes you find the name for the new component hardcoded as a string. This is pretty bad because any typo will result in a runtime crash of your application. When taking the name from the class reference, the compiler can catch any miss-spelling before the application is running.

Here are the three styles you may find. The 3rd form is the preferred one.

```
// Style 1, name is hardcoded (oldest, most ugly way)
Welcome nextPage = (Welcome)pageWithName( "Welcome" );

// Style 2, compile time check on the name possible
Welcome nextPage = (Welcome)pageWithName( Welcome.class.getName() );

// Style 3, the preferred one
Welcome nextPage = pageWithName( Welcome.class );
```

As you now have a standard java object your can call any set-method to initialize your component and set it up properly. When your component object is ready you hand it over to the framework. The framework will then ask the component object to do whatever it is supposed to do (namely generate the necessary html code).

7.3.4 The view part of a component

The view part of a component resides inside the html file. This file contains standard html code as well as inclusions of other components and dynamic elements. Both components and dynamic elements generate html fragments at runtime. For our purpose we can simply say, a dynamic element is similar to a component. The main difference lies in their internal structure and implementation optimization. In the context of this book a component is something that you create whereas a dynamic element is something ready made and available in the frameworks. There is no difference in their usage.

Albeit originally WebObjects, as its name implies, was created to generate html responses and thus the template file is supposed to contain html code, one can actually put anything into the template. So instead of generating html, the result could be pure xml or just plain text or anything else. The ERExcelLook and ExcelGenerator frameworks in Wonder for instance use this method to generate real Microsoft Excel files. With the ERPDFGeneration framework you can generate PDF files.

When you want to include a component or dynamic element into your template you do this with a special tag: <webobject>. We have already used this several times. Here are some examples:

Tag	Description
<webobject name = "hi">Say ↵ Hi</webobject>	we used this to include a WOHyperlink dynamic element
<webobject name = "maincount" />	this created a WOString dynamic element for the display of a counter variable

Part of the view is the bindings file with extension .wod. The bindings file is used to describe exactly what those <webobject> things are. We need to tell the framework not only what kind of element we use, but in many cases, we need to provide some data to the element. For a WOString we need to tell it where to get the value from for display, a WOHyperlink needs to know which action must be triggered when the hyperlink is clicked, and so on.

The classic way to specify what a webobject tag needs is the use of the bindings file. Each webobject tag must have a name. This name is referenced in the bindings file. For the two examples above we have

```
hi : WOHyperlink {
    action = sayHi;
}

maincount : WOString {
    value = application.mainPageCounter;
}
```

Wonder allows a more compact way for specifying this information. You can use a mechanism called inline-bindings. Instead of specifying element type and bindings in the .wod file, Wonder has a special kind of tags.

Compare the classic way with the new Wonder way:

Classic Bindings	New Wonder style
<webobject name = "hi">Say Hi</webobject>	<wo:hyperlink action = "$sayHi">Say Hi</wo:hyperlink>
<webobject name = "maincount" />	<wo:string value = "$application.mainPageCounter" />

When using the <webobject> tag, you must use the bindings file. The shortened <wo:...> tag allows inline bindings. No need for the bindings file. Both styles have their pros and cons. The inline style may become confusing when more than one or two bindings need to be given, whereas in simple cases, inline style can make your code easier to read. Wonder is smart enough that you can mix and match both styles as you want. Use whichever style makes the most sense for any given element you want to include in your template. In this book we will mostly use the classic style, but sometimes when it is convenient you might encounter inline bindings style. I recommend you look up inline bindings in the WOCommunity wiki.

7.3.5 Other parts of a component

There are two more parts to a component. If you look inside Main.wo folder, there is a Main.woo file. This is a text file that is mostly empty. You do not have to be concerned with it for the moment.

```
{
    "WebObjects Release" = "WebObjects 5.0";
    encoding = "UTF-8";
}
```

When you have weird characters showing in your html template, like umlauts not displaying correctly, you want to verify that the text encoding specified in the .woo file matches the one for your template file. Sometimes when you copy a file from a different platform the resulting file encoding may not match the .woo file entry. I strongly recommend using utf-8 character encoding throughout everything from the database to your Eclipse workbench to all project text files.

There is however one important case where the .woo file is heavily used. When using objects of class WODisplayGroup the display group specification will go into the .woo file. Display groups will be covered in their own chapter towards the end of this book.

Yet another file might be part of a component. This file resides in the Components folder in Eclipse alongside the .wo folder. It has the same name as the component with the extension .api. This .api file usually only exists for components that publicize their instance variables as bindings. We will later on create our own nested components.

8   Flow of control

So far we have simply used Wonder and things magically worked. Now let us look a bit deeper and figure out what is going on behind the curtain.

During processing of one pass through the request-response-loop several messages are being sent to application, session, and component objects. All these messages trigger methods that we may sometimes want to override to customize the processing behavior. In any case it is important for a developer to understand the flow of control and the sequence of method calls

Here is the big picture. We'll dissect it step by step.

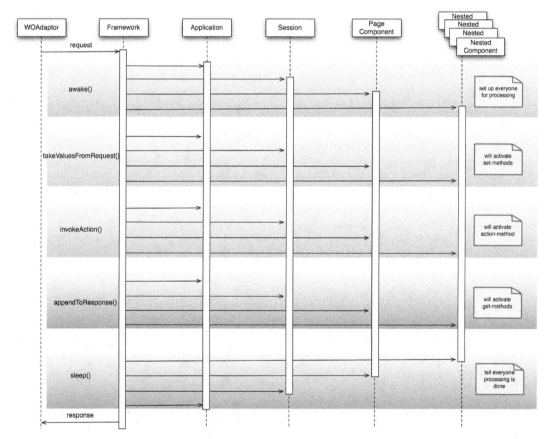

Picture 8-1   Sequence diagram for the simple request-response processing

8.1   awake() and sleep() methods

When the application receives a request coming in from the *WOAdaptor* the following sequence starts:

Flow of control

1 The application object will be woken up

2 The application object either creates a new session or restores an existing one depending on the availability of a session id in the request.

3 The session will be told to get ready for work

4 The session object will then either create a new page component or revive an existing one that should handle the request

5 In any case the page component will be told to get ready

6 The page component passes the get ready message recursively down to all its nested components

This get ready message activates a method that we can override and do whatever we want to prepare for request processing. Here is the signature for this method. It is appropriately called awake():

```
public void awake();
```

Every class starting from the application to the session down to all components can implement this awake() method. The basic idea is that any object can prepare for request processing.

When the whole request processing has been done, every object that was woken up at the beginning, is now put to sleep. This happens in the reverse order from components up to session and application. There is also a method for this with a nice name:

```
public void sleep();
```

We can easily see this in action. Implement the following two methods in the three classes Application, Session, and Main. Here is the code that goes into the Main class.

```
public void awake() {
    super.awake();
    System.out.println("Main awake()");
}

public void sleep() {
    super.sleep();
    System.out.println("Main sleep()");
}
```

Adapt the System.out.println() text accordingly for the other classes, so that you can see which object gets the awake and sleep call. Run your application and observe the output in the console window.

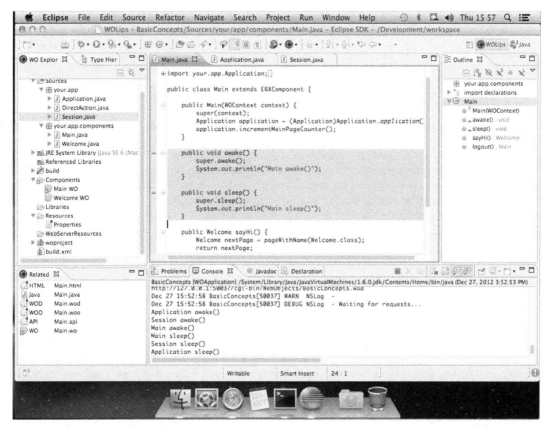

Picture 8-2   Awake and Sleep calls

awake() and sleep() are for preparing for request processing and cleaning up afterwards, but what happens in between? What happens during request processing?

8.2   Processing the request

This is where the real fun is. Here we have the following three methods:

```
public void takeValuesFromRequest(WORequest aRequest, WOContext aContext);

public WOActionResults invokeAction(WORequest aRequest, WOContext aContext);

public void appendToResponse(WORespone aRespone, WOContext aContext);
```

These three methods correspond to three distinct phases in processing.

8.2.1 Phase 1, getting input data from the request

The call to takeValuesFromRequest() is the first phase of the actual processing. This method will only be activated when there is form data available, when a form has been submitted. Each object receiving this message extracts from the request only the data it is interested in. The values are put into the object's instance variables by activating the respective setter methods.

When no form has been sent, this phase will not happen.

We will go into form data details a bit later.

8.2.2 Phase 2, acting upon the request, processing the data

Only after all involved objects had the chance to set their instance variables, the second phase of the request processing starts. Oftentimes the user has clicked a hyperlink or a submit button on a page. As we already have seen this results in an action method being activated. The message invokeAction() is now sent to all objects. Each object will check if it is responsible for taking action. Exactly one object will finally react and tell the calling framework, "hey, it's me over here". The framework will then call the appropriate action method. Of course this search for an acting object is only performed when there is an action click in the request.

When no action has been requested, e.g. when the front door URL has been used, there is no action to take. So this phase will be skipped.

8.2.3 Phase 3, generating the response

Only after the action method has been activated, the third phase starts. Now the response is to be assembled. For this to happen, the framework sends the appendToResponse() message from application down to all involved objects. Each object (usually a component) will add its particular part to the response. So a WOString object will just add some text to the html response, whereas a WOHyperlink will generate the respective <a href...> html snippet. Each object adds just what it is responsible for. At the end, the application sends the now fully assembled response back to the *WOAdaptor* for delivery to the user.

This phase three, generating the response, will always be executed (it would not make sense otherwise).

From the signature of the three methods you see, that each method takes the current context object as the second input parameter. The first two methods receive the current request object and the third one the current response object as the first parameter. Request and response could be found from the context object. It is not clear why those parameters are being passed in in addition to the context object, but that is the way it is.

One very important point here is, that every phase is completely finished before the next phase starts. So during action processing, the component implementing the action method can be sure that all instance variables have been properly set. And when appendToResponse() is called every (action) processing has been performed. This staging ensures that all instance variables are always in a consistent state.

8.3   Handling of navigation

The basic flow of control must be extended a bit when navigation comes into play. The following picture will show what happens when the request results in navigation to a new component. For not overloading the picture, Application and Session have been left out of the drawing. Of course they do get all the messages as well.

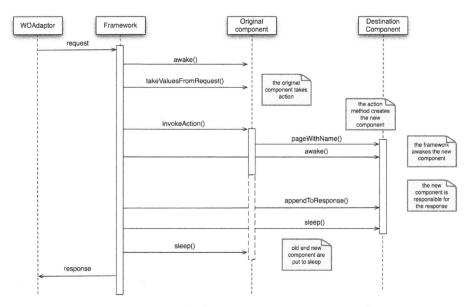

Picture 8-3   Sequence Diagram for the Request-Response-Loop with Navigation

From this diagram, you can see that a component is often involved in two passes through the request-response-loop. The first time, it generates the response that includes a navigation action element (a hyperlink or a submit button for a form). During the following request processing, this component will be told to invokeAction(). The action method creates the destination page by calling pageWithName(). This activates the constructor for the new page. At that time, the new page is not yet part of the request processing. When the destination page has been fully created, the framework will call awake() on it. When the framework finally sends the appendToResponse() message, the new page will receive it. Now the destination page generates the response, which is exactly what the user intended, when he clicked the navigation element. Both the original page, and the destination page, will then get the sleep() message.

Let's see this in action. You probably still have the awake() and sleep() methods in your Application, Session, and Main class.

Add the following two methods to your Main class:

```java
public WOActionResults invokeAction(WORequest request, WOContext context) {
    System.out.println("Main invokeAction()");
    return super.invokeAction(request, context);
}

public void appendToResponse(WOResponse response, WOContext context) {
    System.out.println("Main appendToResponse()");
    super.appendToResponse(response, context);
}
```

Add similar awake(), sleep(), and appendToResponse() methods to your Welcome class in file Welcome.java. Also put a log output line into the constructor.

```
public Welcome(WOContext context) {
    super(context);
    System.out.println("Welcome constructor()");
}

public void awake() {
    super.awake();
    System.out.println("Welcome awake()");
}

public void sleep() {
    super.sleep();
    System.out.println("Welcome sleep()");
}

public void appendToResponse(WOResponse response, WOContext context) {
    System.out.println("Welcome appendToResponse()");
    super.appendToResponse(response, context);
}
```

Restart the *BasicConcepts* application and notice the sequence of calls from the output you get in the Eclipse console view.

Picture 8-4   First part of sequence, before clicking the navigation link.

Click the *Say Hi* link and check what happens now.

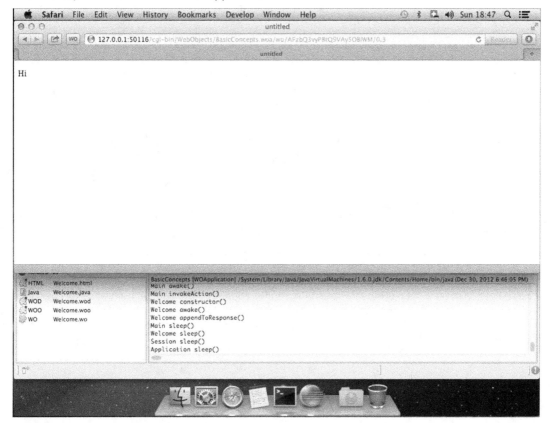

Picture 8-5   Call sequence with navigation

It is obvious from the output that both components, Main and Welcome, are involved.

8.4   The page cache and backtracking

For the navigation to work, the application must store the page object that generated a response somewhere, because this object needs to be around the next time when a request comes in. It is this object that will eventually respond to invokeAction().

Something else can happen. You know, there is that back button in your browser that allows the user to go back to a previous page. This back button is completely local to the browser; your Wonder application will not be notified that the user went back. This is called backtracking and is a problem for every web application, no matter what environment is used.

Play again with the *BasicConcepts* application. When you navigate to the Welcome page, this page is generating the response and of course this page is shown in the browser window. What happens when the user goes back to the Main page by clicking the back button? The browser will gladly display the previous page from its local internal cache. Great, but now try to imagine what happens when the user clicks the *Say Hi* hyperlink again. The browser sends a nice request to the application, telling it to navigate from the Main page to the Welcome page. But it is the Welcome page object, that is current (at least that is what your application knows), and that Welcome page does not have a navigation method. Will your application be in trouble? Of course not! So how does the application do it?

Remember? We already mentioned the class WOContext once. Look at the constructor of a component. A WOContext object is passed to it. The application maintains a context for each pass through the request-response-loop. Part of this context are the two page components that are active, the previous component and the destination component. The application caches the last 30 contexts per session. 30 is the default number and can be changed in your application constructor. Simply add a call to setPageCacheSize(numberOfPages).

Each context has its own id that ends up being part of the URL. Consider again the above example with the user going back to the Main page and clicking Say Hi again. From the URL that is sent to the server, the session realizes that a previous context was responsible for generating the page that the user clicked the link, than what the application thinks is shown in the browser. The session can go back through its cache and find the correct context. The pages stored in that context of course can then react properly to the invokeAction() message. This cache is per session and is called page cache despite its content being context, not individual pages.

After a while in a real application, where many pages are being created and the user navigates from one to the next, the page cache will eventually fill up. In that case, the oldest cached context is thrown away. But what happens when the user goes back further? The session will not find the required context in its page cache and thus cannot continue. The user will get an error message. To show this effect, set the page cache size for the *BasicConcepts* application to 1. Restart the application, click Say Hi, then use the browser back button to go back to the Main page and click Say Hi again.

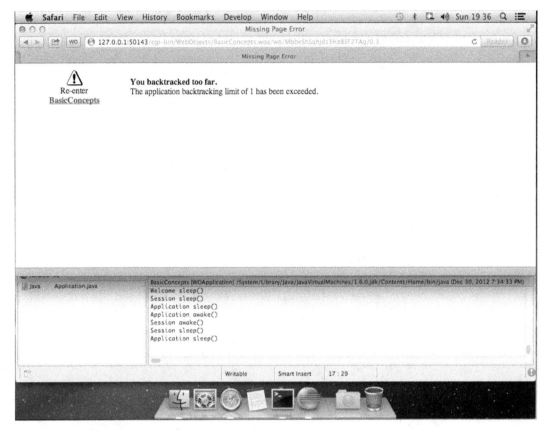

Picture 8-6   Backtracked too far error

The Main page is the first one that generates a response. Its context gets put into the page cache. The Welcome page is the second page and it also gets into the page cache. As we have set the cache size to 1, the context for the Main page is pushed out to make room for that second context. When you backtrack to Main (remember, the browser retrieves the Main page from its internal cache without requesting it from the server) and click Say Hi again, the session cannot find the corresponding context in the page cache – boom!

The default cache size of 30 is a good compromise. It is probably not so common that a user steps back 30 pages; so this should be sufficient. However, the page cache requires memory space. When your application has to handle many concurrent users (many concurrent sessions) and your components are complex and large objects, you may want to reduce the cache size (or add more memory to the server machine).

9 Advanced Collection Classes in Wonder

As WebObjects, the underlying framework to Wonder, is actually older than the Java language, it implements special collection classes that are similar, but not identical, to what a Java programmer is used to work with. When working with Wonder, you as a programmer will be confronted with these classes all the time. They are so important that they warrant their own chapter in this book.

9.1 Array-like classes NSArray and NSMutableArray

NSArray implements an ordered collection of objects. An NSArray is immutable. Once it is created, you cannot change its size nor can you replace referenced objects.

NSMutableArray is an extension of NSArray and adds the ability to change the size of the array at any time. You can replace objects, remove objects from the array and you can add and insert objects as you like.

An NSMutableArray is in many ways similar to a java.util.Vector. There is no immutable equivalent to NSArray available out-of-the-box in Java. However NSArray and NSMutableArray implement the standard Java collection interfaces.

Both classes support templates.

9.2 Playing with NSArray and NSMutableArray

Let's first crate an NSArray of Strings. There are various constructors available. One way to create an NSArray is to supply a plain object array.

```
NSArray<String> strings =
    new NSArray<String>( new String[]{"one", "two", "three"} );
```

You can ask for the number of elements.

```
int elementCount = strings.count();
```

You can get the n-th element (in our case allowed values are 0, 1, 2)

```
String aString = strings.objectAt(2); // this would return the string "three"
```

Of course you could also use the get() method that is specified by the java.util.List interface

```
String aString = strings.get(2);      // also returns the string "three"
```

You can ask for a java.util.Enumerator or a java.util.ListIterator

```
Enumeration enu = strings.objectEnumerator();
while (enu.hasMoreElements()) {
    String aString = enu.nextElement();
    // ... do whatever you want with aString
}
```

Both NSArray and NSMutableArray provide a reverse enumerator, strings.reverseObjectEnumerator(). This allows you to step through an NSArray from last to first element.

NSMutableArray is an extension of NSArray and thus supports the same functionality. Additionally you can add, insert, and remove objects.

You can create a NSMutableArray in the same way as an NSArray. You can also start with an empty NSMutableArray and add objects to it. Or you can take an NSArray and create an NSMutableArray from it. Let's build upon the previous examples.

Create an NSMutableArray from an NSArray:

```
NSMutableArray<String> mutableStrings = new NSMutableArray<String>(strings);
```

Add one more element

```
mutableStrings.add("four");
```

Insert an object

```
mutableStrings.insertObjectAtIndex("two and a half", 2);
```

This will put the new object into position 2 (the 3rd element in the array. All objects from position 2 up will be moved one position higher. Let's output that array. Because NS(Mutable)Array implements the java.lang.Iterable interface, we can use the extended for-loop:

```
for (String aString : mutableStrings) {
    System.out.println(aString);
}
```

9.3   HashMap-like classes NSDictionary **and** NSMutableDictionary

As with NSArray and NSMutableArray, there are two classes for dictionaries, an immutable and a mutable one. NSMutableDictionary is an extension of NSDictionary.

NSDictionary is similar to a Java HashMap or Hashtable. It stores objects associated with a key. The key is typically a string, but could be almost any type of object. Remember the chapter about key-value-coding? NSDictionary is the prototype for key-value-coding. Each entry in a dictionary is the association of a key and a value. The key identifies the value. Therefore the keys in a dictionary are unique.

Both classes implement the java.util.Map interface and support templates.

9.4   Playing with NSDictionary and NSMutableDictionary

Let's first create an empty NSMutableDictionary. For our purpose it should use strings for keys and the objects we want to put into the dictionary should be of type java.math.BigInteger.

```
NSMutableDictionary<String, BigInteger> largeNumbers =
    new NSMutableDictionary<String, BigInteger>();
```

Let's put some potentially big numbers into the dictionary.

```
largeNumbers.setObjectForKey(new BigInteger("100", "one hundred");
largeNumbers.setObjectForKey(new BigInteger("2000", "two thousand");
largeNumbers.setObjectForKey(new BigInteger("3000000", "three million");
largeNumbers.setObjectForKey(new BigInteger("4000000000000000", "too much");
```

We can ask how many entries there are in a dictionary:

```
int thatMany = largeNumbers.count();
```

We can get any value by specifying its key:

```
BigDecimal value = largeNumbers.get("three million");
```

We can replace a value by using the key of that value to identify the new value:

```
largeNumbers.setObjectForKey(new BigInteger("99999999999999999999",
                             "too much");
```

We can ask for an NSArray of all the keys or all the values:

```
NSArray<String> keys = largeNumbers.allKeys();
NSArray<String> values = largeNumbers.allValues();
```

Advanced Collection Classes in Wonder

We can get a key or a value enumerator:

```
Enumeration keyEnu = largeNumbers.keyEnumerator();
while (keyEnu.hasMoreElements()) {
    BigDecimal aValue = largeNumbers.get( keyEnu.nextElement);
    // … do whatever you need to do with the value
}
```

As has been mentioned above, NS(Mutable)Dictionary is the perfect showcase for key-value-coding. You will see the use of dictionaries in many places throughout all of Wonder, exactly because key-value-coding is such an important concept in Wonder and WebObjects.

10 Repeating and Conditional HTML

Repeating html and conditionally showing and hiding html fragments are important techniques that Wonder helps you a lot with.

10.1 Repeating Data in a Web Page with WORepetiton

Assume you need to show data from a database. Depending on the selection criteria, there can be none, one or many records. The number of records is clearly not known upfront. So we need to be able to repeat things like table rows depending on the data. The WORepetition element is what can do this.

Every programmer uses loop constructions like for(...) or while(...) to iterate over a list of things (usually an array). Such loops also need a loop variable that contains or references the current element per pass through the loop. A WORepetition dynamic element builds the equivalent of a loop. It has two bindings. You must give it a list of objects to loop over, and you must provide it with a loop variable. Let's look at this with an example.

We create a simple class Person. Each person has a first name and a last name. In the constructor of our application we are going to populate an NSArray with some person objects. These persons will then be shown in a table on our Main page, each person in a row.

Here is the code for the Person class.

```
package your.app;

public class Person {

    private String lastName;
    private String firstName;

    public Person(String firstName, String lastName) {
        super();
        this.firstName = firstName;
        this.lastName = lastName;
    }

    public String lastName() {
        return lastName;
    }
    public void setLastName(String lastName) {
        this.lastName = lastName;
    }
    public String firstName() {
        return firstName;
    }
    public void setFirstName(String firstName) {
        this.firstName = firstName;
    }
}
```

A person has a first and a last name. We create a constructor that takes the first and last name as a parameter.

Modify the Application class to look like this:

```
package your.app;

import com.webobjects.foundation.NSMutableArray;
import er.extensions.appserver.ERXApplication;

public class Application extends ERXApplication {

    public static void main(String[] argv) {
        ERXApplication.main(argv, Application.class);
    }

    private NSMutableArray<Person> persons;

    public Application() {
        ERXApplication.log.info("Welcome to " + name() + " !");
        /* ** put your initialization code in here ** */
        setAllowsConcurrentRequestHandling(true);

        persons = new NSMutableArray<Person>();
        persons.add(new Person("Jack", "Smith"));
        persons.add(new Person("Peter", "Pan"));
        persons.add(new Person("Loretta", "Meyers"));
        persons.add(new Person("Patty", "Miller"));
    }

    public NSMutableArray<Person> persons() {
        return persons;
    }
}
```

We have cleaned up things a bit and removed all the code from the previous examples. We added an NSMutableArray instance variable with a getter method. In the constructor we create some persons and add them to the persons array.

Now edit the Main component. We want to display the persons in a table, a table row for each person. The html for this would look something like the following:

```
<table>
    <tr>
        <th>First Name</th>
        <th>Last Name</th>
    </tr>
    <tr>
        <td>...</td>
        <td>...</td>
    </tr>
    ...
    ...
</table>
```

You see, the <tr> tags are repeated, one for each person. Inside the <tr> there are two <td> tags for the first and last name respectively.

Let's make this table dynamic. We need to repeat the whole table row and put the correct values for first and last name into the <td> fields.

Here is the Main component (again, we have cleaned up a bit and removed all the contents from the previous examples)

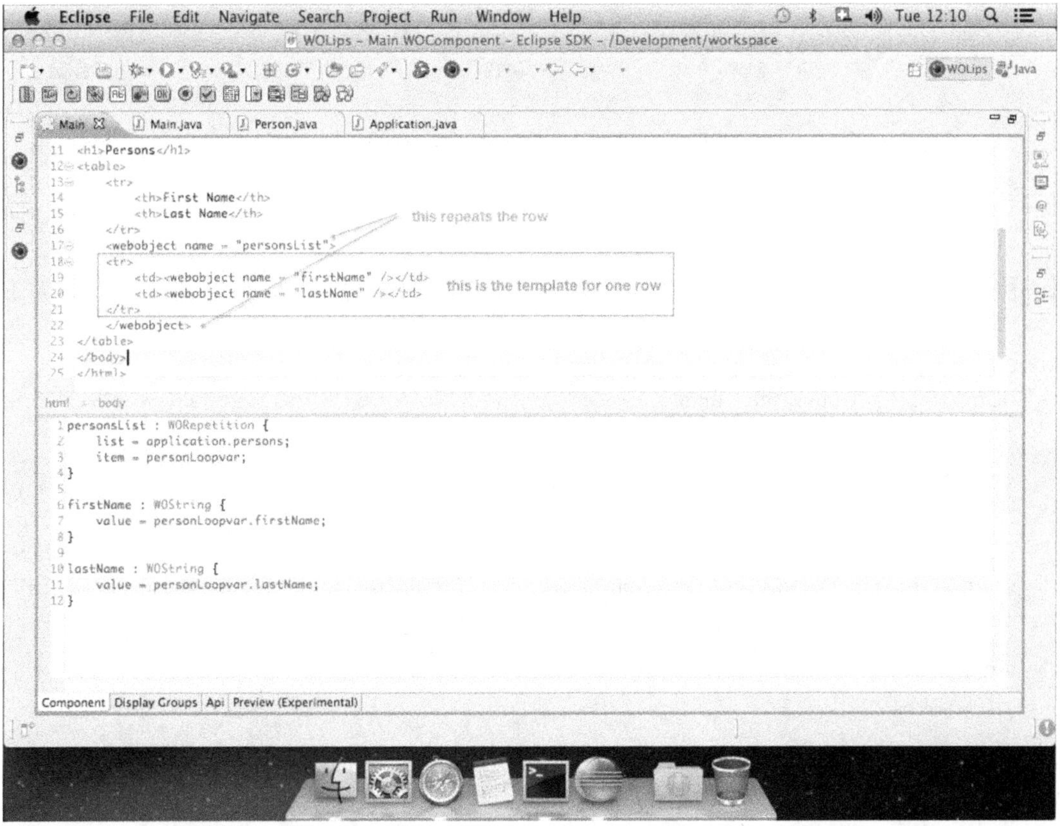

Picture 10-1   Using a WORepetition

Look at the html part first. We have one table row as a template for all rows. It contains dynamic elements for the display of the names. A <webobject> tag with the name personsList wraps the table row template. This element is responsible for repeating the table row as many times as needed.

Let's now see what the bindings are. First there is the wrapper around the table row. This is an object of type WORepetition. A WORepetition is responsible for repeating its contents. It has a list to iterate over (the persons array from the Application object), and a binding for the loop variable. In our case, the loop variable is an instance variable with accessor methods in Main. Here is the code for Main:

```
package your.app.components;

import your.app.Person;
import com.webobjects.appserver.WOContext;
```

```
import er.extensions.components.ERXComponent;

public class Main extends ERXComponent {

    public Main(WOContext context) {
        super(context);
    }

    private Person personLoopvar;

    public Person personLoopvar() {
        return personLoopvar;
    }

    public void setPersonLoopvar(Person personLoopvar) {
        this.personLoopvar = personLoopvar;
    }
}
```

Of course the instance variable used as loop variable must be of the correct type. Here it must be Person.

When the page is rendered, the framework makes sure that the correct number of table rows are being created. During the building process for the table, for each row, the framework will correctly set the value of the loop variable. This allows us to simply bind the WOStrings for first and last name to personLoopvar.firstName and personLoopvar.lastName respectively.

Note

Did you notice? Here is key-value-coding at its best. Person is a plain Java class, nothing to do whatsoever with Wonder, but the framework finds the setter and getter for the instance variables without any problems.

WORepetition has some more interesting bindings.

count

With this binding you can repeat some contents count times without the need of a list. The count and list bindings are mutually exclusive.

index

This binding can be used as a running counter (mind you, the counter starts with 0 up to total counts -1).

There are additional more exotic bindings you can look up yourself in the documentation.

10.2 Conditional HTML

Imagine from the last example what happens, when the list of persons is empty. What would you expect?

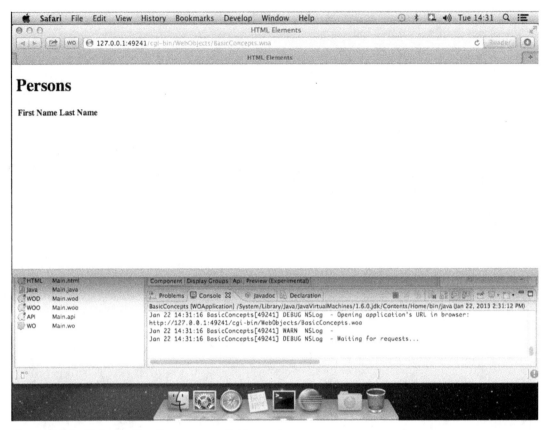

Picture 10-2   Ugly display when persons list is empty

Nothing bad happens, but the resulting page does not look good. We can change this with an element of type WOConditional. As its name implies, it allows us to include or exclude html from the result, depending on a condition.

Here is how to do it.

The html part:

```
<webobject name = "hasNoPersons">        <!-- if there are no persons -->
    <p>There are no persons to show</p>
</webobject>

<webobject name = "hasPersons              <!-- else show the table -->
    <table>
    ...
    ...
    </table>
</webobject>
```

and the bindings:

```
hasNoPersons : WOConditional {
    condition = application.persons.isEmpty;
}
hasPersons : WOConditional {
    condition = application.persons.isEmpty;
    negate = true;
}
```

We wrap the complete table with a <webobject> element of type WOConditional. A WOConditional shows its contents, when the condition binding has a value of true. When the condition binding receives false, the WOConditional will not allow its contents to render, thus nothing will be shown. WOConditional is like an if statement. However it does not have an else part. If we want an else part, we need a second WOConditional, where we negate its action. In this example, we can ask the person list if it has elements or not, and use the return value as the condition.

11 HTML forms and gathering user input

A web application is all about getting input from a user and then acting upon it, retrieving and storing data, and performing actions. This chapter will tell you all about how to get user input.

11.1 The WOForm element

When you need to get user input, you must use an HTML form and put various user input elements into it. When the user is done with filling in all the data, the form must be submitted. This is plain html functionality. In Wonder you need a WOForm and some dynamic input elements. The WOForm is pretty simple.

HTML part:

```
<webobject name = "myForm">
    <!-- here goes the contents of the form -->
</webobject>
```

and the bindings in the WOD:

```
myForm : WOForm {
    multipleSubmit = true;
}
```

The multipleSubmit binding is optional. It allows for more than one submit button in the form. I recommend that you make it a custom to set multipleSubmit = true for all forms.

A WOForm can have an action binding, but one usually binds the action to the submit button and leaves action on WOForm unbound.

The only way in html to submit a form, is by a submit button (<input type = "submit" ...>). You cannot submit form data with a hyperlink (at least not without the help of JavaScript). In Wonder we use a WOSubmitButton for submitting forms.

A WOSubmitButton has two important bindings. One is action and the other one is value. You use value to set the text of the button (like "Send", "Ok", whatever). The action binding is identical to what we have seen earlier for WOHyperlinks. It must bind to a method that takes no input, and returns a WOComponent object. We have seen in Chapter 8.2.1, that the framework will call takeValuesFromRequest() when user data is available. This is what happens when a form is submitted. The invokeAction() method will then call the proper action we have bound to the submit button. At that moment, all instance variables have been properly set with the correct data from the user input.

11.2 Text input fields

Wonder has the following elements for text input WOTextField, WOPasswordField, and WOText.

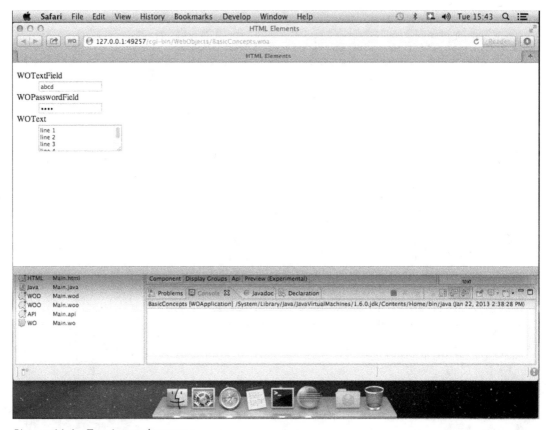

Picture 11-1   Text input elements

11.2.1 WOTextField

A WOTextField represents itself as a text input field. It corresponds to the HTML element <input type="text"...>.

Here are the most important bindings for WOTextField:

value

When a page is shown, this binding sets the default value displayed in the single-line text field. When the form is submitted, it holds the value the user entered into the field, or the default value if the user left the field untouched. Value is a mandatory binding.

dateformat

Either bind a method that returns a format string or enter a constant value directly. This specifies how the value should be formatted when it represents a date or date/time. In that case you can use an NSTimestamp object for the value. See the NSTimestampFormatter class specification for a description of the date format syntax.

numberformat

Similar to *dateformat* this string specifies how the value should be formatted as a number. See the NSNumberFormatter class specification for a description of the number format syntax.

disabled

If disabled evaluates to true, the element appears in the page but is not active. That is, the value binding does not contain the user's input when the page is submitted.

11.2.2 WOText

WOText generates a multi-line field for text input and display. It corresponds to the HTML element <textarea>. WOText has two important bindings:

value

When the page is shown this is what is displayed inside the text field. When the form is submitted it contains the data the user has entered. Value is a mandatory binding.

disabled

If disabled evaluates to true, the text area appears in the page but is not active. That is, value does not contain the user's input when the page is submitted.

11.2.3 WOPasswordField

A WOPasswordField represents itself as a text field that doesn't echo the characters that a user enters. It corresponds to the HTML element <input type="password"...>. WOPasswordField has the same bindings as WOText (no formatter like WOTextField!)

value

When the page is show, value sets the default value of the text field. This value is not displayed to the user. During request handling, value holds the value the user entered into the field, or the default value if the user left the field untouched. Value is a mandatory binding.

disabled

If disabled evaluates to true, the element appears in the page but is not active. That is, value does not contain the user's input when the page is submitted.

Here is an important tip!

You can add any binding you like to a WOText (and actually to any other dynamic element), even if Wonder does not know of such a binding. In that case the binding will be put into the resulting html and end up as attribute to the html tag. As an example let's resize a WOText.

Add the two additional bindings for rows and cols in the .wod file:

```
textfield : WOText {
    value = someVariable;
    cols = 70;
    rows = 4;
}
```

This will result in the following html output:

```
<textarea cols="70" rows="4">...</textarea>
```

You can use this trick to add any desired attribute to an html element. This also works with onclick and any other attribute that references JavaScript code.

Did I mention that all such bindings are dynamic? Create any fancy Java method that returns a string and bind it. Create your onclick JavaScript code fully dynamically according to whatever happens right now in you application.

11.3 Checkboxes and Radio Buttons

A checkbox is created by a WOCheckBox element, you use WORadioButton for radio groups. Whereas check boxes can be set and cleared individually, radio buttons in a group are mutually exclusive. Only one radio button can be checked at any time.

Picture 11-2   WOCheckBox and WORadioButton

Both elements have similar bindings, but they are used differently. Let's have a look at how this page was created. First comes the html part.

```
<?xml version="1.0" encoding="UTF-8"?>
<!DOCTYPE html PUBLIC "-//W3C//DTD XHTML 1.1//EN"
    "http://www.w3.org/TR/xhtml11/DTD/xhtml11.dtd">
```

```
<html xmlns="http://www.w3.org/1999/xhtml" xml:lang="en">
<head>
    <meta http-equiv="Content-Type" content="text/html; charset=utf-8"/>
    <title>HTML Elements</title>
</head>
<body>
    <dl>
        <dt>WOCheckBox</dt>
        <dd><webobject name = "checkbox1" /> Item 1</dd>
        <dd><webobject name = "checkbox2" /> Number 2</dd>
        <dd><webobject name = "checkbox3" /> Option 3</dd>
        <dt>WORadioButton</dt>
        <dd><webobject name = "radiobutton1" /> Swimming</dd>
        <dd><webobject name = "radiobutton2" /> Walking</dd>
        <dd><webobject name = "radiobutton3" /> Climbing</dd>
    </dl>
</body>
</html>
```

Here are the bindings. We will split these and look at the bindings for WOCheckBox first:

```
checkbox1 : WOCheckBox {
    checked = checked1;
}
checkbox2 : WOCheckBox {
    checked = checked2;
}
checkbox3 : WOCheckBox {
    checked = checked3;
}
```

Checkboxes are independent of each other. The user can check as many a he or she wants. The checked binding is usually the only binding used. checked must bind to something that results in a boolean value of true or false. The corresponding Java code could look similar to the following:

```
private boolean checked1;

public boolean checked1() {
    return checked1;
}

public void setChecked1(boolean checked1) {
    this.checked1 = checked1;
}
// with similar constructs for buttons 2 and 3
```

If you need a check box initially checked when the page is displayed, simply ensure that the corresponding get-method returns an initial true value.

Radio buttons are in a way similar to checkboxes but are not independent of each other. Radio buttons are usually collected into so called radio groups where only one button per group can be on with all other buttons in the same group off.

119

Here are the bindings of the three radio buttons.

```
radiobutton1 : WORadioButton {
    selection = mySport;
    value = "swimming";
    name = "sports";
}
radiobutton2 : WORadioButton {
    selection = mySport;
    value = "walking";
    name = "sports";
}
radiobutton3 : WORadioButton {
    selection = mySport;
    value = "climbing";
    name = "sports";
}
```

Its *name* binding forms a radio group. All radio buttons with the same name are in the same radio group. Here we have one group with three radio buttons. The name of the group is sports.

Each radio button represents exactly one value. This value is bound to *value*. In our example we use hard coded values swimming, walking, and climbing. In most cases however we bind value to some key that resolves to the correct value. We'll see an example right next. But first there is that *selection* binding. As there is exactly one value possible for a radio group (only one button can be active at any time) the selection binding usually binds to the same key for all buttons. Here it is the key *mySport*. The corresponding Java code might look something like this:

```
private String mySport;

public String mySport() {
    return mySport;
}

public void setMySport(String mySport) {
    this.mySport = mySport;
}
```

When a form is submitted that contains such a radio group, there will be exactly one radio button set. This button will then push its value (either "swimming", "walking", or "climbing" in this example) into the *selection* binding

And of course if you need to set an initial button, simply make sure that the getter method returns the correct value that corresponds to the desired button.

11.4 Popup Buttons and Selection Lists

Recall chapter 10.1 where we displayed a list of Person objects? We used a WORepetition to repeat html. Look at the html for a popup button:

```
<select name="currencies">
    <option>US Dollar</option>
    <option>Euro</option>
    <option>Swiss Franc</option>
</select>
```

This is composed of repeated html fragments (the *option* tag). Objects of type WOPopupButton and WOBrowser are user input elements that make use of repeating html.

We are reusing the *Person* class and the list of persons generated during application startup from Chapter 10.1 to introduce popup buttons and selection lists.

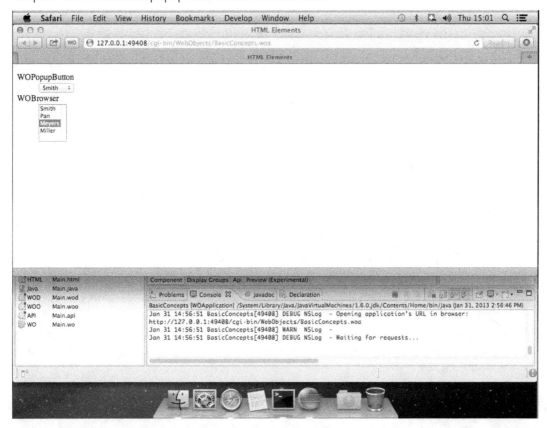

Picture 11-3   WOPopupButton and WOBrowser

Here is the html for this page

```
<?xml version="1.0" encoding="UTF-8"?>
<!DOCTYPE html PUBLIC "-//W3C//DTD XHTML 1.1//EN"
    "http://www.w3.org/TR/xhtml11/DTD/xhtml11.dtd">

<html xmlns="http://www.w3.org/1999/xhtml" xml:lang="en">
<head>
    <meta http-equiv="Content-Type" content="text/html; charset=utf-8"/>
```

```
    <title>HTML Elements</title>
</head>
<body>
<dl>
    <dt>WOPopupButton</dt>
    <dd><webobject name = "popup" /></dd>
    <dt>WOBrowser</dt>
    <dd><webobject name = "browser" /></dd>
</dl>
</body>
</html>
```

and the bindings:

```
popup : WOPopUpButton {
    list = application.persons;
    item = personLoopvar;
    displayString = personLoopvar.lastName;
    selection = selectedPerson;
}

browser : WOBrowser {
    list = application.persons;
    item = personLoopvar;
    displayString = personLoopvar.lastName;
    selections = selectedPersons;
    multiple = true;
}
```

The html for a popup button or a selection list is almost identical, with popup button being a selection list that only shows one item at a time. Thus both WOPopupButton and WOBrowser have very similar bindings. list and item are identical to what we have seen for WORepetition. As a person object has several attributes, we can tell the popup and the browser which attribute to show. We bind displayString to personLoopvar.lastName.

WOPopupButton can return exactly one selected item. This is the one with the check mark. So we have to provide the WOPopupButton with a location where it an put that selection. The Java code might then look something like this:

```
private Person selectedPerson;

public Person selectedPerson() {
    return selectedPerson;
}
public void setSelectedPerson(Person selectedPerson) {
    this.selectedPerson = selectedPerson;
}
```

To have a person already checked when the page is initially displayed simply make sure that the getter for selectedPerson returns a valid person object.

11.5 Arbitrary Dynamic html Elements

There may be cases where an html tag needs some dynamism but there is no ready-made WebObject or Wonder component available. Consider the following case. You want to have a dynamically set font color for a <span>. The html you want should look like this:

```
<span style="color:#ffa000;">...</span>
```

where the color value #ffa000 should be dynamically set. You could write

```
<span style="<webobject name = "color" />">...</span>
```

and then bind color to something that returns the desired color string.

But with this line you will get validation errors. Look at the double quotes and the angle brackets. Double quotes cannot contain other double quotes; angle brackets cannot be nested. This is invalid syntax.

Use a WOGenericContainer! Your html would then be

```
<webobject name = "mySpan">...</webobject>
```

In your .wod file include this definition:

```
mySpan : WOGenericContainer {
    elementName = "span";
    style = colorStyle;
}
```

Then have a colorStyle() method returning the String "color:#ffa000".

WOGenericContainer generates opening and closing tags. Thus you can have any arbitrary content inside the tags. If you want a tag without contents, like an <hr /> you would use WOGenericElement. With WOGenericElement and WOGenericContainer you can sort of make every html tag dynamic.

11.6 Actions make Things happen – Elements that can trigger Actions

We have already seen in Chapter 8.3 how actions work when we looked at navigation and WOHyperlink. Here is a quick recap:

An action is a method in your code with the following signature and typical body

```
public WOComponent myAction() {
    // create the next page to show
```

```
    MyPage nextPage = pageWithName(MyPage.class);
    // set up the next page
    nextPage.setXyz(. . .);
    // pass the newly set up page object to the framework
    return nextPage;
}
```

There are several dynamic elements available to trigger actions. We have already seen WOHyperlink and WOSubmitButton. Both types of elements have an action binding to which you bind your action method.

There are other elements that can trigger an action: WOActiveImage and WOImageButton. Let's first look at WOImageButton.

A WOImageButton allows you to have any image act as a button. In the following example we have drawn a nice looking button. This is a plain PNG image.

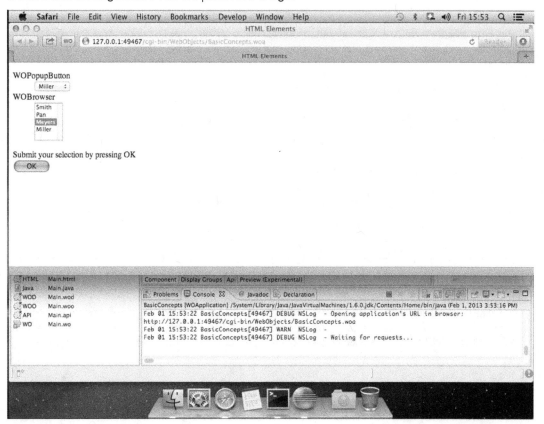

Picture 11-4 Using an image for a button

How did we do this? Here is the html portion

```
<p>Submit your selection by pressing OK <br />
<webobject name = "okbutton" /></p>
```

and the bindings

```
okbutton : WOImageButton {
    action = selectionIsOk;
    filename = "OK Aqua Button.png";
    framework = "app";
}
```

We have first put the graphic file "*OK Aqua Button.png*" into the *WebServerResources* folder of our project. We then added a WOImageButton to our page. The *action* binding specifies the action method being activated when the button is clicked. We use the *filename* binding to just give the name of the image file. No path or any sort of directory is needed. The framework is clever enough and will find the file. There is a third binding, *framework*, that binds to the constant value "app". With this binding we can reference *WebServerResources* in any of the WebObjects and Wonder frameworks. The constant "app" points to our own *WebServerResources* folder where our file resides.

Tip:

For all of these bindings the standard Eclipse control-space magic key combination is available. I have not typed any binding name nor did I have to type any value when I wrote the code.

The last element that can activate an action is WOActiveImage. An active image is also known as an image map. An image map is a graphic where different areas are click-sensitive. Each such area can activate a different action method. In the following image I have marked three areas, a circular area for the lens, a rectangular area for the flash and an arbitrary shaped area covering the body of the camera. The idea is that when the user clicks any of these areas he or she will be taken to a dedicated page for the lens, the flash, or the body.

Note

An image map cannot submit form data; it acts like hyperlinks. If you need data submission, you must use WOImageButton or play with JavaScript.

```
rect toFlashPage 150,30 290,120
circle toLensPage 240,340 320,340
poly toBodyPage 70,220 65,390 112,395 113,360 ...
```

Picture 11-5   Image map graphic with coordinates for clickable areas

An image map can have three types of areas: rectangles, circles, and polygons. Besides the graphic you need a map file. The map file is a plain text file containing descriptions of the areas, one line per clickable area. You need to determine the coordinates of defining points with a graphical editor. Point coordinates are given as number pairs, separated by a comma, with no whitespace between comma and value. All the coordinates are measured in pixel with 0,0 being at the top left. X coordinates run from left to right, and y coordinates run from top to bottom.

The general format for each line is the same:

```
areatype action coordinate-pair coordinate-pair …
```

All items on the line are separated by a space character. Allowed area types are rect, circle, and poly. The second word on each line is the name of the action method that should be triggered by a click in the area, and after another space character come the coordinates for the defining points. For a rectangle (rect) the first point gives the coordinates of the top left corner, the second point specifies the bottom right corner. A circle is defined by the center of the circle and one arbitrary point on the circle itself. A polygon (poly) is simply defined by all its corners; it can have up to 100 points.

You can see the contents of the map file for the camera image in the picture above.

Here is the html and bindings for an active image:

```
<webobject name = "camera" />
```

```
camera : WOActiveImage {
    action = clickOutSide;
    filename = "camera.jpg";
    framework = "appl";
    imageMapFile = "cameraMap.txt";
}
```

The binding for action specifies the action to take when the user clicks outside any mapped area. *filename* and *framework* bindings give the name of the image file and the framework (or here the application itself) where the image file and the map file live. *imageMapFile* binds to the name of the text file that contains all the coordinates that describe the clickable areas.

12 Custom Components

Sometimes you need the same functionality or html fragment in several places. Imagine having a nice header area in each of your pages, showing a logo banner. Or you may want to have the same navigation links on each page. Instead of duplicating html and possibly action methods in each of your page, you can create your own component. This component can then be used like any other Wonder component and dynamic element.

12.1 Creating a custom component

So far when we created a component, it was always a full-blown page component with all the html header and body tags.

Let's create a component that can display a string like a WOString does, but additionally we want to dynamically specify a font weigh like normal, or bold, and a color. Such a component needs a bit of html; but as it is intended to be embedded into a page, it does not need all the bells and whistles of a full page.

We will work with our *BasicConcepts* project. Create a new WOComponent with the name *AttributedString*. Don't check CREATE HTML CONTENTS.

Custom Components

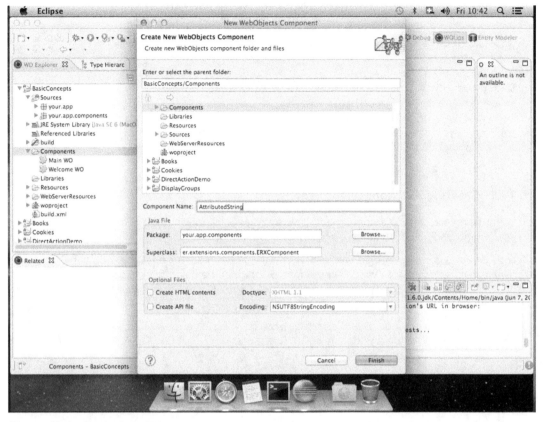

Picture 12-1   Create a custom component

If you accidentally checked CREATE HTML CONTENTs, no harm is done. Simply delete all html from the component.

Put the following into the html part (no other html should be there):

```
<webobject name = "styledSpan"><webobject name = "string" /></webobject>
```

and this is how the bindings should be:

```
styledSpan : WOGenericContainer {
    elementName = "span";
    style = style;
}

string : WOString {
    value = value;
}
```

We are going to use a plain WOString to display the string but we will wrap it with a <span> tag. This <span> gets a style binding we are going to use for the font style and color. To have a dynamic <span> tag, we will use a WOGenericContainer. Have a look at chapter 11.5, where we have done this already.

We need three instance variables. Add the following variable definitions to *AttributedString.java* and create the necessary accessor methods. Value needs a set and a get method; both *color* and *fontWeight* only need a setter.

```
private String color;
private String fontWeight;
private String value;

//... and the public accessor methods
```

We now need a method that composes the style definition.

```
public String style() {
    return "font-weight:" + fontWeight + "; color:" + color;
}
```

Open *Main.wo* and clean out all the html stuff between <body> and </body>. Remove everything from the bindings part, too. Put some <webobject> tags in:

```
<body>
    <p><webobject name = "string1" /></p>
    <p><webobject name = "string2" /></p>
    <p><webobject name = "string3" /></p>
    <p><webobject name = "string4" /></p>
</body>
```

and start typing in the *.wod* part. Type

```
string1 : Att
```

then hit control-<space>.

WOLips knows that there is a WOComponent whose name starts with *Att*. Your *AttributedString* component will be available like any other component or dynamic element. As this is probably the only component available that matches, WOLips will autocomplete right away.

Position your cursor in between the open and close braces and hit control-<space> again. For a standard dynamic element we expect to be presented with the available bindings. This happens here, too. WOLips presents all the publicly available attributes.

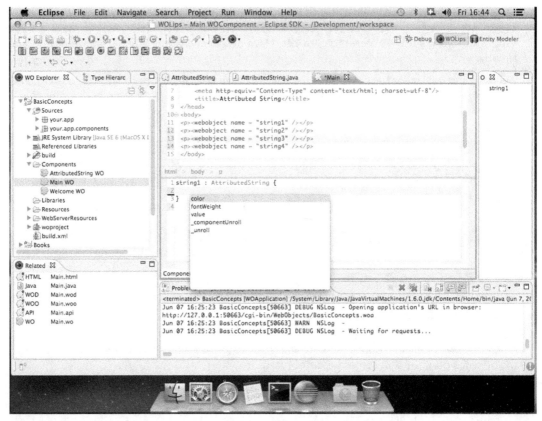

Picture 12-2   Our own attributes are available as bindings

Add bindings for all the strings. This could look like so:

```
string1 : AttributedString {
    color = "black";
    fontWeight = "normal";
    value = "this is a black normal string";
}

string2 : AttributedString {
    color = "red";
    fontWeight = "normal";
    value = "this is a red normal string";
}

string3 : AttributedString {
    color = "blue";
    fontWeight = "bold";
    value = "this is a blue bold string";
}

string4 : AttributedString {
    color = "#0f0";
    fontWeight = "normal";
```

```
    value = "this is a green normal string";
}
```

Run the application.

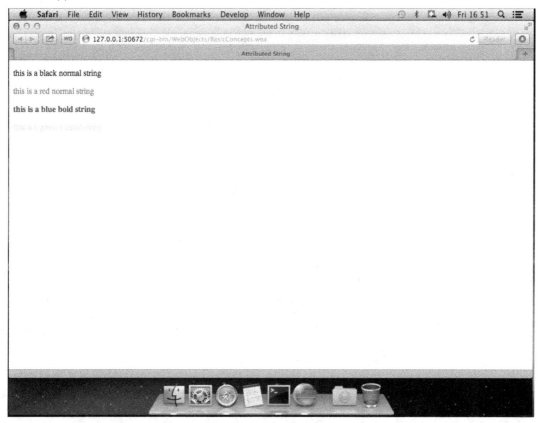

Picture 12-3   AttributedString in action

But wait! That's only the beginning! We can specify rules for the bindings. We can make bindings mandatory, we can make them mutually exclusive, and we can make them allow only certain values.

Open *AttributedString.wo* and note the *API* tab at the bottom.

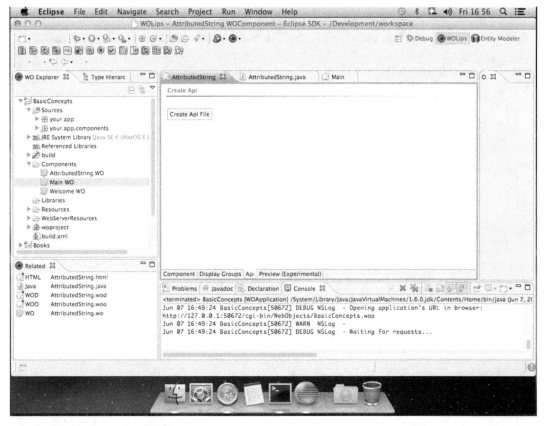

Picture 12-4   Create the Api file

It is here where you can specify the rules for your bindings. Click *CREATE API File*. When you created the *AttributedString* component in the first place, there was a check box labeled *CREATE API FILE*. We did not pay attention to it. In case you checked that box, an *Api* file got created alongside your component and you cannot of course create another one here.

Add one binding by clicking *ADD*:

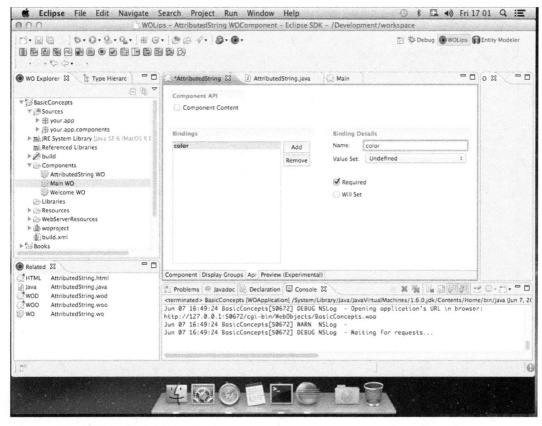

Picture 12-5   Adding the color binding

Give it the name *color* (this name corresponds to the setColor() method) and tick *REQUIRED*. Add two more bindings for *fontWeight* and *value* and also mark them *REQUIRED*.

Setting *REQUIRED* will allow WOLips to flag an error when we forget to bind.

135

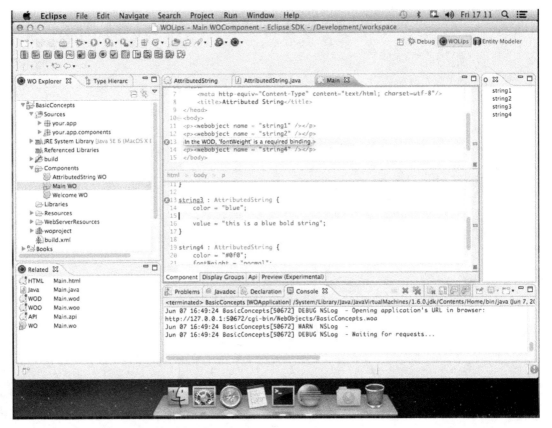

Picture 12-6   We forgot to bind fontWeight

None of our bindings returns a value; we have no get methods. Checking *Will Set* would tell WOLips, that the binding will return a value and thus needs a get method.

Wen you edit a binding there is the *Value Set* popup.

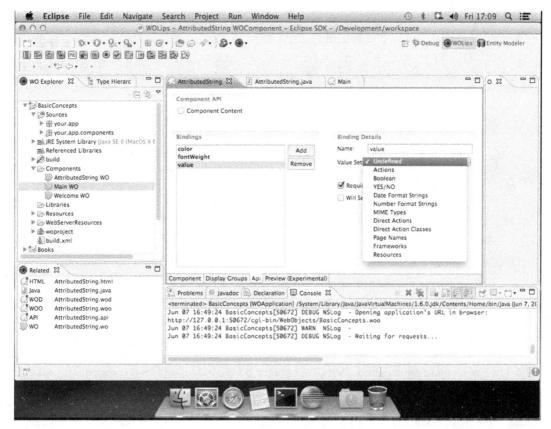

Picture 12-7   The Value Set for a binding

This allows you to specify certain special values the binding requires. Look at the screenshot above. The Api editor in WOLips is a bit limited. The format of the *.api* file is plain XML and allows far more than what the Api editor can do. The *.api* file lives in your *Components* folder alongside the *.wo*. If you cannot see the *.api* file in Eclipse WO Explorer, there is most probably a filter set that hides it. Easiest is to look directly in the file system. Open a Finder window (or an Explorer window in Microsoft Windows). Find *AttributedString.api* and open it with a text editor.

```xml
<?xml version="1.0" encoding="UTF-8" standalone="no"?>
<wodefinitions>
    <wo class="AttributedString" wocomponentcontent="false">
        <binding name="color" />
        <validation message="'color' is a required binding.">
            <unbound name="color" />
        </validation>
        <binding name="fontWeight" />
        <validation message="'fontWeight' is a required binding.">
            <unbound name="fontWeight" />
        </validation>
        <binding name="value" />
        <validation message="'value' is a required binding.">
            <unbound name="value" />
        </validation>
```

```
    </wo>
</wodefinitions>
```

In case you need complex validation rules, you must edit the file manually. Here is an example of a rule that tests, whether exactly one of two bindings is set.

```
<validation message="exactly one of 'color' or 'fontWeight' must be bound.">
    <or>
        <and>
            <unbound name="color" />
            <unbound name="fontWeight">
        </and>
        <and>
            <bound name="color" />
            <bound name="fontWeight">
        </and>
    </or>
</validation>
```

You can create rather complex logical structures. For negating a term surround it with <not>...</not>.

The custom component we have created can be embedded anywhere in a page component. You can even have custom components being embedded inside other custom components, thus forming a tree like embedding structure. This allows you to build small, specialized components, build larger ones from them, and re-use those throughout your application. You can even place those components into a framework and use the framework for several projects.

But wait! There is still more to custom components!

12.2 The WOComponentContent Component

So far we have seen how to create a custom component and embed it into another component. This establishes a component hierarchy. Such a custom component could be used for standard heading or navigation component or anything that should be part of each page. Here is a typical page:

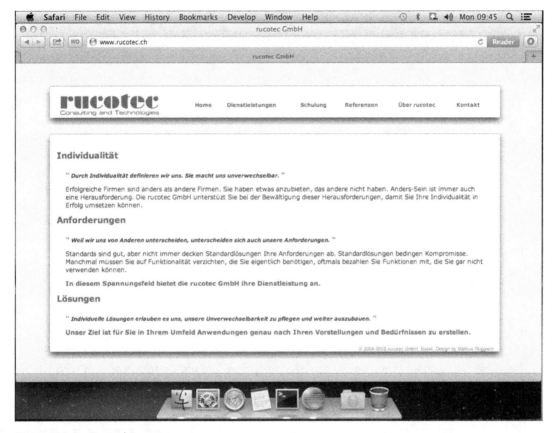

Picture 12-8   Typical Page Layout

There is a top navigation menu and a bottom copyright area. Both are repeated on every page. Oftentimes you also have repeated areas to the left and right of the main content. You would probably create separate components for each part and include them into each page. All your WOComponents need the full html stuff with interspersed custom components. It works but is not particularly elegant. There is better way to do.

Create one custom component that has all the bells and whistles, header, navigation, footer, and side areas. Where the main page content should go you include a WOComponentContent dynamic element. As this component sort of wraps around the contents of the page, we could call it *PageWrapper*. You can of course call it anyway you like.

When you now create any page, create it like a custom component, without any html/head/body stuff. The only thing you need to do is add your super duper page wrapper to it. All the contents of your page then go in between the opening and closing of the <webobject> tag.

For an example we go back to one of our demo projects and modify it a bit. The *DisplayGroups* project is as good as any other one we have.

Create a new component, call it *MySuperDuperPageWrapper* and make it a full page by including all the html stuff.

Add the following between <body> and </body>. Mind you, this is not a beauty contest; it is just to show how things work:

```
<div id = "header" style = "border:solid green 2px" width:100%>
    <p> The Great Page Wrapper Header Part </p>
</div>
<div id = "leftside" style = "float:left; width:20%; border: solid green 2px">
    <p> Here is the great side text. It will be
    the same on each and every page because it is
    included in the page wrapper </p>
</div>
<div id = "content" style="border:solid black 2px; margin-left:20%">
<webobject name = "content" />
</div>
<div id = "footer" style = "border:solid blue 2px; width:100%">
    <p> This is my great footer </p>
</div>
```

We define three <div> areas for header, footer, and a left side area, and a forth <div> will contain the content of the page. Just you can see the different areas we surround them with differently colored borders and put some static text into.

The content area has one <webobject> tag for which we have to specify a definition in the .wod part.

```
content : WOComponentContent {
}
```

Now edit the *Main.wo* html and remove everything from the top down to and including the <body> tag, and remove the </body> tag and everything below it. Just leave the real page content in there. Wrap the page content into a <webobject> </webobject> tag pair

```
<webobject name = "wrapper">
    <webobject name = "form">
    <p>Country <webobject name = "countryQualifier" /></p>
    <p><webobject name = "query" />
    </webobject>
    <webobject name = "batchNav" />
    <ul>
    <webobject name = "countries">
        <li><webobject name = "countryName" /></li>
    </webobject>
    </ul>
</webobject>
```

and add a definition for it to the .wod.

```
wrapper : MySuperDuperPageWrapper {
}
```

Run the application:

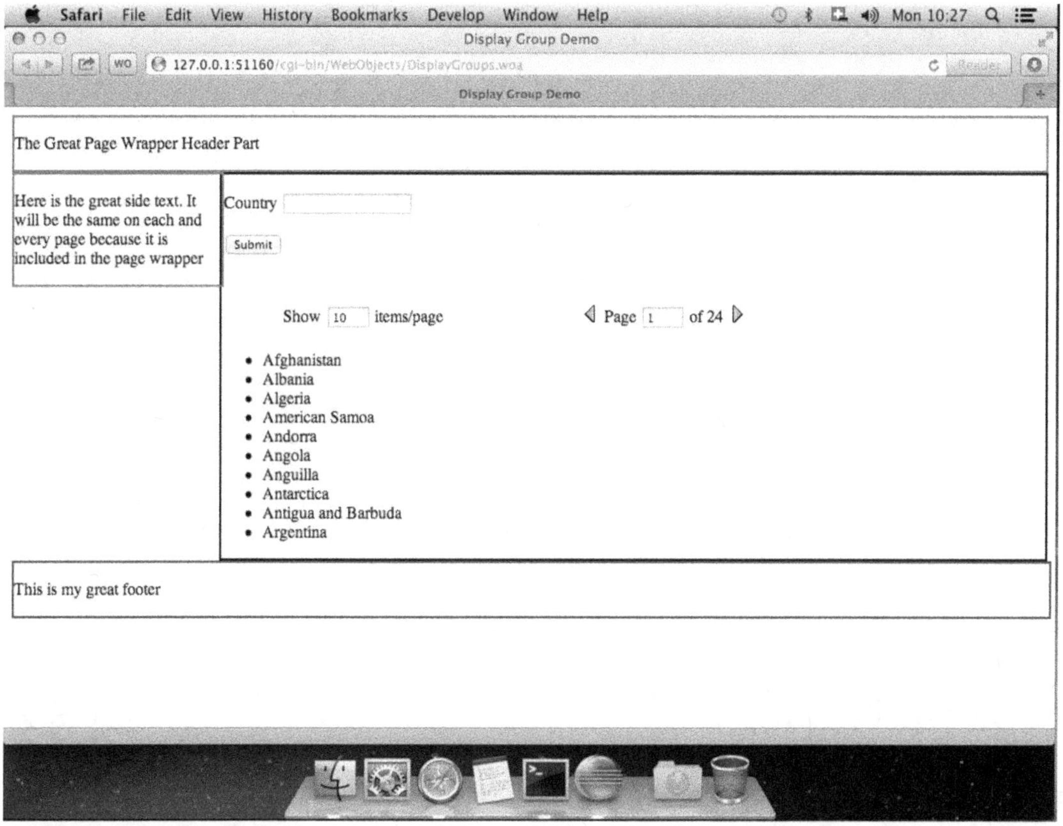

Picture 12-9 WOComponentContent *in action*

You can see two different hierarchies at play. The main page component includes the *MySuperDuperPageWrapper* custom component. Thus *Main.wo* is the parent of *MySuperDuperPageWrapper*! However *MySuperDuperPageWrapper* wraps itself around the main page when the final response is generated. So the visual/html-related hierarchy is just the other way round. This is what the WOComponentContent dynamic element does.

Of course your *MySuperDuperPageWrapper* is just a normal component. You can put anything into it and give it any functionality you like.

You can have at most one WOComponentContent per custom component. The framework would not know which part to wrap around the parent component.

Part C - Enterprise Objects

13 Enterprise Objects

Enterprise Objects, often referred to simply as EOs, are probably the most important things in your application. In this chapter we will see what they are and what you do with them.

13.1 What are Enterprise Objects?

In general an application consists of several types of objects. We have so far met objects that are used to render the user interface (these are Wonder dynamic elements), act as controllers for user interaction (that's what our components derived from ERXComponent are being used for), and objects that provide utility services to our application (based on classes like *Application*, *Session*, NSArray, etc).

But wait, there has to be more...

There are usually objects and classes modeling the business of an application. These are the center parts of every application. In most cases these objects represent persistent data that is usually stored in some form of database. The single most important type of database system to date is still the relational database. New and innovative database paradigms like object oriented databases or NoSQL databases are becoming more and more important, but the majority of applications today use relational databases. This will most probably not change in the near and mid-term future. Thus relational SQL-based databases are what we have to deal with mostly.

Enterprise objects are important to your business. They describe your business and they represent the data your business works with. Usually enterprise objects encapsulate data from the database.

Enterprise objects model the business rules; they should be independent of any user interface or other application functionality. E.g. a login name for a user must be unique no matter how it is displayed or by what means it is entered.

13.2 Enterprise Objects have Behavior

Enterprise objects not only encapsulate data but they can also, and usually do, have behavior. There are many things you can put into your EO classes.

Here is a simple example. Let's say your customer has *firstName* and *lastName* attributes. You could put a small method into the *Customer* class that returns the full name for the customer

```
public String fullName () {
    return lastName() + ", " + firstName();
}
```

This method can be used like any other (get-) method.

Enterprise objects may need to work together to perform some important task. Again an example with our customer object: the *Customer* class could have a method that walks through all the customers orders, and asks each order for its total sum. The class Order will need a method that returns that value. This method should sum up all the prices for each order item and so on. We will see many examples of custom behavior throughout the rest of this book.

13.3 The Technical Side of Enterprise Objects

The Enterprise Objects Framework EOF handles everything database related and thus it also handles all our enterprise objects. For this to be possible, every object, that is supposed to be an enterprise object, must adhere to a set of rules defined by EOF. EOGenericRecord is a generic enterprise object class that can be used in place of custom classes when custom behavior is not needed. It implements the EOEnterpriseObject interface to provide the basic enterprise object behavior. You can thus create and use objects of type EOGenericRecord right away or you can (and usually will) build your own enterprise classes by extending EOGenericRecord.

14 The Editing Context

As we are programming in an object-oriented world we will not work directly with the database. This is the job of the framework. However we do need a notion of a data store where our objects live. In Wonder EOF there is one important class that sort of represents the data store to the application: EOEditingContext. Each and every enterprise object must be associated with an editing context. We interact indirectly with the database by communicating with the editing context. The editing context can be regarded as a high-level abstraction of the database.

The editing context interacts with the underlying frameworks that ultimately generate SQL code and speak to the database. It is responsible to track all enterprise objects and their relationships and it tracks any modifications to the objects. So the editing context knows which objects are new, need to be updated, or are to be deleted. It not only handles the interaction with the database but it is also responsible for transactions and controls the integrity of the data.

14.1 The classes ERXEC and EOEditingContext

The class ERXEC is a Wonder extension of the WebObjects editing context class EOEditingContext. As the underlying Enterprise Objects Framework knows nothing about Wonder it will usually return objects of type EOEditingContext. Of course Wonder ensures that these are actually of type ERXEC. That is the reason you will often see references to simply EOEditingContext.

ERXEC has many methods available, but there is only a handful that you will usually need to call. We will go into more details later on, but here is a list of some often used editing context methods:

Method	Description
objectsWithFetchSpecification()	Accesses the data store and returns objects
insertObject()	Places a newly created enterprise object under the control of the editing context. This will end up as an insert-statement against the database.
deleteObject()	Delete an enterprise object, resulting in a delete-statement against the database.
saveChanges()	Writes any changes back to the database.
revert()	Resets all modifications to all objects made since the last time a saveChanges() call has been made, does not access the database.
refetch()	Similar to revert() but also accesses the database and updates any object with the latest data.

14.2 Accessing the editing context

Because the editing context is such an important thing, every session has a default editing context. You can get a reference to it by calling defaultEditingContext() on the session. You will often have something like the following lines of code:

```
EOEditingContex ec = session().defaultEditingContext();
```

As each enterprise object is associated with an editing context, you can ask any enterprise object for its editing context.

```
Author anAutor = ...  // assume you have an Author object
EOEditingContext authorEc = anAuthor.editingContext();
```

14.3 Working with your own editing context

You can actually have more than one editing context in your application. Why you would want this and what you can do, is an advanced topic that goes beyond the scope of this book. One example however is working session-less with direct actions. Have a look at chapter 0 (

Direct Actions) where we have such a case.

If you need to, you can easily create a new editing context:

```
EOEditingContext newEc = ERCEX.newEditingContext();
```

Be careful here. As the editing context represents a high-level view to the database, we must make sure that different user interactions happening at the same time do not collide. There is an absolute rule saying:

Each editing context must be locked before use and unlocked after using it!

The default editing context is automatically locked at the start of a request-response loop and unlocked when the response has been generated. So we never had to do anything so far.

The Wonder editing context class ERXEC, which is an extension to the base WebObjects EOEditingContext, handles locking and unlocking transparently. However sometimes you work with a plain EOEditingContext object. In that case you are responsible to handle locking yourself.

In the case of using a plain EOEditingContext the following code sequence must be observed:

```
EOEditingContext ec = new EOEditingContext();
// immediately lock the editing context
ec.lock();
// do whatever you need to, fetch, insert, delete objects, save changes, etc.
// when done with using the editing context, release the lock!
// ...
ec.unlock();
```

If you ever forget to correctly lock and unlock your editing context, you can run into all sorts of extremely nasty problems when several users access the same data at the same time. This can result in dead locks, where one database access blocks another and that other one blocks the first access. Often shutting down and restarting the application is the only way to resolve this.

Wonder to the rescue!

The safest way is to always use the Wonder ERXEC editing context! Wonder extends the editing context functionality with auto-locking. No need to take care of locking, no danger to forget to properly handle locking the editing context.

15 Objects and the Relational World – The Data Model

This chapter will establish the concepts of object-oriented access to relational data. From the following chapters you will then learn how Wonder builds upon these concepts in an extremely sophisticated way. We will be dealing with a part of Wonder called EOF, Enterprise Objects Framework. There used to be customers buying expensive WebObjects licenses just because they wanted EOF.

15.1 Entities, Classes, and Relational Tables

The most important thing in EOF is the concept of an *Entity*. An entity in EOF is a logical concept. Entities have a name and attributes. We could talk about a person entity with *Person* being the name of the entity. A person in reality has some attributes like first name, last name, date of birth, gender, eye color, a profession, hobbies, etc.

For any given person we need some place to store the data for that person. In the relational world we probably would have a table PERSON with columns for the attributes like LAST_NAME, FIRST_NAME, BIRTH_DATE, etc. Of course in the database world each table needs a primary key. We may have PERSON_ID to uniquely identify each person entity. As a person may have several hobbies, in the relational database world we probably would then create another table, HOBBY, with columns for HOBBY_ID and HOBBY_TEXT. And you would need a so-called *foreign key* from the hobby table to the person. The foreign key attribute in the hobby table would then contain the person id.

On the other hand in the object oriented world you create a class Person with instance variables to hold the attributes of a person. There are no primary keys; each object has its own identity given by its mere existence. There will probably be a class for hobby objects, and person objects having a relationship with hobby objects. Such relationships could be created in code by an array type instance variable in the Person class, that can hold the list of hobbies for a person.

The Enterprise Objects Framework brings the relational database world and the object oriented Java world together. You as a programmer will not have to deal with a database, you will not have to handle SQL statements, and you will not need to concern yourself with primary and foreign keys. You as a programmer will simply work with objects.

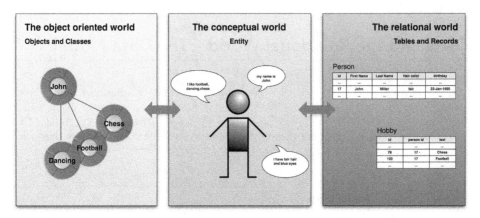

Picture 15-1   OO-World – Conceptual World – Relational World

Here is a comparison of some terms and how they map into the different worlds

Conceptual World	Relational World	Object oriented World
Entity	Table	Class
Attribute	Column	Instance variable with accessor methods
Object identity	Primary key	Location in memory defines object identity
To one relationship	Foreign key	Simple object reference (instance variable)
To many relationship	Foreign key	Simple collection of object references (e.g. Array)
Many to many relationship	Needs intermediate join table with foreign keys	Simple collection of object references

We will see that EOF not only does the mapping between objects and relational data but also handles all the necessary stuff with primary and foreign keys as well as many to many join tables.

For EOF to be able to its job, it must know about all three worlds. It is our responsibility as a programmer to let EOF know how objects and classes are related to the relational database structure. This is done by building the so-called **EOModel**. The EOModel ends up being a folder full of XML files that describe exactly how objects, classes, attributes, datatypes, tables, columns, etc. are mapped. WOLips, the set of development tools we are using, contains a nice editor for this. There is no need for a Wonder programmer to mess with any XML stuff.

15.2 Creating the EOModel

For this and the following chapters we will build upon a simple data model. Have a look at the entity relationship diagram:

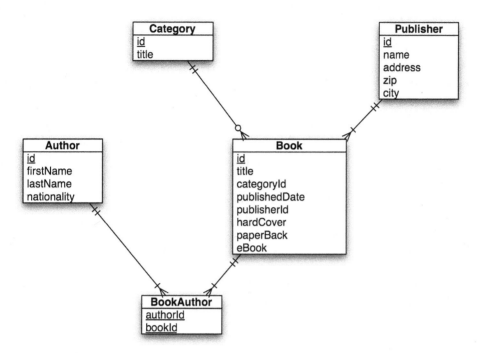

Picture 15-2   Simple data model: Author/Book/Publisher

This **datamodel** is very simple and in real world would need quite some overhaul to be really useful. But it is ideally suited for our purpose to explain the concepts of EOF and how to use EOF.

An author can write several books and a book can have several authors. To be able to model this many to many relationship in a relational database we need a simple **many-to-many join table** (BookAutor). A book has a title, a publishing date and is published in print as hard cover, and/or paper back, and may be published as eBook. Each book has a reference to a category like Crime, SciFi, Fiction, Biography, etc. Of course each book is published by a publisher of whom we note name and address.

So, fire up your development environment and create a new Wonder application called *Books*.

The first thing we need is the model that describes the mapping between objects and database structures.

Use the context menu popup on the Resources folder and select *NEW EOMODEL*.

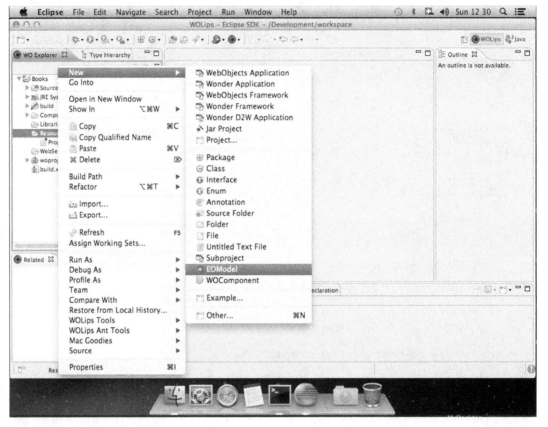

Picture 15-3   Create an EOModel

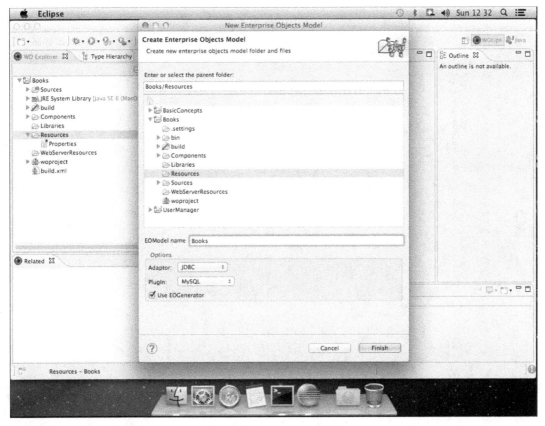

Picture 15-4   Specify necessary information for the new model

Name the model *Books*, set the Adaptor to JDBC, select the correct plugin for your database, and make sure that *Use EOGenerator* is checked. In our example we will work with MySQL. Click *Finish* to create the model. You can change all these values later in case you made an error. After a moment Eclipse will open the *EntityModeler* perpective. Default setting in WOLips is to open a new window for the entity modeler. I personally find this a bit confusing so I changed this in Eclipse preferences under *WOLips -> Entity Modeler*.

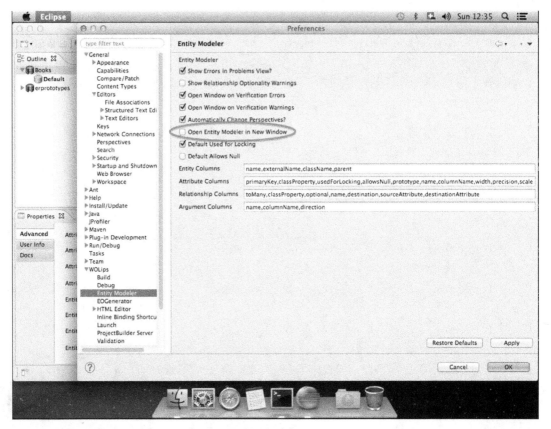

Picture 15-5   WOLips preference for the Entity Modeler

Anyway, here is how the Entity Modeler Perspective looks like:

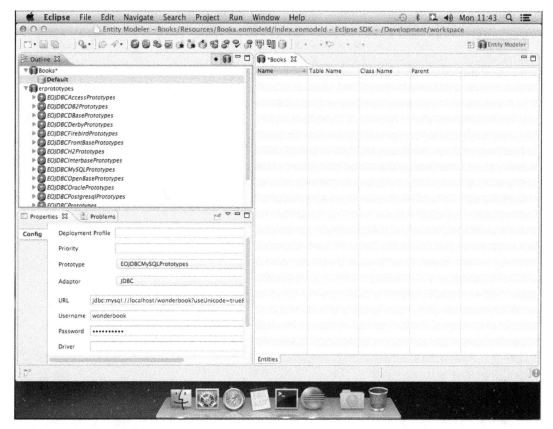

Picture 15-6   Entity Modeler Perspective

The top left view shows two models (yes, we only created one, that is not a bug!). The bottom left view is your properties view and the right side is covered by the editing view.

Why two models? As Wonder EOF supports different databases, Wonder implements a mechanism called **prototype**. You may want to be able to switch the physical database system and the model *erprototypes* allows exactly that. What in MySQL might be a varchar datatype will then become varchar2 datatype for Oracle. So the *erprototypes* model allows a database vendor independent specification of the model. Of course you are not required to use prototypes but I strongly suggest you do! Simply leave *erprototype* alone but set ADAPTOR to EOJDBCMySQLprototypes (or to what ever database system you use).

As you can see from the screenshot I have already started to enter connection data. The application must be able to connect to the database and therefore needs some information. The **connection URL** is database vendor specific. Here is the one I use for accessing a local MySQL database called *wonderbook*.

```
jdbc:mysql://localhost/wonderbook?useUnicode=true&characterEncoding=UTF8
```

Create the database manually and specify the correct USERNAME and PASSWORD for your database. There is no need to enter anything in the DRIVER field.

15.3 Creating entities

Let's first define our entities. Right-click on *Books* and chose *NEW ENTITY* from the context popup menu (or click the leftmost red icon on the toolbar). Create the *Author* entity. Specify *Author* for the name of the entity, you can accept the default name for the table or you can change it, as you like. I tend to use all uppercase names for database elements, so I changed the table name to AUTHOR. Edit the class name so that it includes the package. We want to put all our business classes into the your.app.eo package.

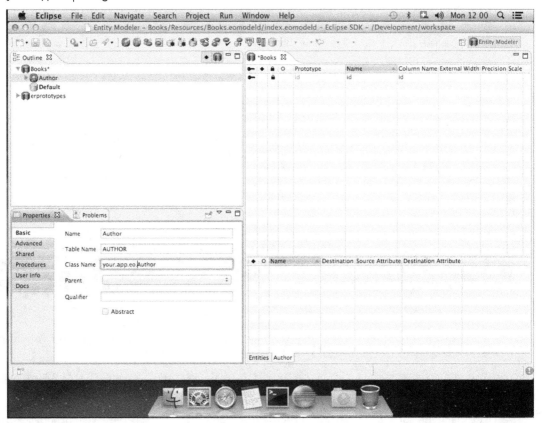

Picture 15-7   Creating a new entity

As you see, the newly created entity has already been setup with a first attribute. Each and every table in the relational world needs a primary key. Open the disclosure triangle for the *Author* entity and select the *id* attribute. The properties view shows that the attribute is called id, that it maps to an id column, and that it is based on a prototype called id. Its logical data type is Integer. Integer maps to INT for the database data type and will be represented in the Java world by objects of class java.lang.Integer.

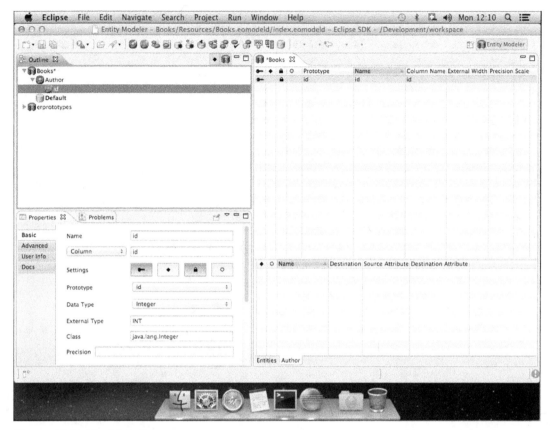

Picture 15-8   The id attribute

15.4   Creating attributes and other entities

Let's add the rest of the *Author* attributes. Select the *Author* entity in the outline view, then select NEW ATTRIBUTE from the context menu popup (or use the second icon from the left in the toolbar). We added the attributes *firstName* and *lastName* (use varchar50 prototype) and the attribute *nationality* (use prototype varchar10, but then manually set the external width to 3).

Add entities for *Book*, *Category*, and *Publisher*. Do not create the *BookAuthor* entity yet! Pick a suitable prototype for each attribute. Also do not add the foreign key attributes *publisherId* and *categoryId* to *Book*. We'll let Wonder handle foreign keys a bit further down. Notice that WOLips remembers the package you added to the Java class for the *Author* entity. Use the boolean prototype for the three Book attributes *hardcover*, *paperback*, and *eBook* respectively.

Here is what the boolean prototype creates:

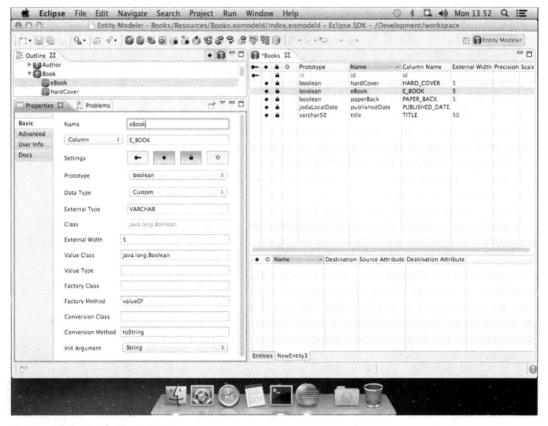

Picture 15-9   Boolean prototype

There are several ways boolean values can be represented in a database. Most database systems do not have a dedicated data type for booleans. The boolean prototype creates a 5 character column that will hold the string values true and false. The Java class java.lang.Boolean has a constructor to create a Boolean object given the string representation true or false, and the the toString() method will return exactly these two character sequences. The *FACTORY METHOD* and the *CONVERSION METHOD* properties are used to specify the methods for converting a java.lang.Boolean from and to the database column's string contents. There are other boolean prototypes available, e.g. to map booleans to numerical values 0, and 1. For the *publishedDate* attribute in *Book* you can use Date prototype.

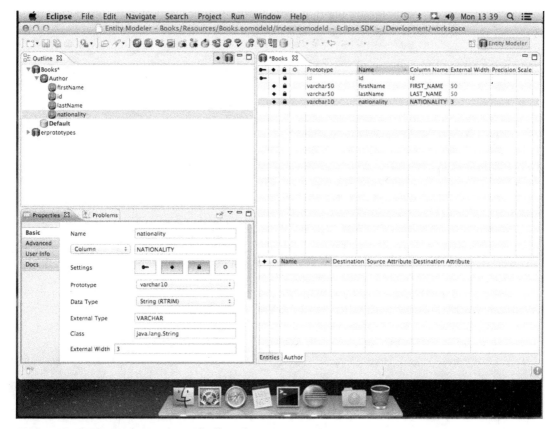

Picture 15-10 The Author entity with all attributes

15.4.1 Attribute Settings

There is a row of four icons in the attribute properties view (called *SETTINGS*). The same icons also appear as column headings in the editor view. We have to have closer look at these now.

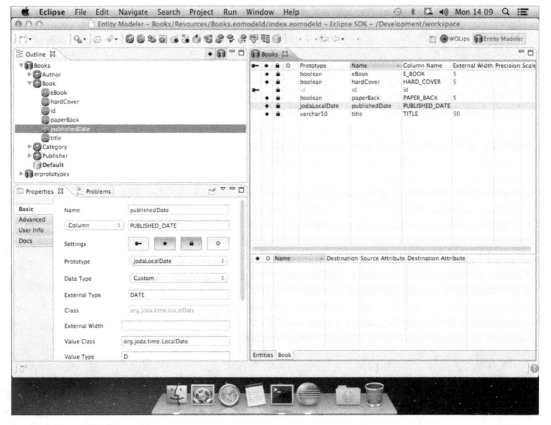

Picture 15-11 Attribute properties

The Settings icons are buttons that can be clicked.

The first icon denotes the primary key. One or more attributes can be marked as being part of the primary key. When we create a new entity it will have an attribute *id* that is marked as being the primary key.

Turning the black square on enables the attribute in Java, turning it off will hide the attribute from the object-oriented world. Primary keys and foreign keys usually should be turned off. There is no need to have primary key attributes modeled in our Java classes. The *id* attribute for instance is not modeled; all the other attributes will be in the Java class.

Wonder EOF uses a strategy for locking called *optimistic locking*. The default is to include each attribute into this strategy. This may not be optimal in certain places like `blob` columns, or `float` and `double` columns where rounding differences might become a problem.

The forth icon denotes whether the attribute must have a value or can be left empty. This icon sets `allows null values`, or `disallows null values`.

Set `allows null` for the *publishedDate* of *Book* to allow null. A book might not yet have a publication date but of course it is already being written and needs to be in our database.

15.5 Adding simple relationships

Now it is time to add the relationship to our model. We will first add the relationship between *Book* and *Publisher*. Use the context popup menu on either one of the two entities and select *New Relationship*.

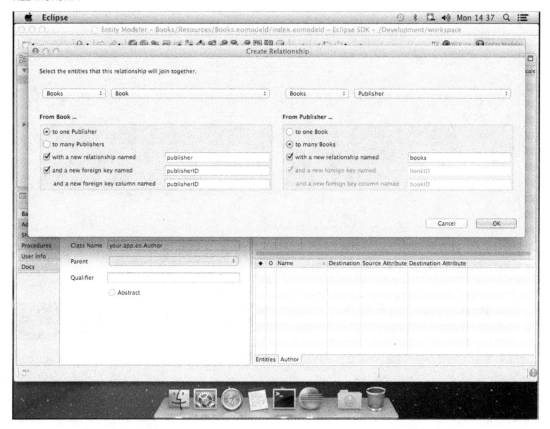

Picture 15-12 New Relationship Dialog

Select the two entities from the popups and activate the correct one to many direction radio buttons. We have relationships from *Book* to one *Publisher* and from *Publisher* to many *Books*. The dialog suggests a name for the relationship based on the entity name. It also asks whether to create the needed foreign key and foreign key column. You can of course edit things to you liking. Then just click *Ok*. The default is a **two-way relationship**. This means that a *Book* object knows its *Publisher* (the to one relationship) and a *Publisher* knows its *Books* (to many relationship). In general you want both ways but you can for performance reasons uncheck one of the directions (check box *with a new relationship named*).

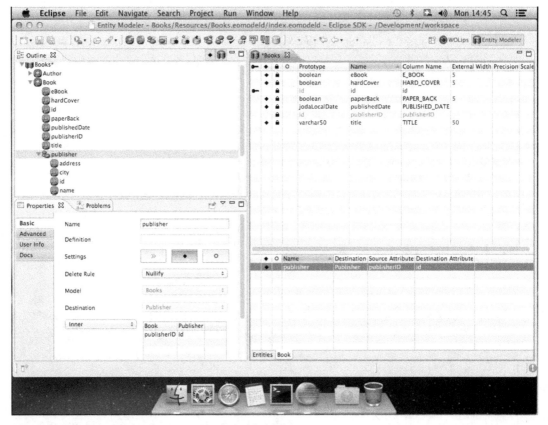

Picture 15-13 Relationship between Book and Publisher

Entity Modeler has created a new attribute in entity *Book*: *publisherId*, based on the *ID* prototype. This is your foreign key from the *BOOK* table to the *PUBLISHER* table. The foreign key attribute is not included in the Java class (the little black square is not set).

Additionally Entity Modeler has created a logical relationship between *Book* and *Publisher*. This is seen in the lower part of the editor view. It is also reflected in the outline view on the top left. You can set the following properties on a relationship:

DELETE RULE allows you to specify cascading deletion of the to-many records when the one-record is deleted. You can also prevent the deletion of database records as long as there are still dependent to-many records, or you can nullify the foreign key.

INNER POPUP specifies that the framework must do an inner join against the database when performing a query operation. You can change this to any kind of outer join (full, left, right outer join). You will probably not change this in most cases.

Now add the relationship from *Book* to *Category* in the same way.

15.6   Adding a many-to-many relationship

There is still that **many-to-many relationship** between *Book* and *Author*. In the database world we need a join table combining two foreign keys. Let's do it the EOF way!

Select *Author* entity and as before from the context menu popup select *New Relationship*. In the dialog select the *Book* entity from the popup.

Now check *From Book to many Authors* and *From Author to many Books* to create a many-to-many relationship. Entity Modeler realizes the need for a join table. It will automatically create one.

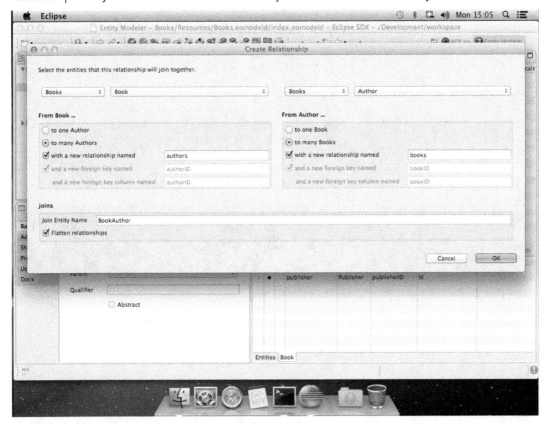

Picture 15-14 Creating a many-to-many relationship

Make sure that *Flatten relationships* is checked. Press Ok.

Look what happened. Entity Modeler has created a new entity, *BookAuthor*, that contains the two foreign keys to *Book* and *Author* respectively and the class name has been set to EOGenericRecord. EOF will handle the join table on its own, no need for us Java programmers to mess with it at all. Thus no need for a specific Java class. EOGenericRecord is a framework class that is sufficient in this case. You can also see that there are relationships but again these are not modeled (no black square) and thus of no interest in the object-oriented world.

Objects and the Relational World – The Data Model

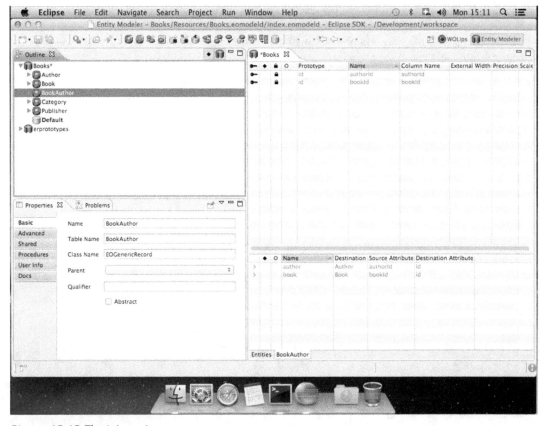

Picture 15-15 The join entity

How do things look on the *Autor* (or *Book*) entity? We see several relationships.

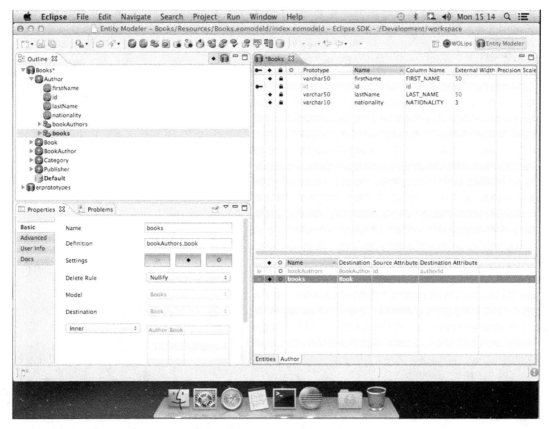

Picture 15-16 Flattened to-many relationship

Author has two relationships. A to-many relationship, that is not modeled (black square not set), to the join entity *BookAuthor*, and a second to-many relationship to *Book*. Look at the DEFINITION property for the relationship to *Book*. It reads bookAuthors.book. This is key value coding again, specifying the key path from *Author* to *Book*. All this is handled for us by EOF, nothing to do for us.

15.7 Add the JDBC driver for your database to the project

Before we can continue we need physical access to the database. Find the JDBC driver for your database. You may have to go to the web and download it from the vendor. Switch to the WOLips perspective and locate the *Libraries* folder in the WO Explorer view. You can drag and drop the driver (it is a *.jar* file) into that folder. Include the driver into the java build path via the context menu popup

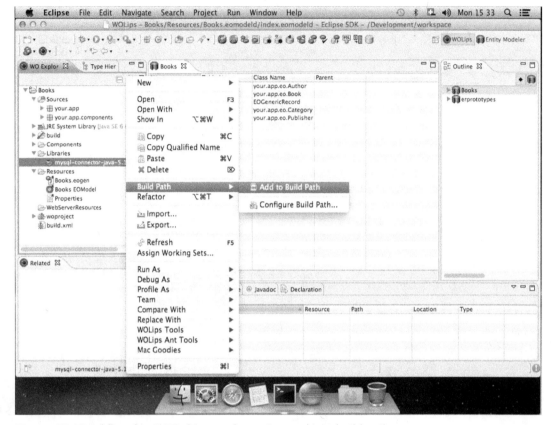

Picture 15-17 Adding the JDBC driver to the project and java build path

Now you are all set.

15.8 Generating the database structure

Our model is complete so far. Entity Modeler can generate the necessary SQL statement to create all the tables in the database. To be able to do this it needs access to the database. If you forgot to include the database driver into the java build path, the SQL generation will fail.

Switch back to Entity Modeler. It is important to save the model first; otherwise the generated SQL will not reflect the whole model.

From the context menu popup on the *Books* model select GENERATE SQL. After a short moment the following window will appear.

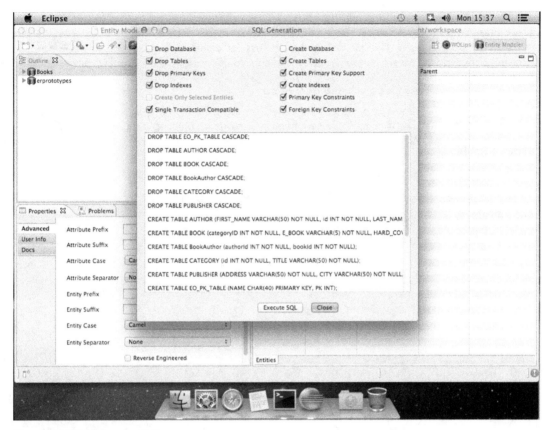

Picture 15-18 Generate SQL

Did you get an error message instead of the SQL statements? Check that the JDBC driver has been included and that the connection info is correctly set in the model (open the model, and check the properties on *Default connection*).

There are some limitations though. First you cannot have the CREATE DATABASE command generated (you can check this but it'll tell you that it can't do it). Secondly, depending on the capabilities of the JDBC driver and the database system, no foreign key constraints will be created. This is the case for MySQL. If you want the foreign key constraints in the database you would have to create them manually afterwards.

For the moment just click EXECUTE SQL. You might want to uncheck DROP TABLES, DROP PRIMARY KEYS, and DROP INDEXES, because there is nothing yet to drop and you will get an error message. The execution however will not fail; you just have to discard the error messages and tell the process to continue.

15.9 Generating the Java class files

The model is finished, the database is up and running, all we lack is the Java classes that implement our entities.

Close the Entity Modeler and switch back to WOLips perspective. Notice that we have not one but two files in our *Resources* folder. *Books EOModel* is our model. You do not need to open the second file called *Books.eogen*. This file drives the process for creating Java classes. There is no need to change anything. If you are curious nobody prevents you from double clicking and have a look.

15.9.1 How Java class files are being generated

The java class files are being generated based on templates. WOLips uses an embedded open source engine that reads a template containing static text, placeholders, and instructions to the engine. Advanced Wonder programmers can (and often do) create their own adapted templates. However we will stick with the defaults.

Select *EOGENERATE* from the context menu popup on the *Books.eogen* file.

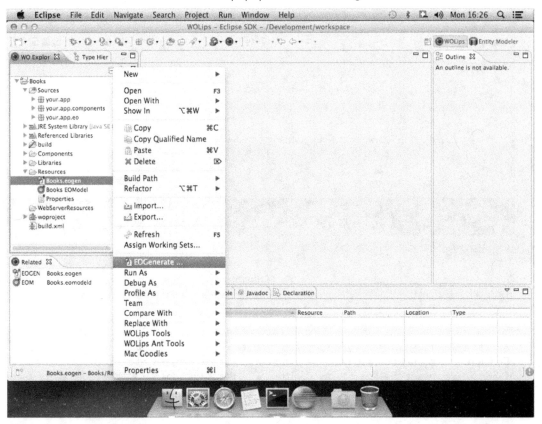

Picture 15-19 Generating the Java Class Files

EOGenerator will create the necessary packages structure and put the generated files into the correct place. If you look closely you see that EOGenerator creates two files per entity.

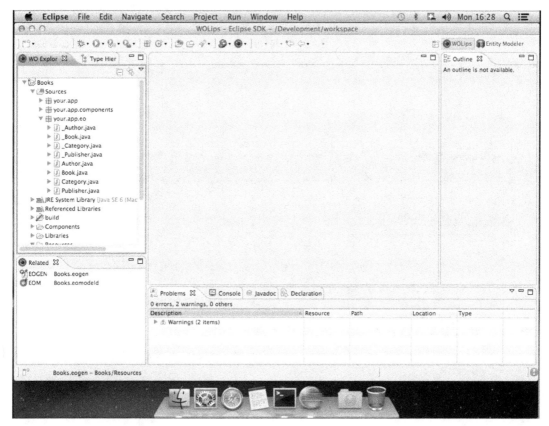

Picture 15-20 Generated Class Files

Let's have a closer look at the files *Author.java* and *_Author.java*.

Here is the content of *Author.java*

```
package your.app.eo;

import org.apache.log4j.Logger;

public class Author extends _Author {
    @SuppressWarnings("unused")
    private static Logger log = Logger.getLogger(Author.class);
}
```

Simple. Basically empty. Class Author extends _Author, nothing else.

EOGenerator uses the so-called **generation gap pattern**. The file *Author.java* will never be overwritten by EOGenerator once it is there, whereas the file *_Author.java* will always unconditionally be recreated. This allows you to make modifications and add business logic to class *Author* without any problems when EOGenerator is run again. So no matter what modifications you will do to the model while working on your application, any customization is save from being overwritten.

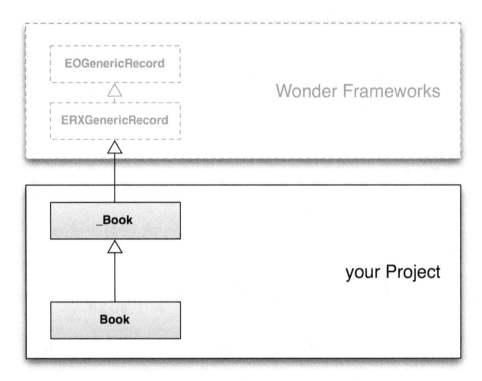

Picture 15-21 Generation Gap Pattern with Classes _Book and Book

So, as *Author.java* is basically empty, the fun must be in *_Author.java*!

Wow, well over 200 lines of code! For such a simple thing like Author? What is going on here? Let's have a closer look at some parts of the file:

```
// DO NOT EDIT.  Make changes to Author.java instead.
package your.app.eo;

import com.webobjects.eoaccess.*;
// ... more imports
public abstract class _Author extends  ERXGenericRecord {
```

First line reads DO NOT EDIT! So we won't. This file will be regenerated whenever EOGenerator is run.

class _Author extends ERXGenericRecord. This is where the frameworks come into play. EOF knows how to handle things because it works with ERXGenericRecords. Our classes are mere extensions to this, so EOF can handle our classes as well.

But what is the rest of those 200+ lines of source code good for? The templates for EOGenerator generate a lot more code than is basically needed. There are a lot of convenience methods and constants in there. You will probably not use most but it is always good to have things around.

Here is the relevant code for the *firstName* attribute of an author:

```
public static final ERXKey<String> FIRST_NAME =
    new ERXKey<String>("firstName");
public static final String FIRST_NAME_KEY = FIRST_NAME.key();

public String firstName() {
  return (String) storedValueForKey(_Author.FIRST_NAME_KEY);
}

public void setFirstName(String value) {
  if (_Author.LOG.isDebugEnabled()) {
    _Author.LOG.debug( "updating firstName from " +
        firstName() + " to " + value);
  }
  takeStoredValueForKey(value, _Author.FIRST_NAME_KEY);
}
```

There are two constants defined for the attribute. These can be used with key value coding. Key value coding needs strings for keys and key paths. Having these constants we can have compile time error checking, as there are many places in the code later on where you have to specify the name of an attribute. They are just a convenience.

There is a get and a set method for the *firstName* attribute. There is however no instance variable. The set and get Methods use inherited key value methods to access the actual *firstName*. How the framework internally stores the values for the attributes is an implementation detail and is of no interest to us.

Here is an example for the to-many relationship from *Author* to *Book*:

```
public NSArray<your.app.eo.Book> books() {
    return (NSArray<your.app.eo.Book>)storedValueForKey(_Author.BOOKS_KEY);
}

public void addToBooks(your.app.eo.Book object) {
    includeObjectIntoPropertyWithKey(object, _Author.BOOKS_KEY);
}

public void removeFromBooks(your.app.eo.Book object) {
    excludeObjectFromPropertyWithKey(object, _Author.BOOKS_KEY);
}
```

You see, actually pretty simple. The accessor methods just call inherited methods from the framework. All the other methods in the file build upon these basic methods, they are not needed but convenient to have nevertheless.

16 Fetching Enterprise Objects

Now that we have a model of our business data structure, we can use EOF to access the database and fetch objects.

Fetching objects from the database is done by using something called **fetch specification**. A fetch specification fully describes what objects should be read from the database. It consists of several parts: a qualifier, some sort orderings, and an object of type ERXFetchSpecification. We will first look at the details of the things we need and then use that knowledge to actually go to the database and retrieve objects.

16.1 Qualifying – How To Build Qualifiers

When we need to fetch objects from a database we need to describe what objects we want. Maybe we need all the customers from a certain city, or we want only those products that have been bought last month. Describing what we want is done by constructing a *qualifier*.

16.1.1 Testing for equality

Let's say, we only want authors from Germany. We need to qualify the fetch by an object of type **EOQualifier**. In Wonder it is very easy to construct a qualifier:

```
EOQualifier qualifier = Author.NATIONALITY.eq("GER");
```

Look into the class definition for _Author. EOGenerator has created the constant NATIONALITY of type ERXKey. The class ERXKey has several methods (like eq() we just used) that create an EOQualifier object.

16.1.2 Wildcard qualifying

If we only wanted German authors whose *lastName* starts with "G", we could extend the qualifier:

```
EOQualifier qualifier =
          Author.NATIONALITY.eq("GER").and(Author.LAST_NAME.like("G*"));
```

We can include the * character as a wildcard. In that case we must use the like() method. There is also a caseInsensitiveLike() available.

16.1.3 Qualifying across a key path

What about all the Authors that have written a book with publication date in the year 2012? Here is a code snippet that shows how to create such a qualifier:

```
NSTimestamp beginOf2012 =
   new NSTimestamp(2012, 1, 1, 0, 0, 0, NSTimeZone.getDefault());
```

```
NSTimestamp endOf2012 =
    new NSTimestamp(2012, 12, 31, 23, 59, 59, NSTimeZone.getDefault());
EOQualifier qualifier =
    Author.BOOKS.dot(Book.PUBLISHED_DATE.between(beginOf2012, endOf2012));
// ... now do the actual fetch
```

The important thing here is, that we basically create a key path from an author to the *publishedDate* of all books. The dot() method help building the key path.

16.1.4 Building an SQL like qualifying string

There are other ways to build qualifiers. Here is one example doing it "the old WebObjects way". The qualifier is built using a string similar to a where-clause in SQL. You can use %@ as a placeholder for an object. The objects must then be provided as elements of an array.

```
NSMutableArray args = new NSMutableArray();
args.addObject(username);
args.addObject(password);
EOQualifier qual = EOQualifier.qualifierWithQualifierFormat(
    "userName = %@ AND password = %@", args);
```

The names of the attributes are included in textual form. It can easily happen that you mistype a name. Such an error will only show at runtime, the compiler cannot catch it.

16.1.5 Qualifying for NULL values

Sometimes it is important to build a qualifier for null-values. There are different ways to do that, too. You could use NSKeyValueCoding.NullValue as the object you stick into the array when using the EOQualifier.qualifierWithQualifierFormat() method or you can use the isNull() or isNotNull() methods of ERXKey. Here is the same example for both ways.

```
// Wonder way
EOQualifier qualifier = Book.PUBLISHED_DATE.isNull();

// building the qualifier by hand (WebObjects way)
NSMutableArray args = new NSMutableArray();
args.addObject(NSKeyValueCoding.NullValue);
EOQualifier qualifier =
    EOQualifier.qualifierWithQualifierFormat("published = %@", args);
```

16.1.6 In-Memory Filtering of an Array

A qualifier is independent of anything database related. It is just a key path with comparisons and logical operations like and and or. It is all key value coding – and NSArray also understands key value coding. This allows us to apply a qualifier to an array for filtering.

```
NSArray<Author> unfilteredList = ...; // assume existing list of authors

EOQualifier qualifier =
    Author.NATIONALITY.eq("GER").and(Author.LAST_NAME.like("B*"));
```

```
// return new filtered Array...
NSArray<Author> filteredList =
    EOQualifier.filteredArrayWithQualifier(unfilteredList, qualifier);

// filter NSMutableArray in place...
EOQualifier.filterArrayWithQualifier(unfilteredList, qual);
```

EOQualifier has two static methods that take an NSArray (or NSMutableArray) and a qualifier and apply that qualifier to the array. One method, filteredArrayWithQualifier(), returns a new NSArray containing only the objects that match the qualifier, the original array is untouched, whereas the second method, filterArrayWithQualifier(), needs an NSMutableArray and applies the filter in place, throwing out all objects that do not match the qualifier.

16.2 What Order Do You Like Your Objects? – Sorting

Very often when we read data from a database we want the resulting list sorted. Relational databases are very good at sorting, so it makes sense to include sort criteria with a fetch specification and offload the job of sorting to the database. Let's retrieve the list of *Authors* sorted by *lastName*, ordered ascending.

```
ERXSortOrdering sortOrdering = Author.LAST_NAME.asc();
```

We can create an ERXSortOrdering in a similar fashion as we have created the qualifier. Want to sort the list of authors by the publication date of their books? It's just a key path away.

```
ERXSortOrdering sortOrdering = Author.BOOKS.dot(Book.PUBLISHED_DATE.asc());
```

Note

Sorting can include more than one attribute, thus we need an array of sortOrderings. *The examples so far specified one attribute for sorting. Therefore we use the class* ERXSortOrdering *(singular name). You can call the* array()*-method on it to create an array.*

And what about the combination? First we sort ascending by the author's last name, then by the first name descending. Here we need the plural form ERXSortOrderings because we have more than one sort attribute.

```
ERXSortOrderings sortOrderings =
Author.LAST_NAME.asc().then(Author.FIRST_NAME.desc());
```

EOSortOrderings is something like an NSArray containing sort criteria.

16.2.1 In-Memory Sorting of an Array

Like with the qualifier above we can use sort orderings to sort any array.

```
// create a new sorted array
NSArray sorted =
    EOSortOrdering.sortedArrayUsingKeyOrderArray(myArray, sortOrderings);

// sort existing array in place
EOSortOrdering.sortArrayUsingKeyOrderArray(myMutableArray, sortOrderings);
```

Again there are two methods, one returns a new array, leaving the original array untouched, the other one needs an NSMutableArray as input and sorts this one in place.

Note

Check the documentation for the classes ERXSortOrdering, ERXKey, ERXQ. These classes contain tons of interesting and useful methods. You do not however have to learn them by heart. But it is good to know what is there, so in case you need something you know where to look.

16.3   The Fetch Specification ERXFetchSpecification

The fetch specification is the final object we need for getting objects from the database. There are various ways to create a fetch specification. You can create one manually in code, create a fetch specification with Entity Modeler, or use convenience methods for fetching.

16.3.1 Building a Fetch Specification Manually in Code

A fetch specification is always associated with an entity. So the most basic form is

```
ERXFetchSpecification<Author> fs =
        new ERXFetchSpecification<Author>(Author.ENTITY_NAME);
```

The only required parameter is the name of the associated entity. Here we can make use of the constant ENTITY_NAME that EOGenerator has put into _Author. This fetch specification allows for an unqualified fetch. We select every available *Author* object.

There is a second constructor for a fetch specification. You use this second form when you need to qualify the data and/or sort the resulting NSArray.

```
EOQualifier qualifier = ...           // build your qualifier as needed
ERXSOrtOrderings sortOrderings = ...  // build your sort orderings as needed
ERXFetchSpecification<Author> fs =
        new ERXFetchSpecification<Author>(
                            Author.ENTITY_NAME, qualifier, sortOrderings);
```

qualifier as well as sortOrderings are allowed to be null.

16.4 FetchSpecification in the Model

You can build a fetch specification with Entity Modeler and store it right in the EOModel. Let's create an author fetch specification. Open the EOModel and from the context menu popup on Author select *New Fetch Specification*.

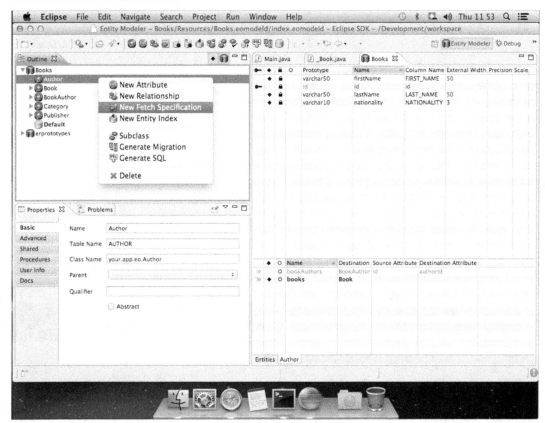

Picture 16-1   Creating a fetch specification in the model

We want to create a fetch specification for fetching authors by their first and last name. Give the fetch specification a descriptive name.

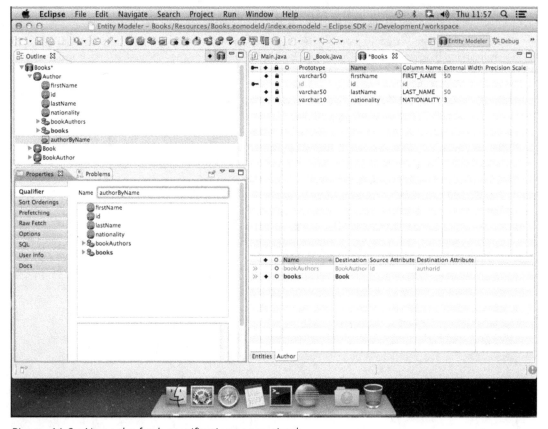

Picture 16-2   Name the fetch specification appropriately

Below the name of the fetch specification you see the list of attributes and relationship of Author. Click on them to put the attribute into the lower area where you build your qualifier. Using the disclosure triangles you can build key paths. Where you need a query parameter you simply invent something. Just prefix the name with a $. You can use the words and, or and not to form quite complex logical expressions, as well as parentheses to group parts of your expression. If you want to include constant values, enclose strings with single ticks " ' ".

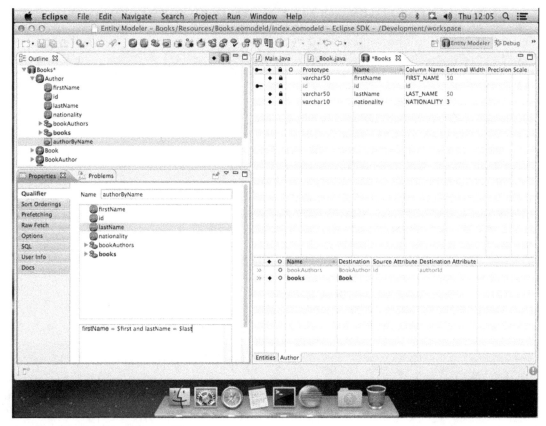

Picture 16-3   Building the qualifier

In our example we have created two placeholders for the selection criteria. You will see later on when we use this fetch specification, we simply have to provide an NSDictionary containing the keys first and last (without $) with the values for qualifying the fetch. The framework is clever enough that when you do not provide a key of one of the $placeholders it will not build that part of the qualifier. So just have a dictionary containing a key *last* and the fetch will only qualify on *lastName*.

Switch to the *SORT ORDERINGS* tab and enter any sort criteria. Click the desired attribute (or key path across relationships), then click *ADD*. You can switch between ascending and descending order and you can specify that you want to order case sensitive (s) or case insensitive (i). Just click the symbols to toggle.

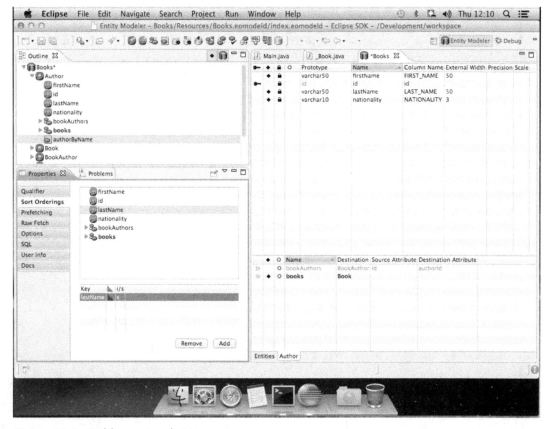

Picture 16-4   Building sort orderings

There are many more options you can set for a fetch specification. Have a look at the documentation for the class ERXFetchSpecification when you have a minute to spare.

Using a model based fetch specification is simple. Have a look at some typical code:

```
// load the fetch spec from the model
EOFetchSpecification fetchSpec = EOFetchSpecification.fetchSpecificationNamed
    ("authorByName", Author.ENTITY_NAME);

// prepare the bindings dict for the parameters
NSMutableDictionary<String, Object> bindings =
    new NSMutableDictionary<String, Object>();

// we fetch Ken Follet, our fetch spec has two
// parameters "$first" and "$last"
bindings.takeValueForKey("Ken", "first");
bindings.takeValueForKey("Follet", "last");

// replace the parameters with actual query values
fetchSpec = fetchSpec.fetchSpecificationWithQualifierBindings(bindings);
```

The static method fetchSpecificationNamed() on class EOFetchSpecification retrieves the named fetch specification from the model. The call to fetchSpecificationWithQualifierBindings() will then use the key value pairs from the dictionary to replace the *$placeholders* in the fetch specification with actual values.

After creating or modifying a fetch specification you must regenerate the java class files. The templates are setup in a way that a handful of convenience methods are created that work with fetch specifications. We'll have a look at these a bit further down.

16.5 Putting it all together

The first step is always to create a fetch specification. We have seen various ways to do this and we have seen that a fetch specification can include qualifiers and sort orderings.

The second step is accessing the editing context. You can use the session's default editing context or you can create a new one.

In the third step you tell the editing context to execute the fetch specification.

Here is the outline of the necessary code.

```
ERXFetchSpecification<Author> fetchSpec = ... // wherever this comes from

// get a reference to the session's default editing context
// (or create a new one)
EOEditingContext ec = session().defaultEditingContext();

// tell the editing context to execute the fetch
NSArray<Author> authors = ec.objectsWithFetchSpecification(fetchSpec);
```

16.6 Using the Wonder Convenience Methods for Fetching

Every fetch requires a similar sequence of code lines. Because of this the Wonder templates for the generation of class files generate convenience methods that you can use.

We'll have a look at some of these. All the examples are from class _Author.

Here is one that does an unqualified fetch. It simply returns all *Authors* from the database.

```
public static NSArray<Author> fetchAllAuthors(EOEditingContext editingContext) {
    return _Author.fetchAllAuthors(editingContext, null);
}
```

Use this like so:

```
NSArray<Author> authors =
    Author.fetchAllAuthors(session().defaultEditingContext());
```

Fetching Enterprise Objects

There are variants of this method that take qualifiers and sortOrderings as additional parameters. These will be called fetchAuthorsXXX(). Note the plural form. Other variants (with singular name fetchAuthorXXX) return exactly one Author object. Yet others will handle the cases where none or more than one Author is/can be found.

There are also some methods particularly specific to our fetch specification in the model. You remember, in the example above, we have created a fetch specification with name fetchAuthorByName. The generated code will then contain methods with the name fetchAuthorByName. Here are two examples copied directly from the file _Author.java. The first one takes an NSDictionary for the bindings in the fetch specification:

```
public static NSArray<your.app.eo.Author> fetchAuthorByName(
    EOEditingContext editingContext,
    NSDictionary<String, Object> bindings) {

    EOFetchSpecification fetchSpec =
        EOFetchSpecification.fetchSpecificationNamed(
            "authorByName", _Author.ENTITY_NAME);
    fetchSpec =
        fetchSpec.fetchSpecificationWithQualifierBindings(bindings);
    return (NSArray<your.app.eo.Author>)
        editingContext.objectsWithFetchSpecification(fetchSpec);
}
```

And the second one takes one value for each of the parameters in the fetch specification:

```
public static NSArray<your.app.eo.Author> fetchAuthorByName(
    EOEditingContext editingContext,
    String firstBinding,
    String lastBinding) {

    EOFetchSpecification fetchSpec =
        EOFetchSpecification.fetchSpecificationNamed
            ("authorByName", _Author.ENTITY_NAME);

    NSMutableDictionary<String, Object> bindings =
        new NSMutableDictionary<String, Object>();

    bindings.takeValueForKey(firstBinding, "first");
    bindings.takeValueForKey(lastBinding, "last");

    fetchSpec =
        fetchSpec.fetchSpecificationWithQualifierBindings(bindings);
    return (NSArray<your.app.eo.Author>)
        editingContext.objectsWithFetchSpecification(fetchSpec);
}
```

From this code you see how the fetch specification from the model is being used. The first method takes an NSDictionary containing the two keys for last and first, whereas the second method takes the values for the two placeholders in the fetch specification individually.

16.7 Using EOUtilities Convenience Methods

There is also a class `EOUtilities` that has several convenience methods for fetching. All of the methods are static and most of them take an editing context reference as the first parameter. Here are some methods that might come handy eventually:

```
objectMatchingKeyAndValue(EOEditingContext ec, String name, String key, Object value)
```

Creates an EOKeyValueQualifier with the specified key and value and returns the matching enterprise object.

```
objectMatchingValues(EOEditingContext ec, String name, NSDictionary values)
```

Creates EOKeyValueQualifiers for each key-value pair in the specified dictionary, ANDs these qualifiers together into an EOAndQualifier, and returns the matching enterprise object.

```
objectWithFetchSpecificationAndBindings(
    EOEditingContext ec,
    String entityName,
    String fetchSpecName,
    NSDictionary bindings)
```

Fetches the enterprise object retrieved with the specified fetch specification and bindings.

There are many more. Most of the fetch-methods are available in singular and plural form. The singular form of the name returns exactly one object, whereas the methods with plural forms can return zero or many objects. Go and have a look in the documentation. You never know when one or another method could be just what you need.

16.8 A Complete Fetch Example

Let's build a simple functioning example. We want to fetch *Authors* and allow the user to specify query parameters for first and last name.

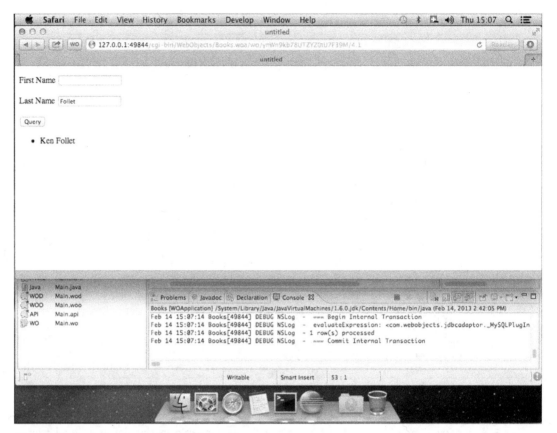

Picture 16-5   *A simple query page for authors*

The html and the bindings are very simple. Put this into your *Main.wo*

```
<?xml version="1.0" encoding="UTF-8"?>
<!DOCTYPE html PUBLIC "-//W3C//DTD XHTML 1.1//EN"
    "http://www.w3.org/TR/xhtml11/DTD/xhtml11.dtd">

<html xmlns="http://www.w3.org/1999/xhtml" xml:lang="en">
<head>
    <meta http-equiv="Content-Type" content="text/html; charset=utf-8"/>
    <title>untitled</title>
</head>
<body>
<webobject name = "form">
    <p>First Name <webobject name = "firstName" /></p>
    <p>Last Name <webobject name = "lastName" /></p>
    <p><webobject name = "queryDb" /></p>
</webobject>
<ul>
<webobject name = "list">
    <li><webobject name = "authorFirst" /> <webobject name = "authorLast" /></li>
</webobject>
</ul>
</body>
```

```
</html>
```

And the bindings

```
form : WOForm {
    multipleSubmit = true;
}

firstName : WOTextField {
    value = queryBindings.first;
}

lastName : WOTextField {
    value = queryBindings.last;
}

queryDb : WOSubmitButton {
    value = "Query";
    action = reload;
}
list : WORepetition {
    list = authors;
    item = authorsLoopvar;
}

authorFirst : WOString {
    value = authorsLoopvar.firstName;
}

authorLast : WOString {
    value = authorsLoopvar.lastName;
}
```

The values for firstName and lastName bind to keys *first* and *last* respectively in an NSMutableDictionary. As these keys do not (yet) exist in the dictionary WOLips will probably warn you about that. This is a warning you can safely ignore.

Here is key value coding again. Look at the firstName and lastName bindings. During takeValuesFromRequest(), when the form has been submitted, the framework will first ask for an object for the key queryBindings. This is an NSMutableDictionary (see the Java code just below). The framework will then ask this object to setObjectForKey() with key being either *first* or *last*. That is exactly what a dictionary is supposed to do. That way, the query values the user has entered, end up in the queryBindings dictionary

Now look at the java code:

```
package your.app.components;

import your.app.eo.Author;

import com.webobjects.appserver.WOComponent;
import com.webobjects.appserver.WOContext;
import com.webobjects.foundation.NSArray;
import com.webobjects.foundation.NSMutableDictionary;
```

```
import er.extensions.components.ERXComponent;

public class Main extends ERXComponent {

    public Main(WOContext context) {
        super(context);
    }

    public void awake() {
        super.awake();
        queryBindings = new NSMutableDictionary<String, Object>();
    }

    private NSArray<Author> authors;
    private Author authorsLoopvar;

    private NSMutableDictionary<String, Object> queryBindings;

    public WOComponent reload() {
        authors = Author.fetchAuthorByName(
            session().defaultEditingContext(), queryBindings);
        return null;
    }
    // bunch of accessor methods, left out for brevity

}
```

During awake() we reset the queryBindings dictionary. When takeValuesFromRequest() happens the values from the form fields are pushed into the dictionary. Next phase in processing is invokeAction(). The action method uses the loaded dictionary to qualify the fetch specification, then the fetch is performed and the resulting list of fetched Authors is put into the authors instance variable. Next step in the request-response-loop is appendToResponse(), which will access the list of authors to build the html.

While playing with this little example you may realize that there is one problem. There is no way to specify wildcards. You might think you can enter "M*" for the last name and get all authors whose name begins with "M". But your application does not find anything and returns an empty list.

What is wrong here?

Let's go back to Entity Modeler and have a closer look at our fetch specification. We have the qualifier written as

```
firstName = $first and lastName = $last
```

This tests equality of the entered criteria. You probably do not have an author with a name containing an asterisk. If you want to be able to use wildcards you can replace the equals sign in the fetch specification by either *like* or *caseInsensitiveLike*.

```
firstName like $first and lastName like $last
```

Now it works!

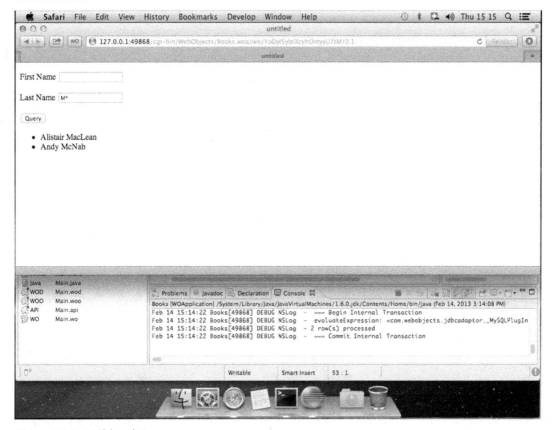

Picture 16-6   Wildcards in query

17 Editing Enterprise Objects

In the previous chapter you have seen how to access a database and retrieve objects. In this chapter we are going to have a closer look at these objects as well as what the role of the editing context is.

17.1 The Editing Context revisited

We have already seen that the editing context is a very important thing. It kind of represents the database in our object oriented world. So far we have used the editing context to fetch enterprise objects. There is a lot of interaction going on between editing context and an enterprise object. This interaction happens mostly through two important methods in the generated class files.

Let's have a closer look at some of the generated methods in the Java class files for our entities, namely the accessor methods for an attribute like *firstName* in the *Customer* entity.

```
public String firstName() {
  return (String) storedValueForKey(_Author.FIRST_NAME_KEY);
}

public void setFirstName(String value) {
  if (_Author.LOG.isDebugEnabled()) {
    _Author.LOG.debug( "updating firstName from " + firstName() +
      " to " + value);
  }
  takeStoredValueForKey(value, _Author.FIRST_NAME_KEY);
}
```

There are these two methods storedValueForKey() and takeStoredValueForKey() that are of interest here. Both methods are inherited from EOEnterpriseObject. These methods interact directly with the editing context that this enterprise object is associated with. Whenever you access the *firstName* attribute, the method storedValueForKey() will return the first name of the customer. But it will also keep the editing context updated. More importantly, when you assign a new first name to that customer, you do this by calling the setFirstName() method. This method will then call takeStoredValueForKey(). takeStoredValueForKey() will not only take the new value, but it will inform the editing context about the change. Through the use of the standard accessor methods for any attribute the editing context will be able to keep track of any change in the objects properties. The editing context knows at all times the exact state of your enterprise objects.

There are some typical tasks one has to perform when using a database: **select** data, **insert** new records, **update** columns, and **delete** existing records. After you are done you tell the database to **commit** your changes. With EOF this works a bit differently.

The following table shows how these SQL tasks map to EOF tasks. You also see some sample code, which we will discuss next.

SQL	EOF	Example Code
SELECT	tell editing context to fetch	ec.objectsWithFetchSpecification();

UPDATE	edit your enterprise object, tell editing context	`customer.setFirstName("John");`
INSERT	create an new enterprise object and associate with an editing context	`Customer customer = new Customer();` `ec.insertObject(customer);`
DELETE	tell editing context	`ec.deleteObject(customer);`
COMMIT	tell editing context	`ec.saveChanges();`

Selecting objects has been covered in the previous chapter. Updating objects is described right above that table. So let's concentrate on the other tasks.

17.2 Creating New Enterprise Objects

Enterprise objects are plain java objects. You create them with the new operator. There is only one important thing you must never forget: each and every enterprise object must be associated with an editing context! There is that typical sequence when you create a new enterprise object:

```
Customer aNewCustomer = new Customer();
editingContext.insertObject (aNewCustomer);
```

The first line creates a new customer object and the second line inserts this object into the editing context.

Note

Inserting an object into the editing context does not insert any data into the database. The editing context merely starts to observe the object and track all modifications to it. Only later will the record get created in the database.

A silly error that often happens is when you create the object but forget to associate it with an editing context. There is a simple cover method in `EOUtilities` that does both steps. We strongly recommend to always using this method.

```
Customer aNewCustomer = (Customer)EOUtilities.createAndInsertInstance (
                                editingContext, Customer.ENTITY_NAME);
```

By using this method your enterprise objects will always be associated with an editing context.

17.3 Deleting Enterprise Objects

When you need to delete an enterprise object (and its data from the database) you simply tell the editing context.

```
editingContext.deleteObject(customer);
```

Make sure to not touch that object anymore. The editing context will make sure that the corresponding data will be removed from the database. Again, as with creating a new object, the editing context keeps track of any deletion but the delete statement against the database will not yet be issued.

17.4 Saving Changes, Reverting Enterprise Objects to Previous State

Eventually you are done with your edits. Now comes the time you need to make your changes permanent.

```
editingContext.saveChanges();
```

Simply tell the editing context to save all changes. When you do this, the editing context will then generate all the necessary SQL statement. It will create INSERT, UPDATE, and DELETE as needed. As all modifications to any enterprise object have been tracked by the editing context it knows exactly what has changed. It will only issue the required SQL statements.

There are situations where you decide you want to rollback all changes to your enterprise objects (that is, before making them permanent). There are two methods available:

```
editingContext.revert();
```

revert() will throw away all modifications since the last time saveChanges() was called. Any edits will be forgotten.

```
editingContext.refetch();
```

This call goes even further. Whereas revert() simply forgets any changes made, refetch() will do the same but then go to the database and reload everything. This might bring in new data from edits other users may have made in the mean time.

Sometimes saveChanges() fails. This can happen, if the underlying database record has been changed be another user. Saving your modifications will then collide with those changes. Another typical problem could be a unique constraint violation.

Therefore you will often wrap saveChanges() within a try/catch block.

```
try {
    editingContext.saveChanges();
}
catch (Exception ex) {

    // tell the user that saving has failed
    // (ex.getMessage() will tell you why)
    // System.out.println(…) or whatever other way makes sense
```

```
    // then revert or refetch as needed
    editingContext.revert();    // or maybe refetch()
}
```

In addition to saving and reverting, the editing context also has undo() an redo() methods. However, be careful with these. They can make your edits complicated and, in conjunction with back tracking, can create a mess. During the many years I have been using WebObjects and Wonder I have never used undo() and redo(). But they are there and available if you need them. Read the documentation!

18 Working with Relationships

We have already worked quite a bit with relationships. We created relationships in the model and we have seen, that we can bind to key paths when fetching and displaying objects. Key paths span relationships.

In the database primary keys and foreign keys express relationships. In the object oriented world object relationships are usually realized in code with a class instance variable for a to-one relationship and arrays (or other kinds of collection) for to-many relationships.

Here is the dialog from Entity Modeler that pops up when you create a relationship between two entities. We have already seen this.

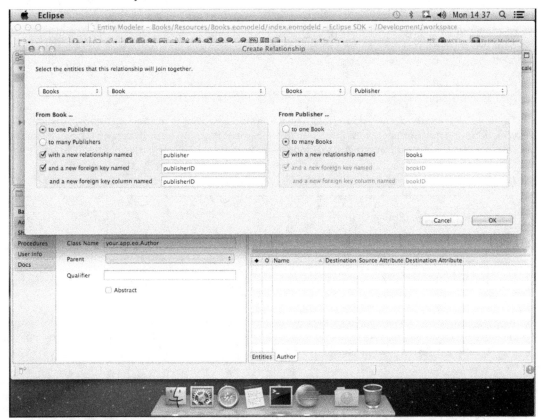

Picture 18-1   Creating a Relationship in Entity Modeler

In general the created relationship is two-way. This means that in the above example there is a relationship being created from entity *Book* to entity *Publisher* and a second inverse relationship from *Publisher* to *Book*. The option WITH A NEW RELATIONSHIP NAMED is checked on both sides. Sometimes you do not want a two-way relationship. Just don't tick the respective check box then! Imagine having a relationship between *Customer* and *ZIPCode*. Resolving a relationship in the database requires join operations between two or more tables. Such operations are rather costly performance wise. For a *Customer* you may need his address and thus the to-one relationship to *ZIPCode* is important. However you may never want to find all Customers given a certain *ZIPCode* (of course something like this depends on the particular requirements of your business).

But be aware that you can only navigate relationships that are modeled. So if you need it, then model it!

18.1 Adding an Object to a Relationship

There are several methods available to join objects. For a to-one relationship you basically just set an instance variable to point to the to-one object. Of course you have to tell the editing context about the changes. For a to-many relationship you add the newly referenced object to the array of many-objects. And again you need to tell the editing context. By the way, you are aware of the fact that with any relationship there are two objects involved, so both must notify the editing context about the changes. And then there is the thing with the direction of the relationship. For a two-way relationship both objects are involved whereas for a one-way relationship only on object takes active part. Which one? You have to be aware of quite some things from your model so you do not forget anything when connecting objects.

So far you should know that something that complicated cannot be the end of the issue in Wonder. And of course it is not!

There is one method that does it all. This method reads the model and knows exactly which directions the relation ship runs. It will call the right things for both objects on both sides of the relationship, no matter how things are modeled. So here is the one and only method you need to know to connect objects.

```
Book aBook = ...;
Publisher aPublisher = ...;
aBook.addObjectToBothSidesOfRelationshipWithKey(
        aPublisher, Book.PUBLISHER_KEY);
```

A method doing that much deserves a long name, wouldn't you agree? Just don't forget, in Eclipse control-space is your friend, no need to type it out all the time.

But what about a many-to-many relationship, you may ask. We have one in our *Books* example between *Book* an *Author*. There is that join table sitting in between which is needed in the relational world. Let the EOF framework do all the work.

```
Book aBook = ...;
Author anAuthor = ...;
aBook.addObjectToBothSidesOfRelationshipWithKey(
        anAutor, Book.AUTHOR_KEY);
```

See? No need to do anything differently. I strongly recommend to only ever using this method. In case you wonder about all the other relationship methods, in class ERXGenericRecord and generated by *eogen*... Wonder does (almost) everything for you, but it allows you to intercept, control, and alter the behavior of the frameworks. Do you need more control for debugging? Do you want to implement custom behavior? Simply do it, the hooks are there. Override those methods and put your custom code in.

Note

There is also a method with plural form in its name that allows to add more than one object to a relationship with one call: addObjectsToBothSidesOfRelationshipWithKey(). This method takes an NSArray of objects and calls addObjectToBothSidesOfRelationshipWithKey() for each one.

18.2 Breaking the Relationship between Objects

Again, as with establishing a relationship between two objects, breaking it is done with a similar one-knows-all method. But again, what was said for creating relationships, is also true for removing objects from relationships: there are methods that let you intercept things and do it manually; but you don't have to.

```
aBook.removeObjectFromBothSidesOfRelationshipWithKey(
        aPublisher, Book.PUBLISHER_KEY);
```

Again the EOF framework handles the case of many-to-many relationship and join table. And again for this method, too, there is a plural form name: removeObjects FromBothSidesOfRelationshipWithKey(). Check out the documentation.

18.3 WOToOneRelationship and WOToManyRelationship Components

It is very common to have user interface elements like popups or selection lists so the user can easily change relationships.

Assume editing a *Book* object. A book has a to-one relationship to a *Category*. You can add a WOToOneRelationship component to your editing page. It will then show up as a popup button, by default listing all available *Categories*. Simply select the one you want and submit your changes.

Picture 18-2   WOToOneRelationship Component in Action

We are still playing with the *Books* project. Here is the code for the above example:

In the *Main.html* you put

```
<webobject name = "category" />
```

and in the *.wod* for the bindings you should have:

```
category : WOToOneRelationship {
    sourceObject = book;
    sourceEntityName = "Book";
    relationshipKey = "category";
    destinationDisplayKey = "title";
    uiStyle = "popup";
}
```

That's all there is. Nothing else needed. The framework will see from `sourceEntityName` and `relationshipKey` that the list of possible *Categories* is needed, so it will go and fetch that list automatically. It will then build the popup menu. The sourceObject binding and the relationshipKey tell the framework how to connect the book and the selected category. The destinationDisplayKey binding specifies what to use from the *Categories* to display in the popup.

There is another binding, uiStyle, that controls the way the list is shown. Default is popup but you can also specify radio or browser.

Very similar to WOToOneRelationship is the ready-made component WOToManyRelationship. It has the same bindings as WOToOneRelationship. Possible values for uiStyle are checkbox or browser. If you don't bind uiStyle, the component will select a style suitable for the number of entries in the list (default is for 5 entries or less: use checkboxes; more than 5 entries: use a browser).

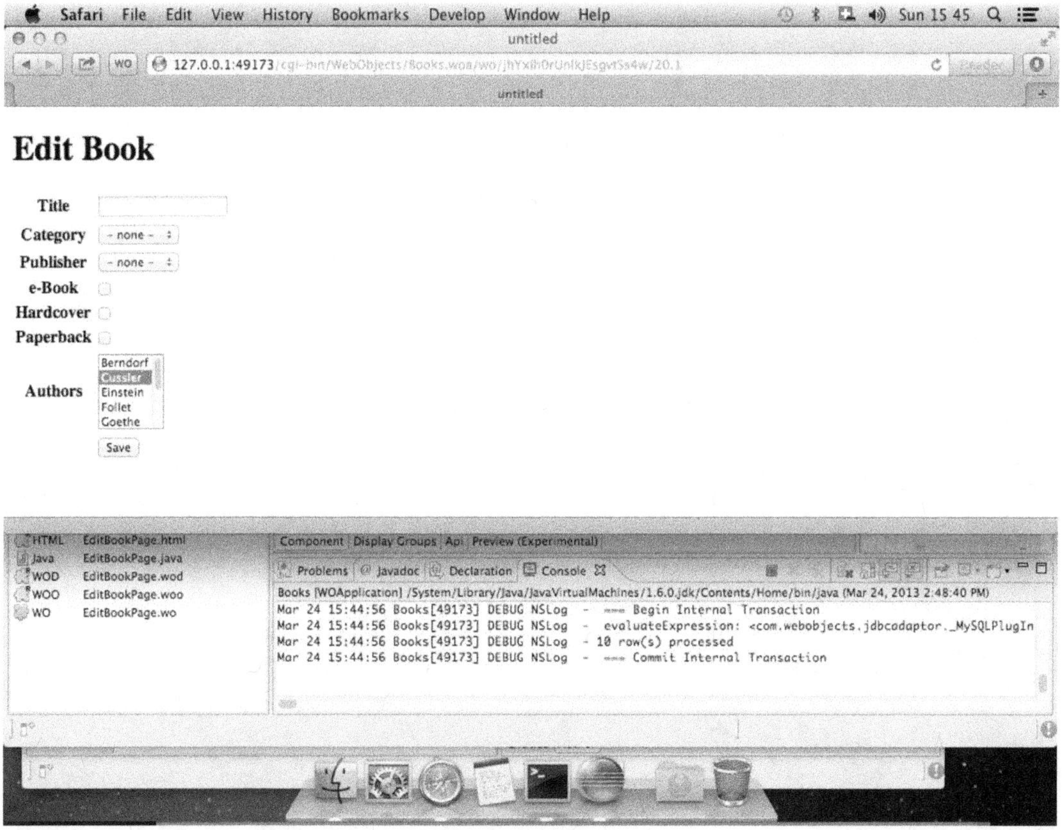

Picture 18-3   WOToManyRelationship displaying as a Browser

Part D - More Wonder

19 Working with Cookies

Cookies are bad! Or are they?

Well, first of all a **Cookie** is just a piece of data. No executable code, nothing that can harm your computer in any way or turn your fresh milk into bad smelling greenish stuff. Basically a Cookie is a key-value pair of strings. A Cookie cannot do anything on its own.

A Cookie can be sent from the web server to your browser. It is part of the http header. The browser does not interpret the cookie data in any way; it simply stores the cookie. Each cookie has two main attributes associated, a lifetime and a domain where it comes from. As long as the lifetime of the cookie has not yet expired, the browser sends the cookie back to the server it came from whenever the user makes a request to that server.

A response from a server can contain more than one cookie. All the cookies are sent as part of the response headers. Therefore a request to a server can also contain several cookies. These are again part of the request header.

When cookies were invented, the idea was to give the server the ability to recognize a user, to link one request from a user to a previously sent response. As we have seen in chapter 7.2, the http protocol is stateless, so there is no inherent way for a web server to logically connect one request-response loop with another one. Cookies give the server a means to pass information around to the user and back to the server. What gave cookies a somewhat bad reputation is not that fact that a cookie exists but how clever servers use cookies to track users, usually for advertising purposes. Besides that, cookies have their legitimate uses.

Working with cookies in Wonder is very easy.

19.1 Sending cookies in the response

You can add a cookie (or several) to a response at any time. Create the cookie giving a key and a value, then add the cookie to the response object. The class WOCookie helps in creating cookies.

```
WOCookie aCookie = new WOCookie("emailForLogin", "john@hotmail.com");
context().response().addCookie(aCookie);
```

In this example we create a cookie with name *emailForLogin*, and the value for this name is john@example.com.

As has been mentioned above, cookies do have some attributes of their own. You can set those easily using the following methods on your cookie:

```
aCookie.setDomain("www.example.com");    // a String
aCookie.setPath("/login");               // a String
aCookie.setExpires(expires);             // an NSTimestamp
aCookie.setIsSecure(true);               // a boolean
```

Working with Cookies

The *domain* specifies which host or subdomain can receive the cookie. The *path* controls which application or CGI path is valid for that domain. The *expires* attribute determines how long the cookie itself is valid. The *secure* attribute, when set to true, requires an HTTPS connection for the cookie to be sent.

19.2 Receiving cookies in the request

Any cookie sent to the server is simply sent as a key/value pair of strings. You do not get back a WOCookie object. Also the domain, path and expiration information is not sent back to the server. However it is very easy to get at the cookie value:

```
String emailAddress = context().request().cookieValueForKey("emailForLogin");
```

If there was a cookie with the name *emailForLogin* sent, the variable will receive the value (in this example it will be john@hotmail.com). Otherwise *emailAddress* will be null.

You can get a dictionary of all cookies in a request at once:

```
NSDictionary cookies = context().request().cookieValues();
```

19.3 A cookie example

To demonstrate how to use cookies we will develop a small application. The *Main.wo* page should display a simple text field and a submit button when no cookie has been received. The user can then submit a name. The application will send a cookie back containing this name. With the next request to the server from the same window this cookie will go back to the server. When the server receives a cookie it will show the name in a WOString and hide the text field and the submit button.

Create a new Wonder application with name *Cookies*. Here is the code for the *Main*-component:

Main.html

```
<?xml version="1.0" encoding="UTF-8"?>
<!DOCTYPE html PUBLIC "-//W3C//DTD XHTML 1.1//EN"
    "http://www.w3.org/TR/xhtml11/DTD/xhtml11.dtd">

<html xmlns="http://www.w3.org/1999/xhtml" xml:lang="en">
<head>
    <meta http-equiv="Content-Type" content="text/html; charset=utf-8"/>
    <title>Cookies Demo</title>
</head>
<body>
    <webobject name = "hasCookie">
    Welcome <webobject name = "lastnameString" />
    </webobject>
    <webobject name = "hasNoCookie">
    <webobject name = "form">
        <p>Name <webobject name = "lastnameField" /> <webobject name = "setCookie"
/>
```

```
    </webobject>
    </webobject>
</body>
</html>
```

Main.wod

```
form : WOForm {
    multipleSubmit = true;
}

lastnameString : WOString {
    value = lastname;
}

lastnameField : WOTextField {
    value = lastname;
}

hasCookie : WOConditional {
    condition = hasCookie;
}

hasNoCookie : WOConditional {
    condition = hasCookie;
    negate = true;
}

setCookie : WOSubmitButton {
    action = setCookie;
}
```

Main.java

```
package your.app.components;

import com.webobjects.appserver.WOComponent;
import com.webobjects.appserver.WOContext;
import com.webobjects.appserver.WOCookie;

import er.extensions.components.ERXComponent;

public class Main extends ERXComponent {

    private String lastname;
    private boolean hasCookie = false;

    public void awake() {
        super.awake();
        String name = context().request().cookieValueForKey("lastname");
        if (name != null && name.length() > 0) {
            lastname = name;
            hasCookie = true;
        }
    }
```

Working with Cookies

```
public WOComponent setCookie() {
    WOCookie aCookie = new WOCookie("lastname", lastname);
    context().response().addCookie(aCookie);
    return null;
}

public boolean hasCookie() {
    return hasCookie;
}

public Main(WOContext context) {
    super(context);
}

public String lastname() {
    return lastname;
}

public void setLastname(String lastname) {
    this.lastname = lastname;
}
}
```

Run the application. We are going to use Firefox in this example because Firefox can better show us the cookies than what Safari can do.

Picture 19-1   The initial window asking for an input.

After submitting the text the application will respond with the same page. However the response will contain the cookie. This can be seen when you go into Firefox preferences. Select the *PRIVACY* Section and click on *REMOVE INDIVIDUAL COOKIES*.

Working with Cookies

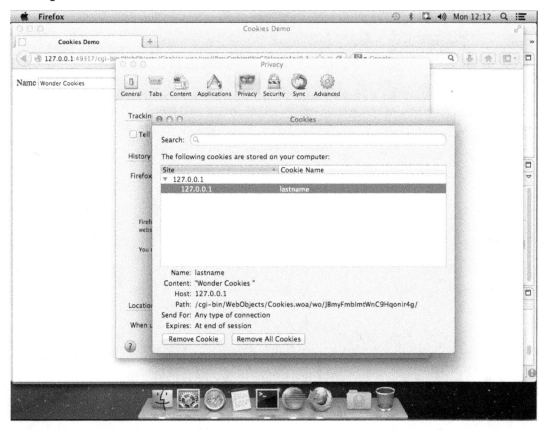

Picture 19-2   Firefox showing the cookie.

Why does the window still show the text input field? Of course it has to because the browser has received a cookie but not yet sent the cookie back to the server. Only with the next click on the button will the cookie be sent back to the application. And only now the application can respond to the cookie.

Picture 19-3   Application has received the cookie back

19.4 Issues with cookies

Cookies have some inherent problems. The allowed length of key and value is limited and browser dependent. Ok, a couple hundred bytes will always fit but you my run into problems when you try to stuff kilo- or even megabytes into a cookie.

Any cookie is just plain text and the browser usually stores cookies for later use somewhere in the file system where they can be altered with any text editor. The user can also disable the reception of cookies completely in the browser. So you will not have any guarantee to get a cookie back after sending one, or that what you get back is what you sent out.

Keeping these limitations in mind cookies can be a good choice in your application.

20 Display Groups and Batch Navigation

While we have seen how to fetch and display data from a database, there is one problem we have silently ignored so far. How would you handle the case where there are many database records in your selection but you only want to show ten at a time and allow the user to show the next batch of ten and so on?

There is one class in the frameworks that allows exactly such behavior: ERXDisplayGroup and its descendant ERXBatchingDisplayGroup.

20.1 What is a display group?

The display group can be seen as kind of a very high abstraction of a list of objects fetched from a database. Let me re-use some sentences from an old Apple document[4]:

"The details of fetching at the editing-context level are encapsulated within the display group to let component designers think at a higher level of abstraction. Part of fetching is the effect of sorting and qualifying, the net effect being a filtering of the displayed objects. The display group also handles these details, often without too much explicit control of the component designer. Altogether, the display group represents the highest, most abstract level of access that EOF provides for database operations. For common types of database access, the display group is often the easiest way for developers to implement solutions."

There are two main types of display groups. The simple (or master) display group is used to work with a list of objects, while the master detail display group is used to work with a list of objects dependent on one master object. An example for the simple type is a list of customers. A typical use case for the master detail display group is the list of orders (the details) for one customer (the master).

A display group can do a lot for you. There are many configuration options for a display group. WOLips also has a special graphical editor for display groups. We best look at an example for using a display group.

20.2 Using a display group

Suppose we have in our database a table that contains all the countries of the world. For each country we note the 2- and 3-character ISO codes and the international dialing code. Such a list contains well over 200 records.

Here is how the EOModel looks like:

---

[4] Official Training Material from the Apple Course Programming WebObjects I

Display Groups and Batch Navigation

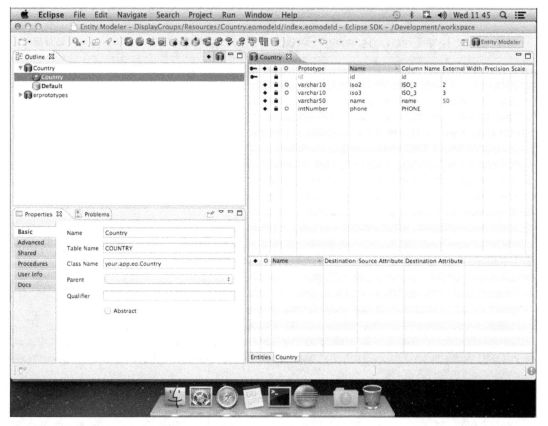

Picture 20-1   EOModel with Country entity

And this is the table definition and some example records from a MySQL database:

```
mysql> describe country;
+--------+--------------+------+-----+---------+-------+
| Field  | Type         | Null | Key | Default | Extra |
+--------+--------------+------+-----+---------+-------+
| NAME   | varchar(255) | NO   |     | NULL    |       |
| ISO_2  | varchar(255) | YES  |     | NULL    |       |
| ISO_3  | varchar(255) | YES  |     | NULL    |       |
| PHONE  | int(11)      | YES  |     | NULL    |       |
| ID     | int(11)      | NO   | PRI | NULL    |       |
+--------+--------------+------+-----+---------+-------+
5 rows in set (0.01 sec)

mysql> select * from country;
+----------------+-------+-------+-------+-----+
| NAME           | ISO_2 | ISO_3 | PHONE | ID  |
+----------------+-------+-------+-------+-----+
| Afghanistan    | AF    | AFG   |    93 | 1   |
| Albania        | AL    | ALB   |   355 | 2   |
| Algeria        | DZ    | DZA   |   213 | 3   |
| American Samoa | AS    | ASM   |     1 | 4   |
| Andorra        | AD    | AND   |   376 | 5   |
```

```
| Angola                              | AO    | AGO   |   244 |   6 |
...

...
| Uzbekistan                          | UZ    | UZB   |   998 | 224 |
| Vanuatu                             | VU    | VUT   |   678 | 225 |
| Venezuela                           | VE    | VEN   |    58 | 226 |
| Vietnam                             | VN    | VNM   |    84 | 227 |
| Wallis and Futuna                   | WF    | WLF   |   681 | 228 |
| Yemen                               | YE    | YEM   |   967 | 229 |
| Zambia                              | ZM    | ZMB   |   260 | 230 |
| Zimbabwe                            | ZW    | ZWE   |   263 | 231 |
+-------------------------------------+-------+-------+-------+-----+
231 rows in set (0.00 sec)
mysql>
```

For this example I have created a simple Wonder application with the EOModel containing just that one *Country* entity.

Let's see what the *Main* component looks like.

In *Main.java* we created two instance variables with corresponding accessor methods, one for the display group and one to be used as loop variable. This is a plain standard *Main* class.

```java
package your.app.components;

import your.app.eo.Country;

import com.webobjects.appserver.WOContext;

import er.extensions.appserver.ERXDisplayGroup;
import er.extensions.components.ERXComponent;

public class Main extends ERXComponent {

    private ERXDisplayGroup<Country> displayGroup;
    private Country countryLoopvar;

    public Main(WOContext context) {
        super(context);
    }

    public ERXDisplayGroup<Country> displayGroup() {
        return displayGroup;
    }

    public void setDisplayGroup(
                ERXDisplayGroup<Country> displayGroup) {
        this.displayGroup = displayGroup;
    }

    public Country countryLoopvar() {
        return countryLoopvar;
    }

    public void setCountryLoopvar(Country countryLoopvar) {
        this.countryLoopvar = countryLoopvar;
    }
}
```

Display Groups and Batch Navigation

More interesting is the html and bindings part:

```
<?xml version="1.0" encoding="UTF-8"?>
<!DOCTYPE html PUBLIC "-//W3C//DTD XHTML 1.1//EN"
    "http://www.w3.org/TR/xhtml11/DTD/xhtml11.dtd">

<html xmlns="http://www.w3.org/1999/xhtml" xml:lang="en">
    <head>
        <meta http-equiv="Content-Type" content="text/html;
                                            charset=utf-8"/>
        <title>Display Group Demo</title>
    </head>
    <body>
        <ul>
        <webobject name = "countries">
            <li><webobject name = "countryName" /></li>
        </webobject>
        </ul>
    </body>
</html>
```

You can see that we have a list (`<ul>`) with list items (`<li>`) wrapped in a repetition called countries. Look at the bindings:

```
countries : WORepetition {
    list = displayGroup.displayedObjects;
    item = countryLoopvar;
}

countryName : WOString {
    value = countryLoopvar.name;
}
```

The interesting thing here is where the list of countries comes from. The `displayGroup` object obviously has a key called *displayedObjects*, which seems to return an `NSArray` which we use to iterate over.

20.3 Defining and Initializing a Display Group with the Graphical Editor

But wait! Where is the display group defined? The only thing we see is an instance variable called *displayGroup*. This must get initialized somewhere. And how does the display group know that it is supposed to fetch *Countries*?

Look at the *Main.wo* editor window. We have used that window so far in split view mode with the upper part showing the html-code and the lower part displaying the bindings. If you look closely at the bottom you can see there are a couple of tabs. The one on the far left called COMPONENT is what we have been working with. There is a second tab called DISPLAY GROUPS. Open your *Main.wo* and click that second tab. I have enlarged the editor window in Eclipse so you can see the full glory of that DISPLAY GROUPS tab.

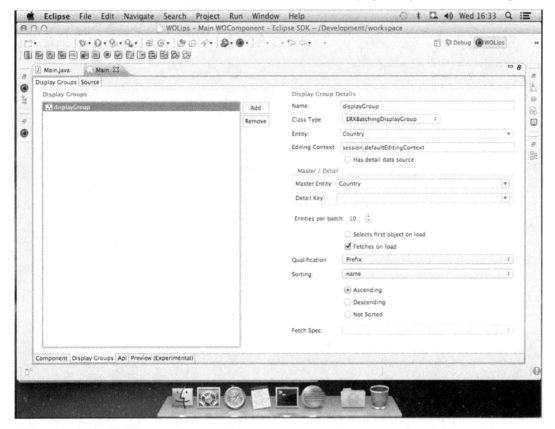

Picture 20-2   Editing Display Group properties

We have defined a display group called *displayGroup*. The right side of the window shows the properties of this display group.

The name is *displayGroup*. This is the name of the instance variable!

The type is ERXBatchingDisplayGroup.

Each display group must be associated with an entity. Here, this the Country entity.

And of course for fetching we need an editing context. We use the default editing context from the session.

We can specify whether this display group is a detail display group or a master display group. When we check *HAS DETAIL DATA SOURCE*, we need to give a key for the details. Assuming for a minute that the master object is a customer (entity *Customer*) and we want to display all the order objects (found via aCustomer.orders()) then we would set the *DETAIL KEY* to *orders*.

A display group has internal variables to hold objects(s) a user selects from the list. We can tick the *SELECT FIRST OBJECT ON LOAD* check box if we want that internal list of selected objects to initially hold the first object from the displayed list. The display group has methods to add to and remove objects from that internal list. This is simply so that we do not need to create any instance variables of our own.

Display Groups and Batch Navigation

FETCHES ON LOAD does exactly what its name implies. When the page is loaded the display group right away goes to the database and fetches the objects. When the box is not checked, we must trigger the fetch action via code. This could be a button whose *action* is bound to displayGroup.qualifyDataSource.

ENTITIES PER BATCH is pretty self-explanatory. The same holds for *QUALIFICATION*, *SORTING*, and *FETCH SPEC*. You can use a fetch specification defined in the model. The corresponding popup button would let you pick the one you want. A display group has a *queryBindings* key that is a NSDictionary. Remember when we talked about fetch specifications in the model having parameters? This is exactly the same. We will see an example a bit further down.

That way you can define one or more display groups in your component. You just need to declare an instance variable and accessor methods for each display group.

The display group editor window has a *SOURCE* tab at the top. Click it and look at what the graphical editor actually generates.

```
{
    "WebObjects Release" = "WebObjects 5.0";
    encoding = "UTF-8";
    variables = {
        displayGroup = {
            class = ERXBatchingDisplayGroup;
            dataSource = {
                class = EODatabaseDataSource;
                editingContext = "session.defaultEditingContext";
                fetchSpecification = {
                    class = EOFetchSpecification;
                    entityName = Country;
                    isDeep = YES;
                    prefetchingRelationshipKeyPaths = ();
                };
            };
            fetchesOnLoad = YES;
            formatForLikeQualifier = "%@*";
            numberOfObjectsPerBatch = 10;
            selectsFirstObjectAfterFetch = NO;
            sortOrdering = ({class = EOSortOrdering;
                key = name; selectorName = "compareAscending:"; });
        };
    };
}
```

You could have written this by hand, but then who wants to! This is the content of the file *Main.woo*. So the *.woo* file is used for display group specifications. When your application is run and the component is created, the framework will read this file and set up your display groups.

Let's run the application!

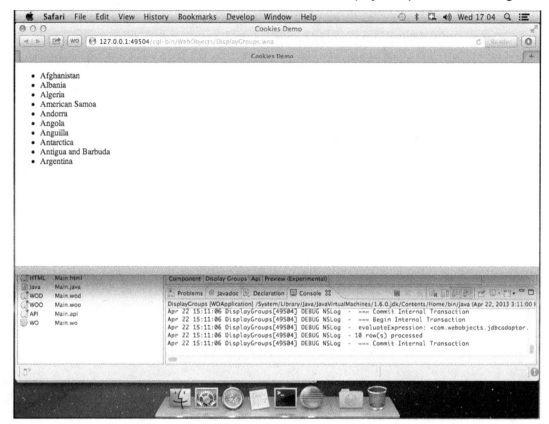

Picture 20-3   Running the display group application

As soon as the main page is created the console window shows that the database is being queried. You can clearly see the message 10 row(s) processed. So with almost no code at all (just two instance variables plus accessor methods) we can display the list of countries (well, the first batch of 10 countries). We know there are more, so how do we let the user see more?

20.4   Batch Navigation with Display Groups

A display group has methods for showing the next or previous batch. You could thus bind the action of a WOHyperlink to these methods. But why do this manually? There is this nice (and highly customizable) ERXBatchNavigationBar. Let's add one to our page.

Simply add an object of class ERXBatchNavigationBar above the country repetition. The only required binding is the *displayGroup*. This tells the batch navigation bar object which display group it should control.

Display Groups and Batch Navigation

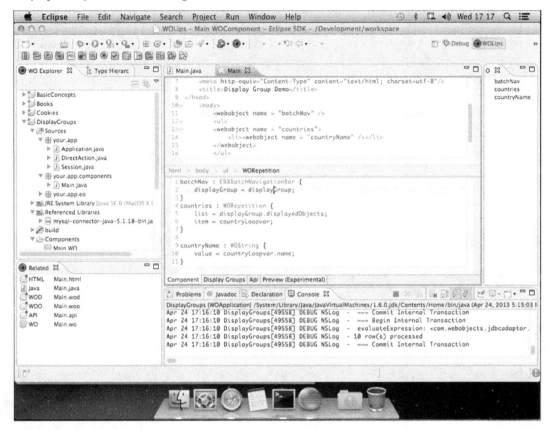

Picture 20-4   Adding the batch navigation bar to Main.wo

Look what we get!

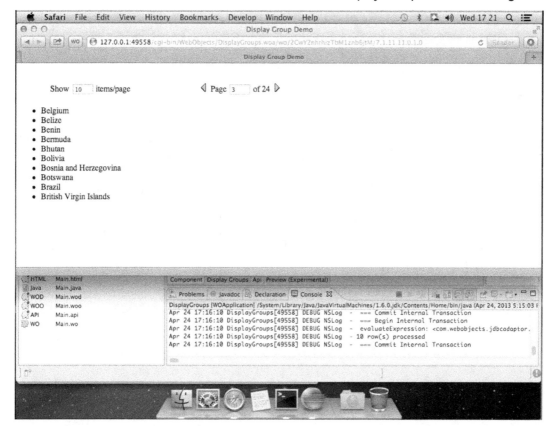

Picture 20-5   Batch navigation bar in action

Pretty cool – and still no code written!

We can do even better. Let's give the user a way to qualify the query.

Add a WOTextField to *Main.wo*, put a WOSubmitButton there and enclose these two objects with a WOForm.

Here are the relevant parts from the html file and the bindings:

```
<body>
    <webobject name = "form">
        <p>Country <webobject name = "countryQualifier" /></p>
        <p><webobject name = "query" />
    </webobject>
    <webobject name = "batchNav" />
    ...
```

```
form : WOForm {
```

```
    multipleSubmit = true;
}

countryQualifier : WOTextField {
    value = displayGroup.queryMatch.name;  // VALID
}

query : WOSubmitButton {
    action = displayGroup.qualifyDataSource;
}
```

We can bind the *countryQualifier* text field directly to the display group's *queryMatch* dictionary. This is similar to the *queryBindings* we used when working with fetch specifications. The *queryMatch* dictionary is internally used to build EOQualifiers. As we want to query by country name we have to specify name for the *queryMatch* key. The WOLips bindings validator will flag a warning because it cannot guarantee the name is a valid key for the *queryMatch* dictionary. We can add // VALID to tell the bindings validator that we know what we do.

At last we bind the action of our submit button to the display group's *qualifyDataSource*. We should probably deactivate the FETCH ON LOAD functionality. This is simply a matter of user interface preference. Do we want to retrieve the first batch of countries right away or do we want the user to (possibly) enter a qualifier and activate the fetch action manually? You decide!

Run the application and play with it.

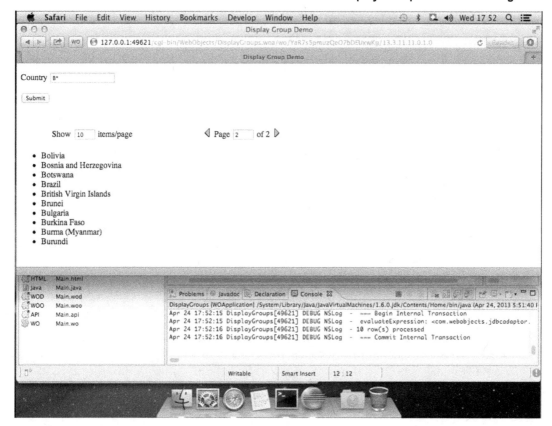

Picture 20-6   Display group with qualifying user input

20.5   How does a display group work under the hood?

Without going too much into details, the master display group is essentially an array manager that uses a fetch specification to get objects from an editing context. There's nothing especially complex here. But because there are different kinds of display group configurations — some that use fetch specifications, some that don't — it makes sense to factor these differences into a separate object called the data source. There are different classes of data sources, depending on the type of display group configuration requested. The master display group uses a database data source, which implies two things: it uses the editing context to go straight to the database and it uses a fetch specification.

20.6   "To DisplayGroup" or not "To DisplayGroup"

Do you have to use display groups at all? No, you don't but then why should you not? The display group is available; someone has already written the code, so why not take advantage of it? Besides when you need to do real batching against the database then the display group is the only thing that can do it. Not having display groups for batching would be a nightmare! You would have to write all the necessary code for keeping track of the current batch, creating the required qualifier for fetching the next batch of objects, etc.

20.7 Initializing a Display Group in Code

Everything (and more) we have done with the graphical editor to set up the display group, can of course be done in code. You don't even have to bind the display group to your user interface at all, just use it from your java code.

Let's see how one would do this.

```
// allocate the display group
ERXDisplayGroup<Country> dg = new ERXDisplayGroup<Country>();

// get an editing context, the default one from the session
// or get one by any other means
EOEditingContext ec = session().defaultEditingContext();

// a master display group needs to have a datasource
EODatabaseDataSource dataSource
    = new EODatabaseDataSource(ec, Country.ENTITY_NAME);
dg.setDataSource(dataSource);

// any other configuration you like
// dg.set...
```

I strongly suggest you read up on display groups in the API documentation (classes WODisplayGroup, ERXDisplayGroup, and descendants thereof). There is a lot more to a display group than what this small example highlights.

21 Direct Actions

Sometimes you do not need the overhead of sessions. In such a case direct actions are your friend.

21.1 Direct Actions – a Lightweight Request-Response-Loop

So far all of our applications used sessions. We have discussed the *Session* class in chapter 7.2. Sessions are very convenient and it is great that Wonder gives us sessions without us having to do anything. However sessions have some overhead. The sessions must be managed by the application and stored somewhere (usually in memory, could be on disk or even in a database) on the server. Sometimes an application does not need sessions at all. Imagine an application that is primarily read-only. This could be a web shop. A user can look up up some articles and products and have the application display detailed information. Such type of functionality does not need a session. A session of some kind is only needed when the user starts to add things to a shopping basket.

Such session-less functionality is available in Wonder. It's called Direct Action. A direct action is rather similar to what other web application environments like PHP provide. There you normally run session-less and you must switch sessions on explicitly. Wonder runs perfectly without sessions, it's just that in Wonder having sessions is the default.

21.2 There are different request handlers to a Wonder application

Let us look again at some Wonder application URLs:

Here is a standard front-door URL. This URL string ends with the name of the application:

```
http://www.example.com/cgi-bin/WebObjects/MySuperApp.woa
```

Now a typical component URL

```
http://www.example.com/cgi-
bin/WebObjects/MySuperApp.woa/wo/YaR7s5pmuzQeO7bDEUxwKg/13.3.11.11.0.1.0
```

We have the session id and the component references. But look closer: between the application name and the session id there is that little .../wo/... thingy. This is the code for the request handler to use. As the name request handler implies a Wonder application will have an object that receives the request from the *WOAdaptor* and figures what to do. A Wonder application can have different types of request handlers. The URL part .../wo/... specifies the default Wonder request handler called the Component Request Handler. This request handler tries to find a session id with the request and either restores the session or creates a new one. It is also responsible to initiate the sequence of calls we have seen in chapter 8, Flow of control: awake(), takeValuesFromRequest(), invokeAction(), generateResponse(), and sleep().

There is another type of request handler readily available in any Wonder application. This request handler is much simpler; it is called the Direct Action Request Handler. The direct action request handler is triggered by .../wa/... in the URL. The sequence of calls the direct action request handler issues is also much simpler. There is no takeValuesFromRequest() and no invokeAction() call involved. The direct request handler requires an object of type ERXDirectAction that must implement the action(s) you want to trigger. You need to subclass ERXDirectAction so you can add you own actions. The direct action request handler looks for a default class called DirectAction. When you create a new Wonder project you automatically get a default DirectAction class.

21.3 Setting the Default Request Handler

The front-door URL for an application does not specify a request handler. The default for any Wonder application is the component request handler. You can easily set a different request handler as your default.

Put the following line into your application constructor:

```
setDefaultRequestHandler(
    requestHandlerForKey(directActionRequestHandlerKey()));
```

With this line, the application will default to use the direct action request handler for the front-door URL.

21.4 Direct Actions in Action

Create a new Wonder application; we will call it *DirectActionDemo*.

The functionality of this application will be somewhat similar to the *DisplayGroups* application. But this time we are going to do everything with direct actions. So no session should be created.

Modify the constructor in the file *Session.java* so that it tells us when a session is being created.

```
public Session() {
    super();
    System.out.println("**** Session created ****");
}
```

We do not want to see this output! Seeing this we will know that something is not right!

Let's add some stuff to the project. We want to play with the same country data we had in the *DisplayGroups* project. Add the EOModel from that project to the *Resources* folder of our new project, use the context menu on the EOModel file *WOLips Tools -> Create EOGenerator File* to create the *eogen* file, the run *eogen* to create the enterprise objects classes.

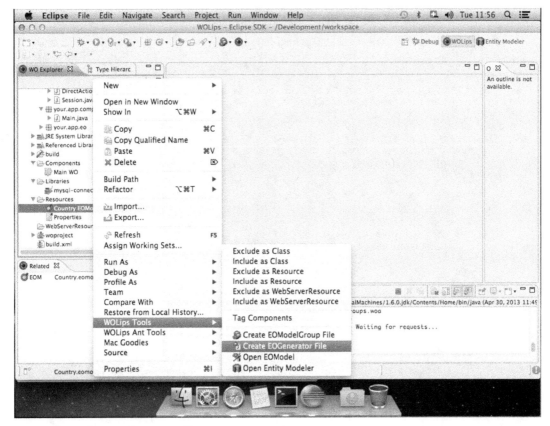

Picture 21-1   Create the eogen file

We want to have a Main page that displays a text entry field and a list of countries. The user enters some search criteria for the country name in the text field. With a click on a button all matching countries are read from the database and listed. This functionality is very similar to what we had in our display groups project. However here we cannot easily use a batching display group because we (or rather the ERXBatchNavigationBar) would have to keep track of the current batch between requests – and that would need a session. Also we cannot have any dynamic element on the page that needs to write back to instance variables in the component because again this would require to have some contextual info preserved through at least two request/response loop passes. You remember? That is where the page cache comes into play – and the page cache is maintained by the session. We can use dynamic elements like WOTextField but we have to handle the passed-in values ourselves, which means a bit more manual coding instead of letting the framework do all the work.

These are the restrictions we face when we want to use session-less direct actions: no dynamic element can automatically send data to an instance variable (or a set-method) in the component! This also applies to action methods. Those are a no-no, too! Whenever we violate these restrictions Wonder will automatically create a session.

21.4.1 The Main component

We create our *Main* component in a combination of plain html and WebObjects tags:

```
<?xml version="1.0" encoding="UTF-8"?>
<!DOCTYPE html PUBLIC "-//W3C//DTD XHTML 1.1//EN"
    "http://www.w3.org/TR/xhtml11/DTD/xhtml11.dtd">

<html xmlns="http://www.w3.org/1999/xhtml" xml:lang="en">
<head>
    <meta http-equiv="Content-Type" content="text/html; charset=utf-8"/>
    <title>Direct Action Demo</title>
</head>
<body>
    <webobject name = "form">
        <p>Enter country name <webobject name = "queryName" />
            <webobject name = "query" /></p>
    </webobject>
    <table>
        <tr>
            <th>Name</th>
            <th>ISO_2</th>
            <th>ISO_3</th>
            <th>Country Code</th>
        </tr>
        <webobject name = "countryList">
        <tr>
            <td><webobject name = "countryName" /></td>
            <td><webobject name = "iso2" /></td>
            <td><webobject name = "iso3" /></td>
            <td><webobject name = "phone" /></td>
        </tr>
        </webobject>
    </table>
</body>
</html>
```

Notice that we use our standard <webobject> tags for the form, the text input and the submit button. However we are not allowed to push values to the Java code in *Main.java* nor can we bind to an action in the class *Main*. The WOTextField has a *value* binding that is bound to an instance variable (and its accessor methods) in *Main.java*, it will however only use the get method. There is no takeValuesFromRequest() phase which would put the value from the html field into the instance variable. Thus we do not need to have a set method.

Also the WOForm is set to use the GET-method. This is just so that any parameter is appended to the URL instead of being submitted in the body of the request. Having the parameters in the URL allows us to bookmark the query.

```
form : WOForm {
    directActionName = "queryCountry";
    method = "GET";
    multipleSubmit = true;
}

query : WOSubmitButton {
    directActionName = "queryCountry";
}

queryName : WOTextField {
    name = "queryName";
    value = queryName;
```

```
}
countryList : WORepetition {
    list = countries;
    item = countryLoopvar;
}

countryName : WOString {
    value = countryLoopvar.name;
}

iso2 : WOString {
    value = countryLoopvar.iso2;
}

iso3 : WOString {
    value = countryLoopvar.iso3;
}

phone : WOString {
    value = countryLoopvar.phone;
}
```

In *Main.java* create the two necessary instance variables for the WORepetition with suitable set and get methods and a get method for the *queryName* text field. This queryName() method is needed so we can connect the value binding of the WOTextField.

```
private Country countryLoopvar;
private NSArray<Country> countries;

public String queryName() {
    return null; // or any sensible default value you like
}

public Country countryLoopvar() {
    return countryLoopvar;
}

public void setCountryLoopvar(Country countryLoopvar) {
    this.countryLoopvar = countryLoopvar;
}

public NSArray<Country> countries() {
    return countries;
}

public void setCountries(NSArray<Country> countries) {
    this.countries = countries;
}
```

21.4.2 Direct Action Methods

Any action method we need cannot be in the component but must be located in a direct action class. We are going to use the default *DirectAction.java* file for this. There is a somewhat weird naming convention for **direct action methods**: the method name is the name of the action with the word *Action* appended. When we want an action called queryCountry, the method name must be queryCountryAction().

Direct Actions

All the dynamic elements with an action binding (WOHyperlink, WOSubmitButton, etc) also have two direct action related bindings:

- *directActionName* is a string specifying the name of the action (without the word *Action* appended).

- *actionClass* is the name of the direct action class. The default is DirectAction.

A direct action method looks like any other action method. Its return value is normally of type WOActionResults. This is a bit more generic than a WOComponent, which inherits from WOActionResults.

21.4.3 Accessing Form Values

During direct action processing there is no takeValuesFromRequest() call. We must therefore access the raw form values directly from the request header.

```
String countryQuery = request().stringFormValueForKey("queryName");
```

We can use a WOTextField with a *name* binding. This would require at least a get method for the value binding (see above). We could also use a plain html form field with a name:

```
<input type = "text" name = "queryName" />
```

In any case the name given becomes the key to use in the call to stringFormValueForKey().

There are several other methods allowing us to get numeric data (numericFormValueForKey()), date and time values (dateFormValueForKey()) and some more generic ones like a general formValueForKey(). We can also get an NSDictionary with all the key/value pairs by calling the method formValues().

21.4.4 Accessing the Database and the Editing Context

For access to the database we need an editing context. However as there is no session, there is no session.defaultEditingContext(). We need to instantiate an editing context.

```
EOEditingContext ec = ERXEC.newEditingContext();
```

With this we can complete the action method that is bound to the WOSubmitButton. This code goes into file *DirectAction.java*:

```
public WOActionResults queryCountryAction() {

    // access the form values
    String countryQuery = request().stringFormValueForKey("cname");

    // build a fetch specification
    EOQualifier qualifier = Country.NAME.ilike(countryQuery);
    ERXSortOrdering ordering = Country.NAME.asc();

    // get a new editing context and fetch the data
    EOEditingContext ec = ERXEC.newEditingContext();
```

```
NSArray<Country> countries =
    Country.fetchCountries(ec, qualifier, ordering.array());

// prepare the response page
Main nextPage = pageWithName(Main.class);
nextPage.setCountries(countries);
return nextPage;
}
```

Build and run the application. You should not see any session created messages in the console!

However, there is one problem with the application. What happens when the user leaves the search field empty? Yep, you are right, the application crashes, because we blindly try to use null, which comes from our call to stringFormValueForKey(), to qualify the database access. Let's fix this right away. Add the following if statement after getting the form value for the query string:

```
if (countryQuery == null) {
    countryQuery = "*";
}
```

Now it works.

21.5 Direct Actions and Sessions

Direct actions and sessions go together quite nicely. Whenever you are in a session and then call a direct action the framework will transparently send the session id with the request. In the case of the GET method the session id is appended to the URL. The session id is named wosid.

A typical direct action URL with a session id might look like this:

```
http://127.0.0.1:49948/cgi-bin/WebObjects/DirectActionDemo.woa/wa/
    queryCountry?cname=*&wosid=YaR7s5pmuzQeO7bDEUxwKg
```

The request handler recognizes the wosid in the request and tries to find a corresponding session in the session store. Whenever the resulting page needs a session, this session will be used. If there is no session found with the given wosid, then a new session will be created.

Assume you have some components in your application that may be used in the context of a session, but also sometimes when you don't want a session. Depending on whether you are in a session or not your component needs to behave differently.

The call to session() will always put you into a session. Either the framework finds a session when a wosid parameter is given in the request or it creates a new session. When you just want to test if you are running in the context of a session, you can call existingSession(). This method will return a reference to the existing session or null, it will not create a new session!

21.6 Creating direct action URLs

Direct actions make most sense for GET requests. The following assumes, you have set your forms to use the GET method.

For a GET URL the parameters to be sent to the server are appended to the URL:

```
http://www.server.com/…..?param1=value1&param2=value2&param3=value3
```

The question mark starts the list of parameters, the ampersand separates the param=value pairs.

WOForm and WOHyperlink accept a custom binding that results in a parameter added to the generated URL. For a WOHyperlink in a repetition you could have the following bindings:

```
countryLink : WOHyperlink {
    directActionName = "showCountry";
    ?countryName = countriesLoopvar.name;
}
```

The weird looking binding (note the question mark) *?countryName* will end up appended to the generated link:

```
http://127.0.0.1:50004/cgi-bin/WebObjects
    /DirectActionDemo.woa/wa/showCountry?countryName=Switzerland
```

Remember, any binding that is not known to Wonder ends up as attribute to the html tag. The exception is the binding starting with a question mark! This will be used as URL parameter.

What if you need more than one parameter? You cannot have two bindings starting with a question mark. Wonder supports another binding: *queryDictionary*. This binding accepts an NSDictionary containing any number of key=value pairs. These end up appended to the generated URL. The *queryDictionary* binding is available for WOHyperlink and WOForm.

21.7 When would you use direct actions?

Direct actions are lightweight. There is (usually) no session involved. The application internal overhead of managing a session, allocating resources for the session, and several message calls like takeValuesFromRequest() and invokeAction() are avoided.

You would use direct actions whenever you do not need the overhead of a session.

With direct actions it makes a lot of sense to submit form data via GET request. This puts the form data into the URL and allows for easy bookmarking.

A typical scenario for a direct action application is our demo project. The user can browse the list of countries and get detailed info about each found country.

Another typical use case is application login. Your application provides a login screen and only when the user successfully logs in, the application actually goes to work. Why would you need to have a session just to tell the user that his credentials are not valid? So you keep the Main page session-less. Bind the login-button to a direct action that checks username and password against the database. Put some nice error message into the main page and show the login again when the credentials are not valid. Only when the user successfully logs in you return the actual starting page of your application from the login direct action method.

Another interesting use case for a direct action is command line access to your application. An application can provide one-shot functionality that can be triggered from a command line, e.g. with a tool like curl or wget. This could allow an external timing program like cron to activate an action. Such an action could then create and return some dump file or initiate a data transfer to a remote system, or send a mailing out, or whatever else you can imagine.

21.8 Example: Using a direct action to generate a CSV file

Create a new component in your *DirectActionDemo* project. Call it *DownloadCountryList*. We are not going to generate html but rather plain text. So replace anything in the *DownloadCountryList.html* with

```
<webobject name = "countryList">
<webobject name = "countryName" />;<webobject name = "iso2" />;<webobject name =
"iso3" />;<webobject name = "phone" />
</webobject>
```

and put the following into the bindings part:

```
countryList : WORepetition {
    list = countries;
    item = countryLoopvar;
}

countryName : WOString {
    value = countryLoopvar.name;
}

iso2 : WOString {
    value = countryLoopvar.iso2;
}

iso3 : WOString {
    value = countryLoopvar.iso3;
}

phone : WOString {
    value = countryLoopvar.phone;
}
```

This whole thing is actually a stripped down version of the *Main* component. We simply leave out the form with the search field and remove all html tags.

Direct Actions

Duplicate the direct action method queryCountryAction() and name the new method downloadCountryListAction(). Of course in a real life project you would not just duplicate code but nicely factor common things out. There is only one modification needed in the new method: replace the references to Main with DownloadCountryList. Here is the code with the changes marked.

```
public WOActionResults downloadCountryListAction() {
    String countryQuery = request().stringFormValueForKey("cname");
    if (countryQuery == null) {
        countryQuery = "*";
    }

    EOQualifier qualifier = Country.NAME.ilike(countryQuery);
    ERXSortOrdering ordering = Country.NAME.asc();
    EOEditingContext ec = ERXEC.newEditingContext();
    NSArray<Country> countries =
        Country.fetchCountries(ec, qualifier, ordering.array());
    DownloadCountryList nextPage =
        pageWithName(DownloadCountryList.class);
    nextPage.setCountries(countries);
    return nextPage;
}
```

Now start a command line session. Here is the example from a Mac OS X terminal. In the background of the screen shot you see the interactive query where we have been searching for countries whose name starts with "D", in the terminal window you see the command line and the results. We used the command curl to access the direct action *downloadCountryList*.

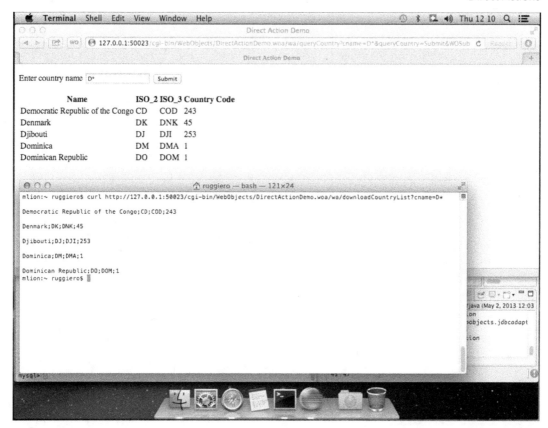

Picture 21-2   Accessing a direct action from the command line

The output goes to the terminal, but a simple i/o-redirection could put the list of countries into a file. You can put any kind of text into your component so that the end result can be formatted any way you want. Instead of html tags place some xml tags there and you generate a nice xml output. Or replace the xml tags by "(", ")", "{", and "}" and build a json formatted output.

22 Debugging and Logging

Sometimes there is a problem with your application. It does not behave like you want it to. No data is shown, or it takes a wrong turn when the user navigates to some page, or, heaven forbid, the application simply crashes and throws an exception. Of course it is never the programmer's fault, it is the application not behaving properly. But no matter, it is you, the programmer, who has to persuade the application to behave. The following will show you some debugging techniques that will help you figure what is going on and how to fix things.

22.1 Generating log output to the console

The simplest way to generate debug output to the console is the good old `System.out.println()` call. As simple as this is, sometimes it is the quickest way to see what is going on when your application runs.

Just don't forget to remove the call before deploying your application.

22.1.1 Using NSLog

A lot better is the use of NSLog. NSLog is the standard WebObjects logging class. You can use NSLog similarly to `System.out.println()`.

```
NSLog.out.appendln("This is a Debug Message");
```

NSLog will put a timestamp in front of the message. Here is the result from above program line:

```
May 04 14:25:03 DirectActionDemo[50049] DEBUG NSLog  - This is a Debug Message
```

However NSLog can do more. It allows you to specify a log level and debug groups. With the log level you say how important a message needs to be before it is being output, with debug groups you can enable certain types of actions in your application. There are three debug levels. You can specify what level you want by calling

```
NSLog.debug.setAllowedDebugLevel(...);
```

This call can be put anywhere you like. Often the constructor of the application or of a component is a good place. Also well suited are `awake()` and `sleep()`.

Setting the debug level to...	will output any message with level...
DebugLevelDetailed	DebugLevelDetailed, DebugLevelInformational, and DebugLevelCritical

Debugging and Logging

Setting the debug level to...	will output any message with level...
`DebugLevelInformational`	`DebugLevelInformational,` `DebugLevelCritical`
`DebugLevelCritical`	`DebugLevelCritical`

In other words, when you set `DebugLevelCritical`, only the most critical information is logged, while the other levels allow more and more information to be output.

Whenever you need some output to the console you decide what level should be required. You might want to set the debug level in your application depending on whether your application is running from within Eclipse (and thus you are in active development and debugging process) or it is running in a productive deployment environment.

Here is an example from the documentation for class NSLog. When an exception is encountered, the exception message should always be output, but the stack trace should only be output if a particular level of debugging is requested:

```
} catch (Exception e) {
    NSLog.err.appendln("Exception encountered: " + e.getMessage());
    if (NSLog.debugLoggingAllowedForLevel(NSLog.DebugLevelCritical) {
        NSLog.debug.appendln(e);
    }
}
```

There are 28 defined debug groups. Your code would have to check whether a certain debug group is enabled before outputting a message. Each of the available debug groups can be activated or deactivated individually. NSLog provides methods to enable/disable a group and to check the current status.

NSLog, being the native WebObjects logging mechanism, is used throughout all WebObjects and EOF frameworks. Please consult the API documentation for NSLog for more details.

22.1.2 Logging with Log4j

Somewhat similar to NSLog is *log4j*. This is an Apache project and is widely used in the Java world for logging. Wonder uses *log4j*. NSLog can be used on top of *log4j*. This is what you get when you create a Wonder application.

Log4j also distinguishes debug levels and has something analogous to debug groups. Describing *log4j* goes way beyond the scope of this book. For details please consult the *log4j* documentation online.

Defined log levels are debug, log, info, error, fatal, and trace. There are corresponding methods available. Working with *log4j* is pretty simple. Here are some examples for using *log4j*.

Let's stay with our *DirectActionDemo* project. You want to have logging in your queryCountryAction() method. All you need to do is acquire a Logger object and use this for output:

```
Logger log = Logger.getLogger(DirectAction.class);
log.info("This is an informational out"); // log level must be set to info
log.debug("This is a debug output");      // log level must be set to debug
```

In your application properties file you can then enable and disable logging on per-class basis and you can specify the required debug level. When you look at the *Properties* file in your *Resources* folder you will find lines like these:

```
# Log4j Categories
# Here are a few log4j sub-categories that are interesting.
# Don't forget that in development mode this file will get reloaded
# everytime it changes, so if you say want to turn adaptor debugging
# on in the middle of the app simply set the below category to debug.
# Very handy.
# Base Category
log4j.logger.er=INFO

# ERExtensions
# Transaction - Switching this to debug will start the sql ouputting.
log4j.logger.er.transaction.adaptor.EOAdaptorDebugEnabled=DEBUG

# Fixes - Turning this on will show all the models that are loaded
log4j.logger.er.extensions.fixes.ERSharedEOLoader=INFO

er.extensions.ERXNSLogLog4jBridge=INFO
#log4j.logger.er.eo.ERXGenericRecord=DEBUG
#log4j.logger.er.validation.ERXEntityClassDescription=DEBUG
#log4j.logger.er.default.ERXEntityClassDescription=DEBUG
log4j.logger.er.extensions.ERXDatabaseContextDelegate=WARN
log4j.logger.er.extensions.ERXConfigurationManager=INFO
#log4j.logger.er.extensions.ERXApplication.RequestHandling=DEBUG
```

If you want to enable debug logging for your *DirectAction* class you would then add the following line to this file:

```
log4j.logger.your.app.DirectAction=DEBUG
```

This would cause all log.debug(...) statements in class DirectAction to generate output. Also all other log.something(...) statement with lower priority like *INFO*, etc. would show.

Setting log4j.logger.your.app.DirectAction=INFO would then not generate output for log.debug(...).

When running in development mode a Wonder application constantly monitors the *Properties* file and reloads it dynamically whenever you make a change. So it is very easy to enable any logging without having to restart the application!

There is an even better way to dynamically configure *log4j*. With a Wonder application you automatically get a special direct action that opens a configuration window for *log4j* directly inside your running application.

Enter the following URL when your application is running (adapt the port number accordingly):

http://127.0.0.1:50049/cgi-bin/WebObjects/DirectActionDemo.woa/wa/ERXDirectAction/log4j

Here is what you get:

Debugging and Logging

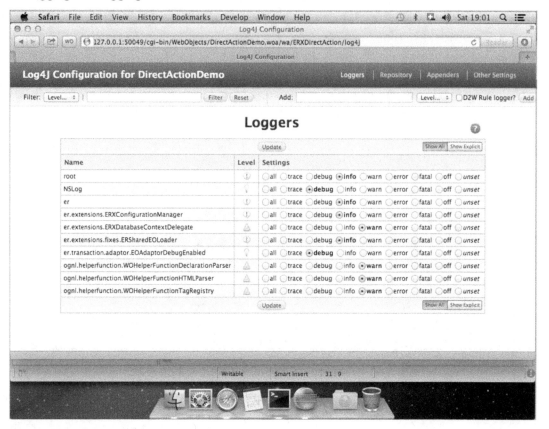

Picture 22-1   log4j configuration page

Not bad! Please consult the *log4j* documentation for more info. There is also built-in help accessible via that nice button towards the upper right corner of the screen.

22.1.3 Logging SQL statements

Very often you do not get the data you expect from the database or something happens to or does not happen to the data. In this case it is a good idea to switch on logging the generated SQL statements. This allows you to see exactly what calls EOF issues to the database and what the outcome is. So you want the EOF adaptor to log the statements. The EOF adaptor is the part of the enterprise objects framework that communicates with the relational database.

There is one property you have to switch on. You can do this in two different ways. One way is to specify a command line parameter. When you have a run- or debug-configuration in Eclipse you can set the necessary parameter in the WO-section. Look at the following screen shot:

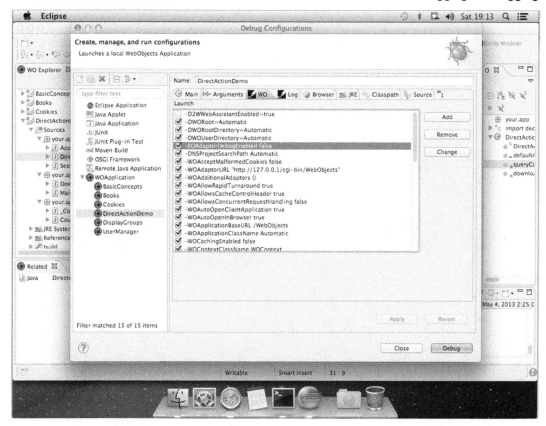

Picture 22-2   Edit Run- and Debug Configurations in Eclipse

There is an entry –EOAdaptorDebugEnabled that is currently set to false. Change it to true and you will get SQL logging.

You can also change this parameter in the *Properties* file (or via the *log4j* direct action configuration). The default *Properties* file already contains the proper line, albeit commented out. Simply remove the comment character (#).

```
# ERExtensions
# Transaction - Switching this to debug will start the sql ouputting.
log4j.logger.er.transaction.adaptor.EOAdaptorDebugEnabled=DEBUG
```

You may have to enable both settings, the one in *Properties* as well as the command line setting to really get the SQL logging. Here is a screen shot of our *DirectActionDemo*. The user has specified "C*" as search criteria.

Debugging and Logging

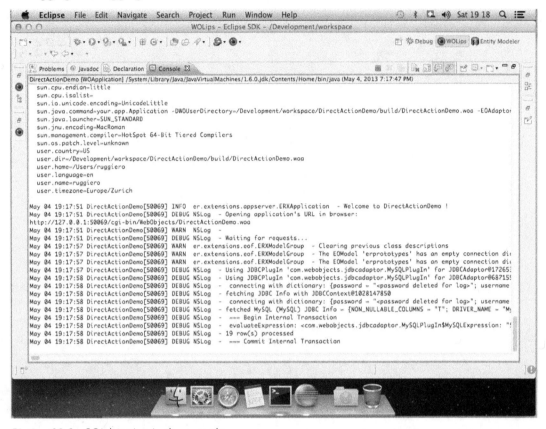

Picture 22-3   SQL logging in the console

By scrolling the console view sideways you can see the complete generated SQL statement with all parameters. Underneath the statement the adaptor tells you that the query resulted in 19 rows. That means the query has found 19 countries having a name starting with "C".

Here is the complete SQL statement, reformatted for better legibility:

```
May 04 19:17:58 DirectActionDemo[50069] DEBUG NSLog  - evaluateExpression:
<com.webobjects.jdbcadaptor.MySQLPlugIn$MySQLExpression: "SELECT t0.id,
RTRIM(t0.ISO_2), RTRIM(t0.ISO_3), RTRIM(t0.name), t0.PHONE FROM COUNTRY t0 WHERE
UPPER(t0.name) LIKE UPPER(?) ESCAPE '|' ORDER BY t0.name ASC" withBindings:
1:"C%"(name)>
```

This is an invaluable aid in debugging. You see the exact statement including all the parameter values. I often copy/paste the generated statement into an SQL console and run it interactively for a test when something seems not right.

Part E - Deployment

23 Introduction to Deployment

You have that great application in your Eclipse workspace, now it is time to put it up on a server for productive use.

Let's go back to the explanation of the request/response loop in chapter 0. We had the following graphic there:

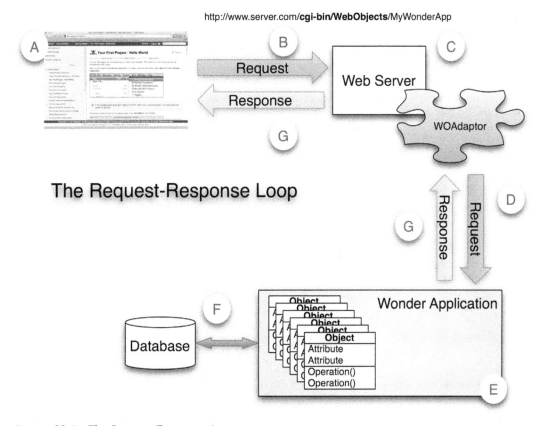

Picture 23-1   The Request/Response Loop

From that picture we saw that we need a Web Server and the *WOAdaptor*. Both have not played any role during our development so far.

For deploying a Wonder application these things become important.

23.1 Requirements

For deployment any computer that can run a recent version of Java can be used for deployment of a Wonder application. People have successfully deployed on a broad variety of computers running various operating systems. It is very difficult to give exact figures for required RAM, disk size, and

CPU speed, as these things largely depend on the specifics of your application. Let me therefore just mention some systems that can be used:

Hardware:

- Apple Mac Mini and Mac Mini Server
- Apple Mac Pro
- Amazon EC2 Cloud (does this count as "hardware"?)
- Any Intel® Core i5 or better desktop machine

Operating Systems

- Apple Mac OS X 10.5 or newer
- Microsoft Windows Vista or newer (no experience with Windows 8 yet)
- Various Linux distributions like Debian, Ubuntu, RedHat Enterprise, and others
- Various Unix incarnations like Solaris, and others

General rules are: you want a server platform, probably no need for a state-of-the-art graphics card, but first and foremost you want RAM! Get as much as you can, Java and Wonder applications tend to eat your RAM for breakfast.

We will cover using Mac OS X as the server platform in this book. Detailed instructions for deploying on Windows and Linux/Unix can be found in the official Wonder wiki on *wiki.wocommunity.org*. The general mechanism for setting up a server however is the same for each platform.

23.2 The Big Picture

The following picture will give you an overall view over the deployment environment for a Wonder application.

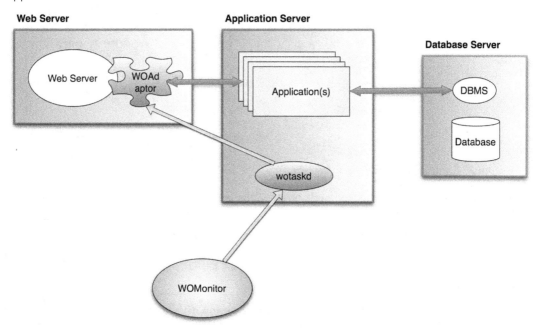

Picture 23-2 Deployment The Big Picture

A Wonder application can be used very small, similar to what we have done so far during development. However a Wonder application can scale very big and serve thousands of requests per second. The beautiful thing is that you do not have to change anything in your application, when you grow. Simply reconfigure your deployment environment.

The following sections will explain how these things work.

23.3 Deployment Architecture

On the left side of the picture above there is a box called Web Server with a bubble inside also marked Web Server. The Web Server bubble is your Apache or Microsoft IIS or whatever web server software you use. In any case the web server process needs to be linked to the Wonder Adaptor. You already know that the *WOAdaptor* is responsible for converting incoming requests to WORequest objects and forwarding those to the Wonder application. It also receives the WOResponse objects and hands their content to the Web Server for delivery to the browser. The *WOAdaptor* and the Web Server must be linked tightly together and thus must be on the same physical computer.

The *WOAdaptor* can communicate with the Wonder application over a network link. This allows you to install your application on the same box as the web server or on a different computer dedicated to hosting the application. Of course the database server can be run on the same system or offloaded to yet another system. The *WOAdaptor* needs to know what applications there are, where in the network they can be reached and how many instances are currently available. It receives all the necessary information through an application called the *JavaMonitor*.

A Wonder application can service many requests in parallel. However for larger installations one might want to start the application more than once on the same computer. This allows for even better performance, because when one application instance is really busy servicing requests, additional incoming requests can be handled by another instance of the same application. And again, these instances of the same application do not even have to run on the same physical computer. Spread the load over as much instances and systems as needed. If you see that the incoming requests start to overrun your application, simply start another instance, and then one more. Eventually you'll reach limitations on I/O and RAM usage on your computer running the application. No problem! Simply add another physical box and have more instances run there.

23.4 Split install

There are two distinct types of resources an application needs, those that are only relevant for the application itself, like the EOModel, and the compiled Java class files, and others like graphics, that are visible to the user. Albeit each Wonder application can serve static web content (we used this functionality during development), graphics and similar things are better served directly through the deployment web server.

In your development project you have two folders, *Resources*, and *WebServer Resources*. *Resources* contains all the things the application needs, whereas *WebServer Resources* contains everything that must be accessible directly to the web server. When we build our application for deployment, the build system inside WOLips will create two deployment packages. One is the application itself with all its resources and one is a package containing only the web server resources. The web server resources need to be put into the web server documents directory. The application itself must not be accessible directly by the web server and should therefore reside outside the document root. Wonder will generate URLs for resources so that the web server can serve these without bothering the application. We will see how this works when we actually deploy one of our applications in chapter 26.

This type of installation, where the web server serves the static resources, and the application serves the dynamically created responses, is called **split install**.

23.5 The Role of *wotaskd*

On each computer where you want to run an instance of a Wonder application you need a Wonder Task Demon process, commonly known as *wotaskd*. There must be one such process per computer.

wotaskd is a background process that is monitoring your applications. It knows what applications are on that particular system and it knows all the running instances of all Wonder applications on the computer. You don't want a Wonder application to lock up or even terminate due to it being overrun by requests. But as a programmer, you know that sometimes things go wrong. In that case, *wotaskd* is responsible for restarting your instance. It is also starting all the configured instances when the computer boots up. With *wotaskd* you can schedule controlled restart of individual application instances. Restarting an instance after some time can free up resources that might otherwise remain allocated but not used anymore.

The Wonder Task Demon is itself a Wonder application. Its source code is freely available.

You can ask *wotaskd* for its configuration. By default *wotaskd* listens on port 1085. When you connect with your browser to that port, it responds with a nicely formatted xml display. We are going to deploy our *DirectActionDemo* application further down in this book in chapter 26, but here is already a screen shot of the corresponding *wotaskd* configuration.

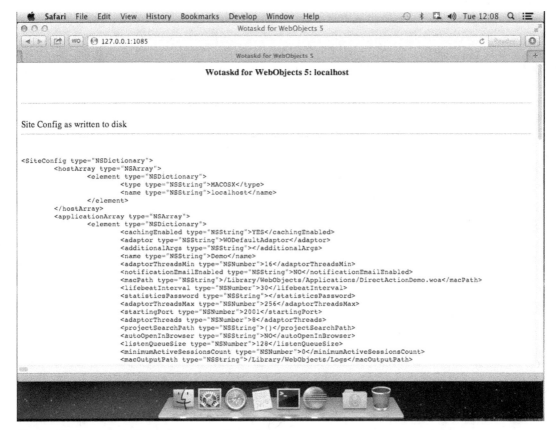

Picture 23-3 wotaskd reporting its configuration.

Judging from the position of the scroll bar it is obvious that there is a lot more being reported. After you have successfully deployed your applications you can have a look yourself. Simply access port 1085 with your browser.

23.6 The Role of *JavaMonitor*

wotaskd knows everything, but who did tell it? And the *WOAdaptor* also needs some information. There is a Wonder application available called *JavaMonitor*. This application knows how to communicate with the Wonder Task Demon. It is also responsible to set up the *WOAdaptor*. It allows you to configure your complete deployment environment through a web based user interface.

Monitor can launch an application or terminate it — immediately or gracefully, waiting until all current sessions have terminated — and monitor the state of an application in terms of runtime statistics, errors, and crashes. We will use *JavaMonitor* to deploy and control our *DirectActionDemo* application.

24 Setting up the Server

In this chapter we are going to set up a computer running Mac OS X as a deployment system. Setting up a computer running another operating system, Microsoft Windows®, Linux, or anything else, is similar.

First of all you need a web server. Mac OS X includes Apache web server software. The same is valid for most Linux distributions. On Windows you can install Apache or use Microsoft IIS. In any case there will be a directory acting as documents root. This is the directory that contains all the html and css files, and any other resource that the web server needs to access and vend out.

On an Apple Macintosh computer it is perfectly possible to use Mac OS X client or Mac OS X Server operating system.

Don't forget to install a Java Runtime environment on Mac OS X 10.8 Mountain Lion. A standard out-of-the-box installation does not install Java!

24.1 Preparing the Directory Structure

You need to create a directory that will hold all the pieces of your Wonder installation. Create the following directory structure (this is on Mac OS X, adapt accordingly when setting up a deployment machine running another operating system). /Library on Mac OS X is where WebObjects deployment tools used to put things. On Windows the standard install location is C:\Apple, and on Linux/Unix it is typically /opt/Apple.

```
/Library/WebObjects
/Library/WebObjects/Configuration
/Library/WebObjects/Logs
/Library/WebObjects/Adaptors
/Library/WebObjects/Deployment
/Library/WebObjects/Applications
/Library/WebObjects/WebServerResources
```

Make these directories owned by _appserver and set the group to _appserveradm

```
$ chown -R _appserver:_appserveradm /Library/WebObjects
$ chmod -R 755 /Library/WebObjects
```

Most of the directory names are self-explanatory. The *Deployment* sub-directory will become home of the *JavaMonitor* and *wotaskd* applications, while *Applications* will be the place where you install your applications. Having a *WebServerResources* sub directory under */Library/WebObjects* is just a convenience. We will link it into the web server documents root so that we can install everything in one place and do not have to hunt about in the file system.

24.2 Installing *JavaMonitor* and *wotaskd*

You can download *JavaMonitor* and *wotaskd* directly from the *wocommunity.org* site or you can build them yourself. When you download the full Wonder source code (see chapter 2.4.2) you also get the source for *JavaMonitor* and *wotaskd*. See the build instructions for how to compile them.

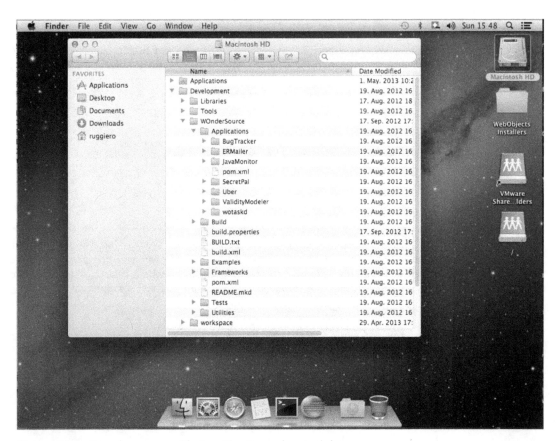

Picture 24-1   *Wonder source with JavaMonitor and wotaskd*

Let's download and put things into the right place. For the fun of it we will do this from the command line (you may need to run the following commands with sudo). Of course you can always point your browser to http://jenkins.wocommunity.org and navigate from there to the download location.

```
$ cd /Library/WebObjects/Deployment
```

Download *wotaskd*. The following should be entered on one line, no line breaks!

```
$ curl -O ↵
http://jenkins.wocommunity.org/job/Wonder/lastSuccessfulBuild/artifact/Root/Roots/wo
taskd.tar.gz
```

Unpack and set ownership and permissions

```
$ tar xzf wotaskd.tar.gz
$ chmod -R 755 wotaskd.woa
$ chown -R _appserver:wheel wotaskd.woa
$ chmod 750 wotaskd.woa/Contents/Resources/SpawnOfWotaskd.sh
$ chmod 750 wotaskd.woa/wotaskd
```

We do the same for *JavaMonitor* (again this should be on one line)

```
$ curl -O ↵
http://jenkins.wocommunity.org/view/Wonder/job/Wonder/lastSuccessfulBuild/artifact/R
oot/Roots/JavaMonitor.tar.gz
```

Unpack and set ownership and permissions

```
$ tar xzf JavaMonitor.tar.gz
$ chmod -R 755 JavaMonitor.woa
$ chown -R _appserver:wheel JavaMonitor.woa
```

We need to start *wotaskd* automatically when the system boots up. Here is a simple *launchd* parameter file to do that. If you want to deploy on Windows or Linux you need to create some startup mechanism suitable to your platform. It is possible to also start *JavaMonitor* with a similar script.

Put the following text into a file called *org.projectwonder.wotaskd.plist* in directory */Library/LaunchDaemons*

```xml
<?xml version="1.0" encoding="UTF-8"?>
<!DOCTYPE plist PUBLIC "-//Apple Computer//DTD PLIST 1.0//EN"
"http://www.apple.com/DTDs/PropertyList-1.0.dtd">
<plist version="1.0">
<dict>
    <key>Disabled</key>
        <false/>
    <key>GroupName</key>
        <string>_appserveradm</string>
    <key>Label</key>
        <string>org.projectwonder.wotaskd</string>
    <key>OnDemand</key>
        <false/>
    <key>Program</key>
        <string>/Library/WebObjects/Deployment/↵
                                wotaskd.woa/wotaskd</string>
    <key>ProgramArguments</key>
        <array>
            <string>wotaskd</string>
            <string>-WOPort</string>
            <string>1085</string>
        </array>
```

```
    <key>ServiceIPC</key>
        <false/>
    <key>UserName</key>
        <string>_appserver</string>
    <key>StandardOutPath</key>
        <string>/Library/WebObjects/Logs/wotaskd.log</string>
    <key>StandardErrorPath</key>
        <string>/Library/WebObjects/Logs/wotaskd.log</string>
</dict>
</plist>
```

If you are not deploying on Mac OS X, you need to create something that issues the following command line upon boot (adapt the path according to your install location)

For Linux/Unix:

```
/Library/WebObjects/Deployment/wotaskd.woa/wotaskd wotaskd -WOPort 1085
```

For Windows:

```
C:\Apple\WebObjects\Deployment\wotaskd.woa\wotaskd.cmd wotaskd -WOPort 1085
```

Do not change the port assignment; leave it at 1085.

Here is the content for the startup plist file for *JavaMonitor*. Name the file *org.projectwonder.womonitor.plist* and put it into */Library/LaunchDeamons*, too.

```
<?xml version="1.0" encoding="UTF-8"?>
<!DOCTYPE plist PUBLIC "-//Apple Computer//DTD PLIST 1.0//EN"
"http://www.apple.com/DTDs/PropertyList-1.0.dtd">
<plist version="1.0">
<dict>
    <key>Disabled</key>
        <false/>
    <key>GroupName</key>
        <string>appserverusr</string>
    <key>Label</key>
        <string>org.projectwonder.womonitor</string>
    <key>OnDemand</key>
        <false/>
    <key>Program</key>
        <string>/Library/WebObjects/Deployment/JavaMonitor.woa/ ↵
                                        JavaMonitor</string>
    <key>ProgramArguments</key>
        <array>
            <string>JavaMonitor</string>
            <string>-WOPort</string>
            <string>56789</string>
        </array>
    <key>ServiceIPC</key>
        <false/>
    <key>UserName</key>
```

```
        <string>_appserver</string>
    <key>StandardOutPath</key>
        <string>/Library/WebObjects/Logs/womonitor.log</string>
    <key>StandardErrorPath</key>
        <string>/Library/WebObjects/Logs/womonitor.log</string>
</dict>
</plist>
```

This file makes *JavaMonitor* reachable on port 56789. This port can be freely set to anything that suits you.

We can startup *wotaskd* and *JavaMonitor* now:

```
$ cd /Library/LaunchDeamons
$ sudo launchctl load -w org.projectwonder.wotaskd.plist
$ sudo launchctl load -w org.projectwonder.womonitor.plist
```

Let's check if these two processes started up:

```
$ ps -ef
  UID    PID  PPID  C STIME    TTY          TIME CMD
    0      1     0  0 10:33AM ??          0:06.23 /sbin/launchd
    0     11     1  0 10:34AM ??          0:00.41 /usr/libexec/UserEventAgent
(System)
......
   79   7307     1  0 11:33AM ??          0:04.10 /usr/bin/java -XX:NewSize=2m -
Xmx64m -Xms32m -DWORootDirectory=/System -DWOLocalRootDirectory= -DWOUserDirectory=/
-DWOEnvClassPath= -
DWOApplicationClass=com.webobjects.monitor.application.Application -
DWOPlatform=MacOS -Dcom.webobjects.pid=7307 -classpath WOBootstrap.jar
com.webobjects._bootstrap.WOBootstrap -WOPort 56789
......
   79   7345     1  0 11:33AM ??          0:03.25 /usr/bin/java -XX:NewSize=2m -
Xmx64m -Xms32m -DWORootDirectory=/System -DWOLocalRootDirectory= -DWOUserDirectory=/
-DWOEnvClassPath= -DWOApplicationClass=com.webobjects.monitor.wotaskd.Application -
DWOPlatform=MacOS -Dcom.webobjects.pid=7345 -classpath WOBootstrap.jar
com.webobjects._bootstrap.WOBootstrap -WOPort 1085
    0   1922  1920  0 11:04AM ttys000     0:00.03 login -pf markus
  502   1923  1922  0 11:04AM ttys000     0:00.07 -bash
    0   7379  1923  0 11:34AM ttys000     0:00.00 ps -ef
    0   6576  1920  0 11:31AM ttys001     0:00.03 login -pf markus
  502   6577  6576  0 11:31AM ttys001     0:00.01 -bash
```

You should see *wotaskd* and *JavaMonitor* running.

24.3 Setting up the Web Server and *WOAdaptor*

We now need the *WOAdaptor* that allows the Web Server to forward request to our Wonder applications. The source code for the *WOAdaptor* is written in plain ANSI-C with no dependencies on any framework. It is included with the Wonder Source distribution. However there is no need to build the adaptor yourself. Prebuilt binaries are available on *http://www.wocommunity.org/documents/tools/mod_WebObjects.*

```
cd /Library/Wonder/Adaptors
curl -O http://www.wocommunity.org/documents/tools/mod_WebObjects/↵
                        Apache2.2/macosx/10.6/mod_WebObjects.so
```

The command starting with curl must be on one line. You may need to prefix the curl command with sudo. This *WOAdaptor* has been compiled for Mac OS X 10.6, but it is still good for the latest version Mac OS X 10.8 Mountain Lion. In the same location you can find various compiled adaptors for other Apache versions and different operating systems.

Next step is to tell the Apache web server about the adaptor. Create the following two configuration files, all in */Library/WebObjects/Adaptors* (if you are in a hurry, you do not need to retype the whole files, just use the lines that do not begin with a hash character #).

File *wo_apache.conf*: This is the main configuration file

```
# WebObjects 5.4: Enable the WebObjects module.
LoadModule WebObjects_module /Library/WebObjects/Adaptors/mod_WebObjects.so

# You can change the 'cgi-bin' part of WebObjectsAlias to whatever you
# prefer (such as Apps), but the 'WebObjects' part is required.
WebObjectsAlias /Apps/WebObjects

# Here are the 3 possible configuration modes.
# The apache module uses one of them to get information
# about your deployed applications.
# 1085 is the reserved port on which wotaskd processes listen to by default.

# Host List Configuration
# wotaskd is started automatically on supported platforms,
# so this is the default mode.
# The apache module gets its configuration from the wotaskds
# listed on the configuration line
# For multiple hosts:
# WebObjectsConfig http://<name-of-a-host>:<port-on-a-host>,http://<name-of-another-
host>:<port-on-a-host> <interval>
# For localhost:
WebObjectsConfig http://localhost:1085 10

# Multicast Configuration
# The apache module gets its configuration from all wotaskds
# that respond to the multicast call on the subnet
# WebObjectsConfig webobjects://239.128.14.2:1085 10

# File Configuration
# The apache module gets its configuration from one file
# WebObjectsConfig file://<path-to-a-xml-config-file> 10

# To enable public access to the WOAdaptorInfo page, uncomment the following line
# WebObjectsAdminUsername public

# To enable the WOAdaptorInfo page with restricted access,
# uncomment the next two lines and set the user and password
# To access the WOAdaptorInfo page with restricted access,
```

```
# use a URL like: http://webserver/cgi-bin/WebObjects/WOAdaptorInfo?user+password.
# WebObjectsAdminUsername user
# WebObjectsAdminPassword password

# To change the logging options, read the following comments:
# The option name is "WebObjectsLog" and the first value indicates the path of the
log file.
# The second value indicates the log level. There are five, in decreasing
informational order:
#       "Debug",     "Info",     "Warn",      "Error",     "User"
#
# Note: To enable logging, touch '/tmp/logWebObjects' as the administrator user
(usually root).
#
# The following line is the default:
# WebObjectsLog /Library/WebObjects/Logs/WebObjects.log Debug
```

The following configuration file sets some expiration options.

File wo_expires.conf

```
## File for Expires
<IfModule mod_expires.c>
  ExpiresActive On
  ExpiresDefault A60
  ExpiresByType image/x-icon A3600
  ExpiresByType application/x-javascript A3600
  ExpiresByType text/css A3600
  ExpiresByType image/gif A3600
  ExpiresByType image/png A3600
  ExpiresByType image/jpeg A3600
  ExpiresByType application/x-shockwave-flash A3600
  ExpiresByType video/x-flv A3600
  ExpiresByType application/pdf A3600
</IfModule>
```

Now set the owner of all files

```
chown -R _appserver:_appserveradm /Library/WebObjects/Adaptors
```

Add the following two lines to the end of your Apache configuration file. On Mac OS X client, this file is */etc/apache2/httpd.conf*. When you configure your Mac with *Server.app*, the configuration file will be */Library/Server/Web/Config/apache2/httpd_server_app.conf*.

```
Include /Library/WebObjects/Adaptors/wo_apache.conf
Include /Library/WebObjects/Adaptors/wo_expires.conf
```

There is another modification you need to make on mac OS X Mountain Lion when running the client version. Edit */etc/apache2/httpd.conf* (you need admin privileges for this). Either add a comment character (#) in front of the two lines marked in the following screenshot ore remove them altogether.

Picture 24-2   Comment out two lines in httpd.config on Mac OS X client

This seems not to be needed on Mac OS X Mountain Lion Server!

Now restart Apache:

On Mac OS X client you do this with the following command:

```
$ sudo apachectl restart
```

With Mac OS X Server you should use *serveradmin* command

```
$ sudo serveradmin stop web
$ sudo serveradmin start web
```

Check to see if Apache has successfully come up:

```
$ ps -ef | grep http
```

```
    0  5641    1   0  1:45PM ??        0:00.26 /usr/sbin/httpd -D FOREGROUND -D
WEBSERVICE_ON
   70  5642 5641   0  1:45PM ??        0:00.00 /usr/sbin/httpd -D FOREGROUND -D
WEBSERVICE_ON
  501  5647 4941   0  1:46PM ttys000   0:00.00 grep http
```

This is from Mac OS X Mountain Lion Server. The display might look a little bit differently when the same command is issued on Mac OS X Mountain Lion Client.

24.4 Creating Symbolic Links for Convenience

There are two small things we can do to make life a bit easier. We want everything Wonder/WebObjects related accessible from one common location. That is why we have created /Library/WebObjects in the first place. Creating some symbolic links to locations outside of this directory will help us find things easier.

Wonder writes its log file into /Library/Logs. We are going to create a symbolic link so that the log file will end up inside our directory structure:

```
$ cd /Library/Logs
$ ln -s /Library/WebObjects/Logs/ WebObjects
```

Another directory outside our structure is the web server documents root. When we install a Wonder application we also need to put the Web Server Resources into the web server documents root. We create a symbolic link inside the web server documents root to point to our directory structure.

```
$ cd <YourSiteFolder>
$ sudo ln -s /Library/WebObjects/WebServerResources WebObjects
```

For <YourSiteFolder> insert the documents root for your web site. On a standard Mac OS X Client this is at /Library/WebServer/Documents whereas with Server.app the default document root is at /Library/Server/Web/Data/Sites/Default.

24.5 Setting up the Server in *JavaMonitor*

Each machine running a Wonder application must have *wotaskd* running. *JavaMonitor* is a Wonder application that is used to configure each *wotaskd* process and the *WOAdaptor*. There needs to be only one *JavaMonitor* running in the whole network. Our demo installation comprises one system that is running all the processes: Apache web server, *wotaskd*, our deployed applications and *JavaMonitor*. However for *JavaMonitor* to be able to do its job, it must know about all the machines in the network running *wotaskd*. This is what we are going to configure next.

Start your browser and point it at http://localhost:56789.

56789 is the port number you have set in the startup script for *JavaMonitor*. Here is what you get:

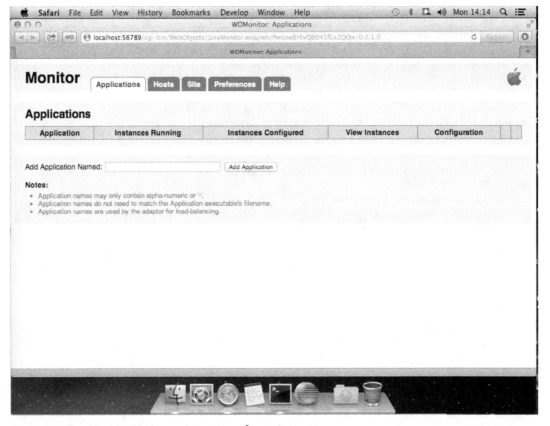

Picture 24-3   *JavaMonitor is running, no configuration yet*

There are some settings we are going to at least look at. No need to change anything for our particular setup.

Click on the *SITE* tab.

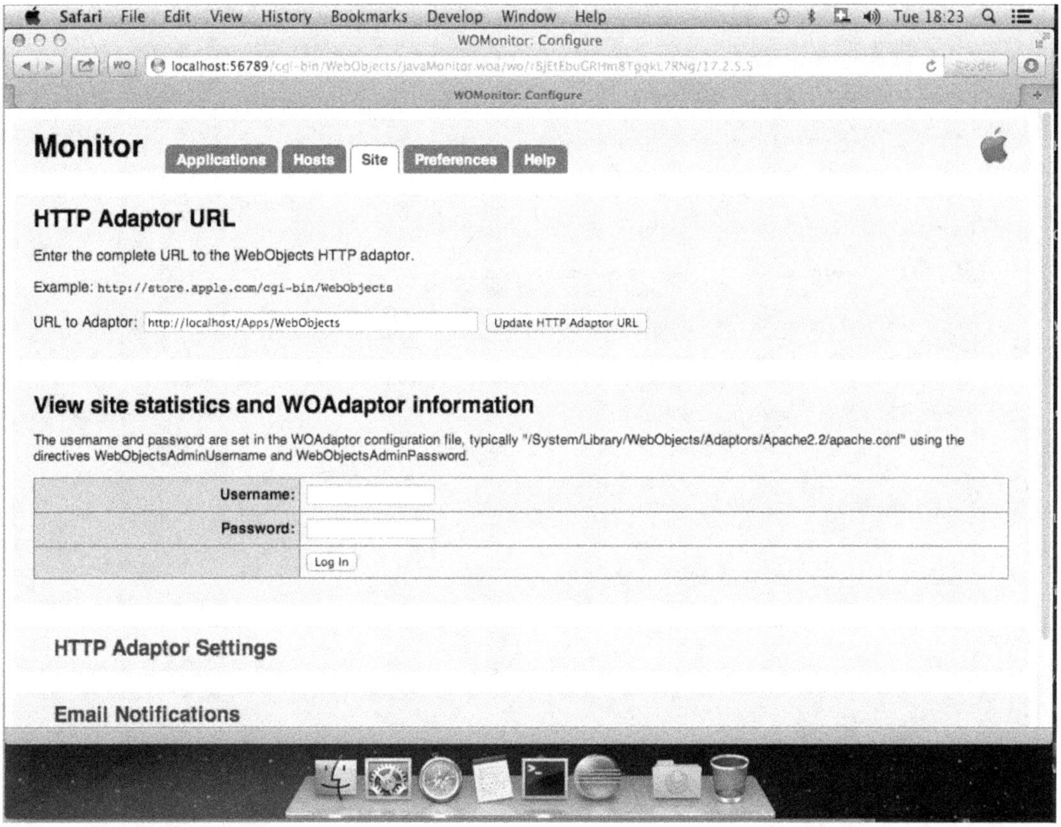

Picture 24-4   Site Settings in *JavaMonitor*

JavaMonitor needs to know where the WOAdapter is. It communicates with *WOAdaptor* through the web server. The default is noted on the page. There is the string *cgi-bin* included in the adaptor URL. Remember when we created the file *wo_apache.conf*? There are the following lines near the top of that file:

```
# You can change the 'cgi-bin' part of WebObjectsAlias to whatever you
# prefer (such as Apps), but the 'WebObjects' part is required.
WebObjectsAlias /Apps/WebObjects
```

Instead of */cgi-bin/WebObjects* it reads */Apps/WebObjects*. It seems that in newer incarnations of Mac OS X *cgi-bin* can cause problems accessing a deployed application. Therefore **Apps** is a better choice. So we have to inform *JavaMonitor* about the changed URL. Enter the following and then push *UPDATE HTTP ADAPTOR URL*.

Other settings in the same screen allow you to specify various timing parameters for the communication between *WOAdaptor* and Wonder applications. Leave all settings to their default, no need to set anything yet.

Let's now activate the *HOSTS* section. Click the corresponding tab at the top of the *JavaMonitor* window.

259

Setting up the Server

It is here where we let *JavaMonitor* know which computers it should control.

Enter "localhost" into the *Add Host* field, select the correct type of deployment system, and then press the *ADD HOST* button. In our case we use MacOSX as the host type.

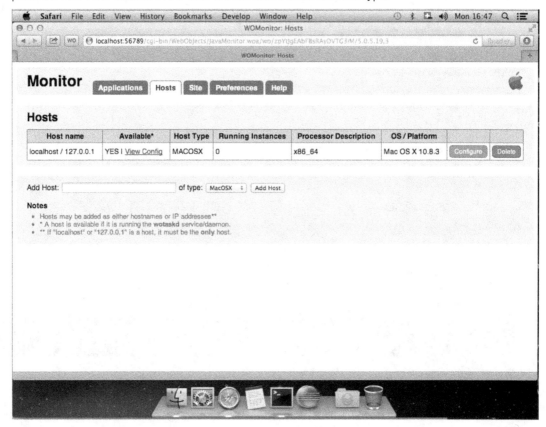

Picture 24-5   *Host localhost added to JavaMonitor*

JavaMonitor shows, that the host is available. This means that there is a *wotaskd* running on that host and *JavaMonitor* was able to communicate with it. We can also see some information about the host like its operating system and how many Wonder application instances are currently running. Clicking on the *VIEW CONFIG* link will bring up something like the following.

Picture 24-6   JavaMonitor showing host config data

With this our deployment system is fully configured and ready for our Wonder application.

25 Building Your Application for Deployment

Go back to Eclipse. There is our great application waiting to be liberated from the development system and deployed to the world.

Our application depends on various things. First of all it's the set of Wonder and WebObjects frameworks. Those are located inside a subdirectory of our development directory. Eclipse knows where to find them through the *wolips.properties* file. These frameworks are shared between all applications inside our development environment.

In the old WebObjects times one had to install the WebObjects frameworks system wide on the deployment machine. As they were in a known location, every application installed did find them. With WOLips it is possible to embed frameworks into the application itself. This has the benefit that nothing Wonder/WebObjects related has to be installed on the deployment system, making it independent of Wonder. In addition this makes it possible to build applications against different versions of the frameworks.

Where there is light, there is darkness – or so to speak! Each application bundles all the frameworks it needs, adding some 50Mbytes to the distribution. Each framework may so end up duplicated inside several applications.

Disk space is not at a premium any more, some 50Mbytes more or less does not count nowadays. So the benefits of having embedded frameworks outweigh the disadvantages. We will build our application with everything embedded.

Open the properties dialog for your project (context click on the project itself) and then select the WOLips Deployment section in the left side bar.

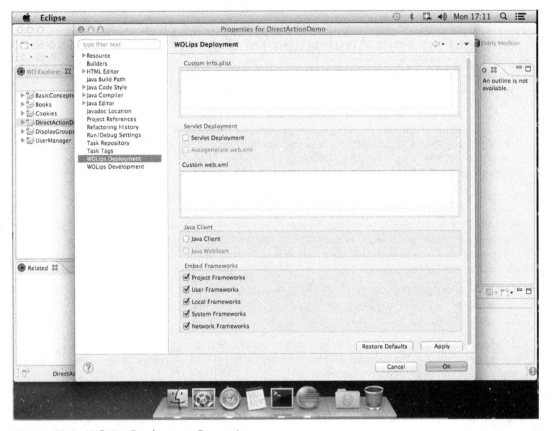

Picture 25-1   WOLips Deployment Properties

Make sure that all five checkboxes for embedding frameworks are checked. Accept your changes and leave the dialog. Now open the file *build.xml*. It is located on the root level of your project. This file contains the instructions to the Eclipse built-in *ant* tool.

From the outline on the right side select the BUILD [DEFAULT] action. Bring up the context menu and select RUN AS -> ANT BUILD.

Picture 25-2   Building the application for deployment with ant

After a minute or so the console will tell you that your build was successful (hopefully!). If you look closely you see a new directory in your project called *dist* (you may have to refresh the *WOExplorer* view for it to show up).

Building Your Application for Deployment

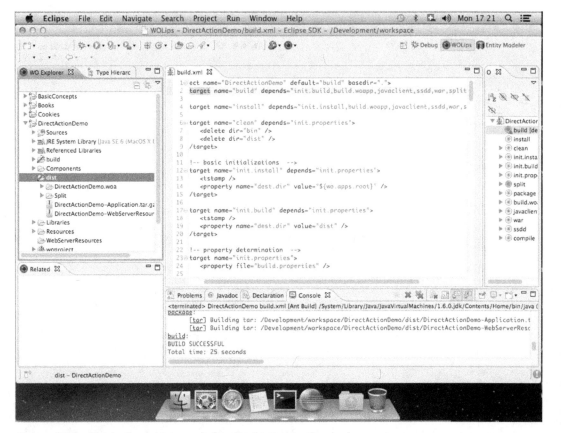

Picture 25-3   The built project, ready for distribution to the deployment server

The build process has created two directories and two compressed tar files. Switch to Finder (or Windows Explorer) and change to the *dist* directory. You can do this right from inside Eclipse. Use the context menu item *MAC GOODIES* or *WINDOWS GOODIES* respectively.

Picture 25-4   Opening the dist folder right in Finder

Here is the (expanded) view of the final built application.

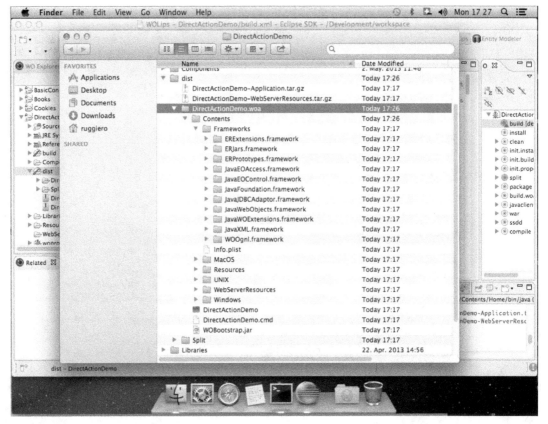

Picture 25-5   Built Application

The name of the project has become the name of a directory with extension *.woa*. Inside this directory you can see several folders that correspond to folders from the project setup in the development environment. These are all inside the *Contents* directory. The *Frameworks* subfolder contains all the frameworks we have included in the build path. While we have checked the EMBED FRAMEWORKS checkboxes in the project properties dialog, WOLips copied these frameworks into the final directory structure. That is one of the reasons the build process takes some time. There are several 10.000s of files to be copied.

Another interesting point to note is that the *Contents* folder contains sub folders *MacOS*, *UNIX*, and *Windows*. The built application can be deployed on any of these platforms; the corresponding folders contain all the necessary platform specific resources.

At the top level of the *DirectActionDemo.woa* are two startup scripts named after the project. The one without a file extension is a Unix shell script, and the one named *DirectActionDemo.cmd* is the corresponding Windows batch file. If you want to run your built application from the command line, simply call the corresponding script file. This is also the file that *wotaskd* will ultimately resort to for starting the deployed application.

Now let's have a look at the second directory created inside *dist*. It is called *Split* because it serves the split install. The build process has collected all the *WebServerResources* from the application and all embedded frameworks into this directory. It contains a sub folder called *DirectActionDemo.woa*. This is the exact same name as the main application directory.

In your Wonder application you have often seen bindings called *filename*. You find them typically on WOImage and other dynamic elements, where you need to bind a (static) resource. Any resource that you want to web server to vend goes into the *WebServerResources* folder in your project. Your Wonder application will at runtime generate a URL relative to the documents root. Here is a typical URL for such a filename binding:

```
<img src="/WebObjects/DirectActionDemo.woa/Contents/ ↵
                    WebServerResources/icon.gif" ... />
```

The structure inside the *Split* directory matches that URL.

For our convenience the build process packs the two directories into a compressed tar archive for easy transporting to the deployment machine.

That's it! We have successfully built our application for deployment.

26 Deploying Your Application

In this chapter we are going to deploy our built application.

26.1 Bring the Application over to the Server

First step is to bring the built application over to the server. The build process has created two compressed archives, which we now copy to their final location on the deployment server. According to our chosen directory layout the application should go into */Library/WebObjects/Applications* and the webserver resources go to */Library/WebObjects/WebServerResources*.

Copy the two archives to their destination folders. You may need admin privileges because we have set the whole directory tree to be owned by *_appserver*. Expand the archives either from the command line or by double clicking the files.

Note

When expanding on Mac OS X by double clicking the archives in the Finder, the result will go to your Downloads folder when you do not have the necessary privileges to directly write to the destination folder. Move the expanded folder manually over and accept the prompt from Finder to authenticate.

Deploying Your Application

Here is how things should look like.

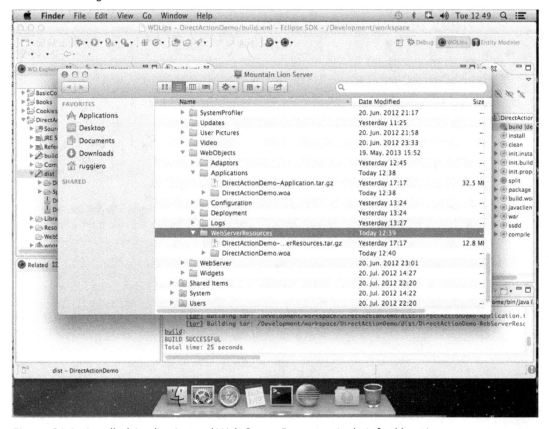

Picture 26-1 Installed Application and Web Server Resources in their final location

Now we have to set the owner correct. This is an important step, as *JavaMonitor* and *wotaskd* won't be able to properly start the application. Checking proper ownership of the files is the first thing to do when your applications do not want to start.

You can do this directly from the command line. Issue the following two commands:

```
$ sudo chown -R _appserver:_appserveradm ↵
         /Library/WebObjects/WebServerResources
$ sudo chown -R _appserver:_appserveradm ↵
         /Library/WebObjects/Applications
```

26.2 Making the Application known to *JavaMonitor* and *wotaskd*

Open your browser and enter the URL for your *JavaMonitor*. Click the APPLICATIONS tab. We are going to set up the just installed application in *JavaMonitor*.

Give your application a name. This does not have to be the name of the project. Note the rules for naming your application stated on the screen. We will use *Demo* as the name for our application. Click *ADD APPLICATION*.

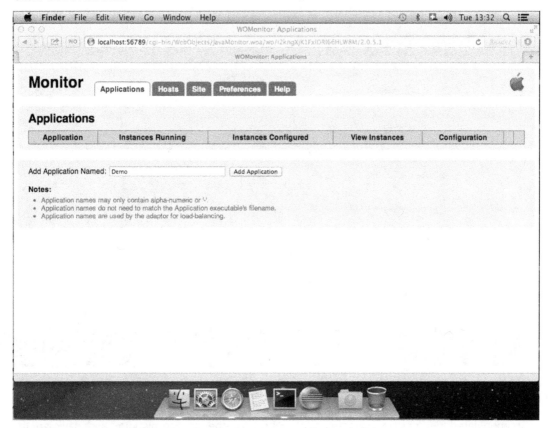

Picture 26-2   Add an Application to JavaMonitor

JavaMonitor changes to the configuration screen for your new application.

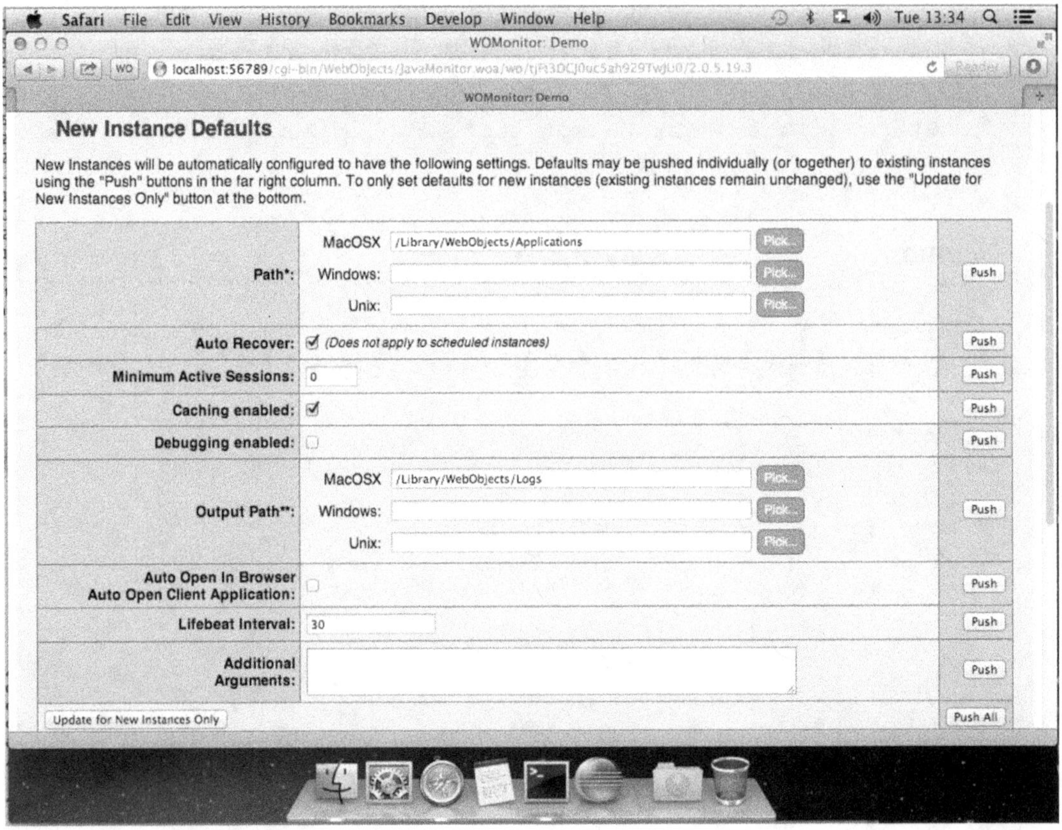

Picture 26-3 Application Settings

The first thing you need to do is point *JavaMonitor* to the executable of your application. The *PATH* is prepopulated but not yet complet. Click *PICK...* for the proper platform and navigate to the executable inside your *.woa* directory.

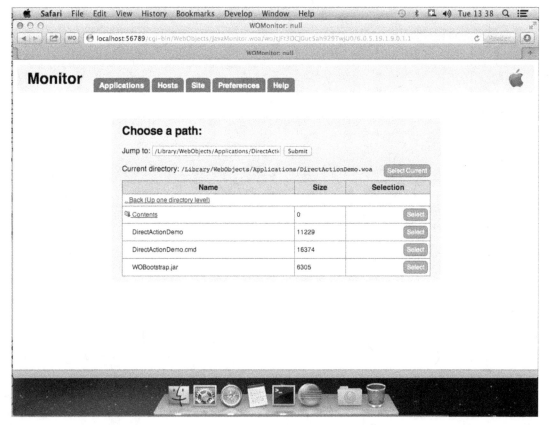

Picture 26-4   Select the Executable

Press *SELECT* on the file *DirectActionDemo* (the startup script we mentioned above) and you are all set.

There are many more possible settings but you do not currently have to change anything else. Push either the *PUSH* button right besides the Path setting or use the *PUSH ALL* button at the bottom.

We will come back later to this screen. For now our goal is to get the application up and running.

At the top of the screen click *DETAIL VIEW*. On the resulting screen add one instance of the *Demo* application.

Picture 26-5   One instance is ready for startup

As *AUTO RECOVER* is set by default, *JavaMonitor* will immediately try to start your application. If it does not, just click the green dot under *START-STOP*. If all goes well the *STATUS* indicator (the large old-fashioned power switch) should stay up and turn a bright green ON.

Your application should now be up and running.

Open a new browser window and enter this address: *http://localhost/Apps/WebObjects/Demo*. The *DirectActionDemo* application should show up.

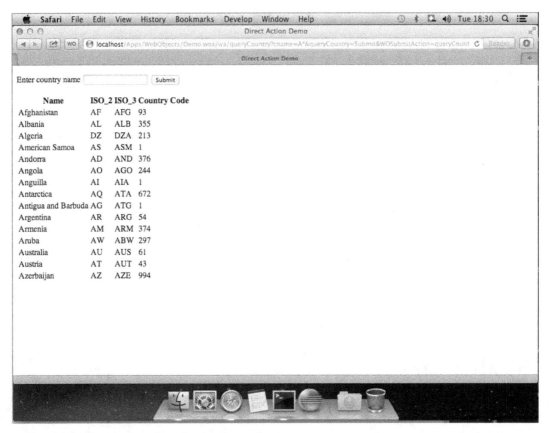

Picture 26-6   The deployed application is running

Lean back and enjoy! You have successfully deployed your first Wonder application!

26.3   Managing the application with *JavaMonitor*

In this chapter we will have a closer look at what *JavaMonitor* can do for you. *JavaMonitor* helps you manage the complete deployment environment.

26.3.1 Configuring the Site

Access *JavaMonitor* with your browser and click the SITE tab. It is here where we configure the *WOAdaptor*. We have already seen the first part, *HTTP ADAPTOR URL*, where we specify how to get to the *WOAdaptor* through the browser.

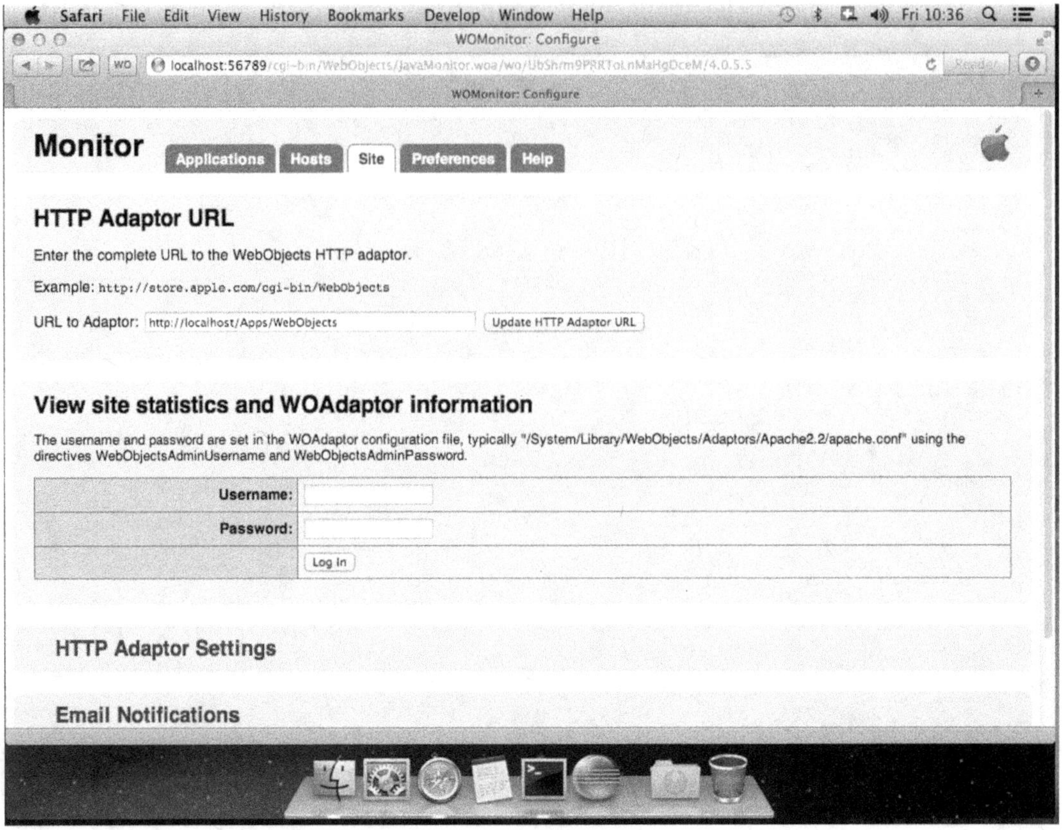

Picture 26-7   Setting Adaptor URL in *JavaMonitor*

The given URL must match the one we have set in the Apache configuration file. We have done this in chapter 24.5, Setting up the Server in *JavaMonitor*.

JavaMonitor collects various statistics for your applications. You need to specify a username and a password. Again these must correspond with the settings in the Apache config file. Edit the file at */Library/WebObjects/Adaptors/wo_apache.conf*. Find the following section and uncomment the two lines with *WebObjectsAdminUsername* and *–password*. Enter whatever you want for the username and give it a nice password. Of course you should pick better values than I have done here.

```
# To enable the WOAdaptorInfo page with restricted access,
# uncomment the next two lines and set the user and password
# To access the WOAdaptorInfo page with restricted access,
# use a URL like: http://webserver/cgi-bin/WebObjects/WOAdaptorInfo?user+password.
WebObjectsAdminUsername admin
WebObjectsAdminPassword demo
```

You need to restart Apache for these changes to take effect.

Now you can enter your chosen username and password and have a look at the statistics and adaptor configuration page.

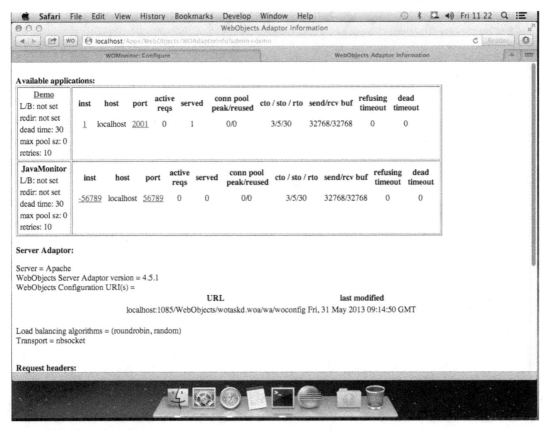

Picture 26-8   JavaMonitor statistics page

We have currently two applications running, our deployed *Demo* and *JavaMonitor* itself. We will not go into all the details that the page shows us.

Back in the *SITE* view of *JavaMonitor* click on *HTTP ADAPTOR SETTINGS*:

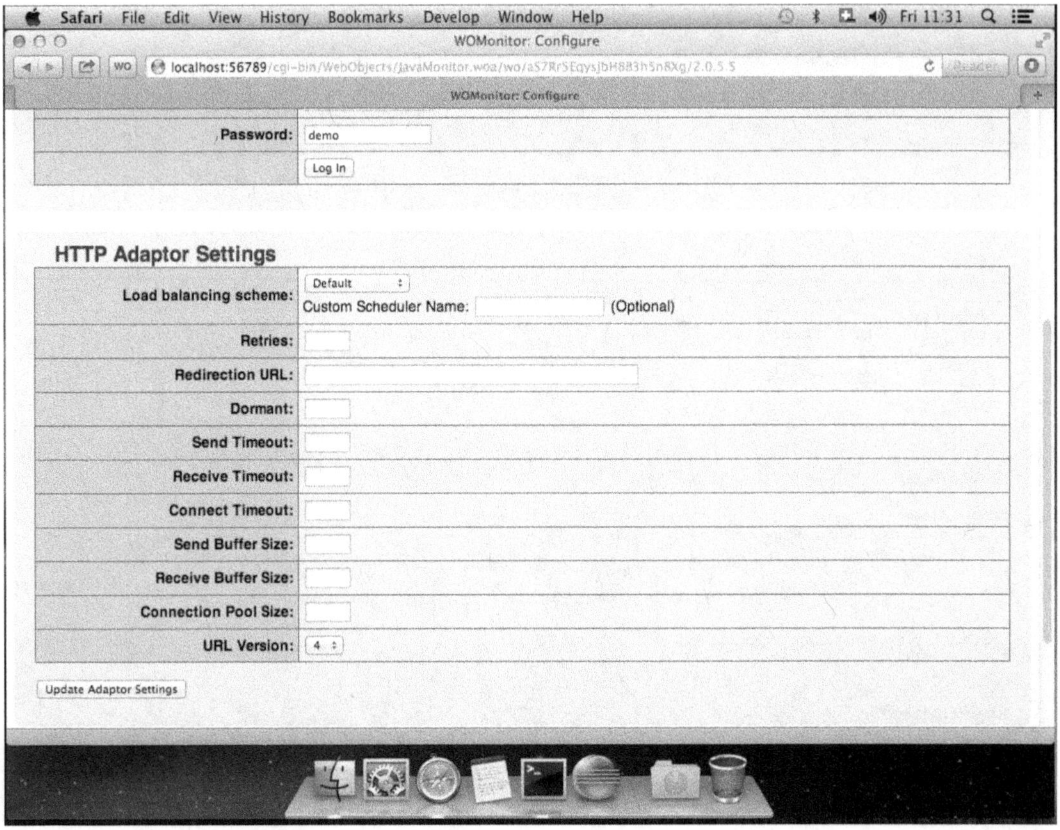

Picture 26-9   HTTP Adaptor Settings

In here you can fine-tune various parameters that affect the communication between the *WOAdaptor* and the deployed applications. Under normal circumstances you should not touch these settings.

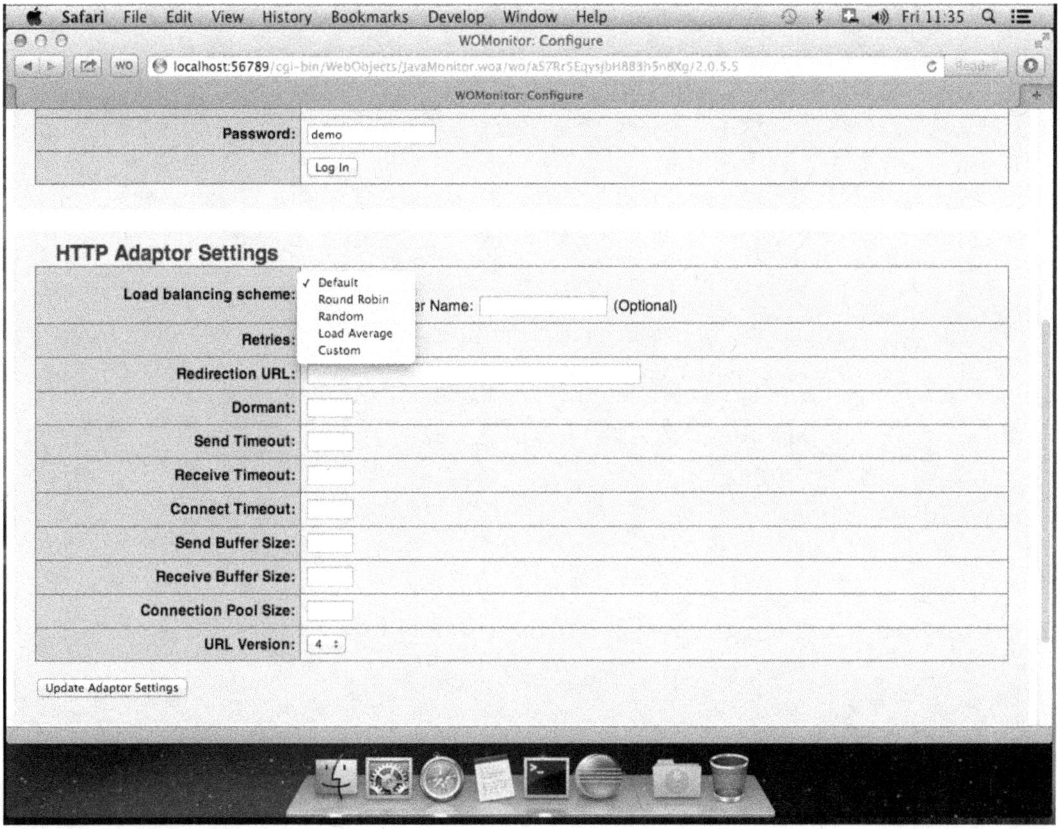

Picture 26-10 Load balancing schemes

LOAD BALANCING SCHEME

When you have more than one instance of an application the *WOAdaptor* tries to distribute the incoming requests.

RETRIES AND TIMEOUT VALUES

How often should the adaptor try to send a request to an application instance before giving up? And how long should it wait until deciding that an instance is not reachable or that there will be no answer coming back?

BUFFER SIZES

In case your applications receives many large requests or sends large answers (think of file up- and downloads) it might make sense to play with buffer sizes.

As I said above, under normal circumstances you should leave the adaptor settings alone.

Further down on the *SITE* page is the *EMAIL NOTIFICATIONS* section:

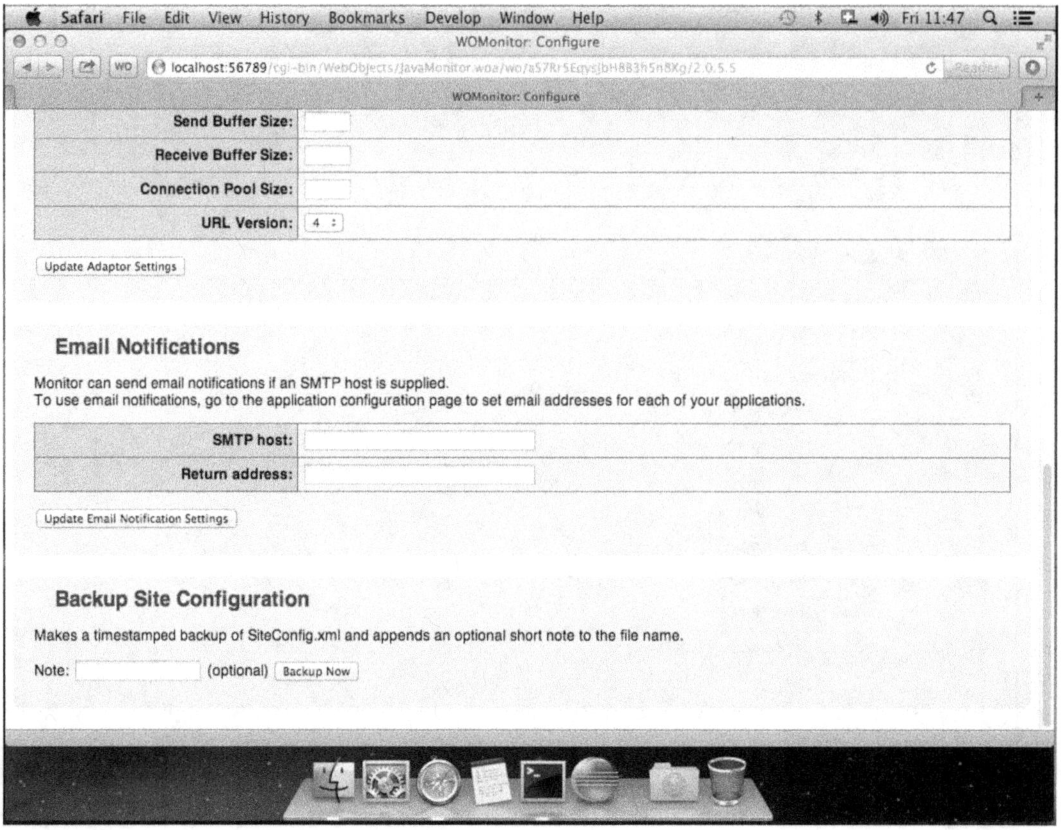

Picture 26-11 Email Notifications

As the text in *JavaMonitor* reads you can specify the *SMTP HOST* and a *RETURN ADDRESS*. *JavaMonitor* can send various notification emails. Here you tell it how to do that.

26.3.2 Application Settings

From the main navigation tabs at the top of *JavaMonitor* select *APPLICATIONS*, then click the *CONFIGURE* button. Here you can configure several properties for an application. This screen is used for configuring settings that apply to all instances. To the right of each setting is a *PUSH* button. With this button you only push that particular setting. At the bottom of the page are buttons that allow you to save the settings for new not-yet created instances and fully update all already configured instances.

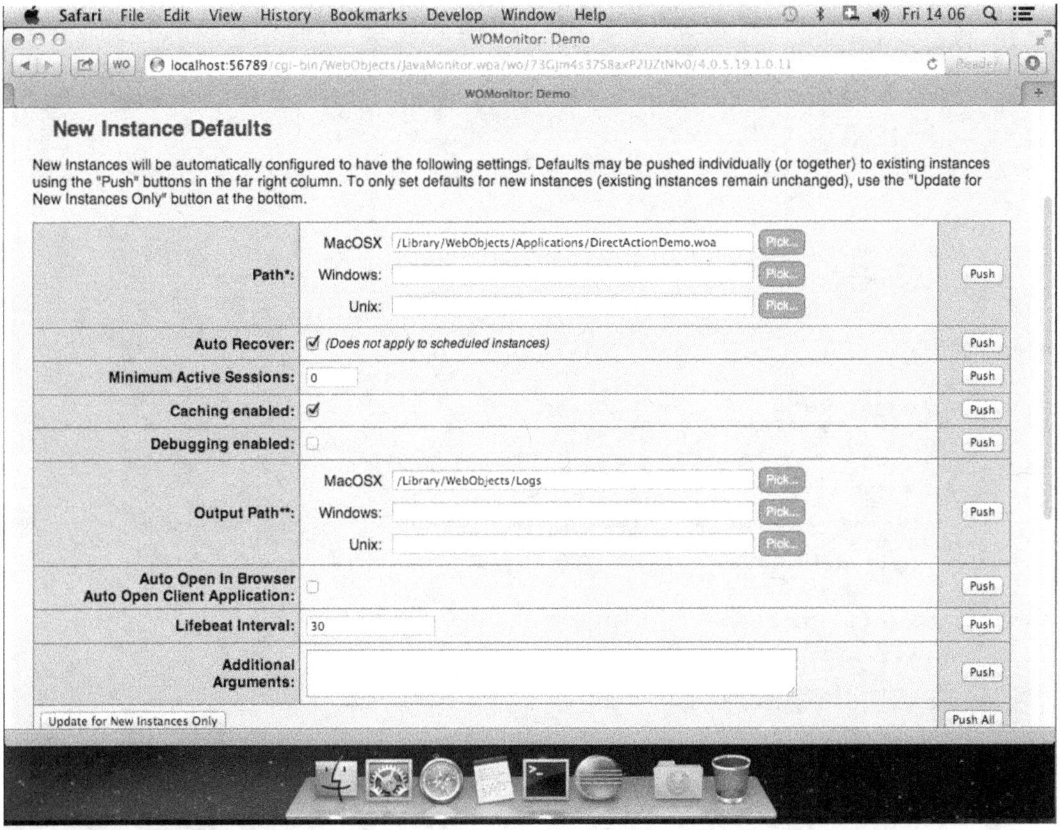

Picture 26-12 New Instance Defaults

We have already used the *PATH* section when we created our first deployment. It tells *JavaMonitor* where the executable file for the application is.

You can find a detailed description of all settings directly in *JavaMonitor*. Click the *HELP* tab and look under the heading *WHAT INSTANCE DEFAULTS AND SETTINGS ARE AVAILABLE THROUGH MONITOR?*

During development you have found that changing a WOComponent's *.html* or *.wod* part did immediately take effect without having to restart the application. A Wonder application under development does not cache the component but reads it from disk every time it needs it. This is good for the developer but a deployed application should not do this for performance reasons. By default the *CACHING ENABLED* check box is checked.

During development you usually want much more debugging output than when you deploy. In case you need to activate debug output for a deployed application you can check the *DEBUGGING ENABLED* box.

Your application calls back into *wotaskd* in regular intervals to let it know that it is still alive. How often this happens is given in *LIFEBEAT INTERVAL*. After that many seconds without a call from the application *wotaskd* will consider it dead (aka crashed or hanging) and try to restart it.

In the *ADDITIONAL ARGUMENTS* box you can enter any other command line arguments you want to pass to your application. A typical scenario could be memory management settings for the Java virtual machine.

The next section on that *JavaMonitor* page lets you specify global settings for the deployed application.

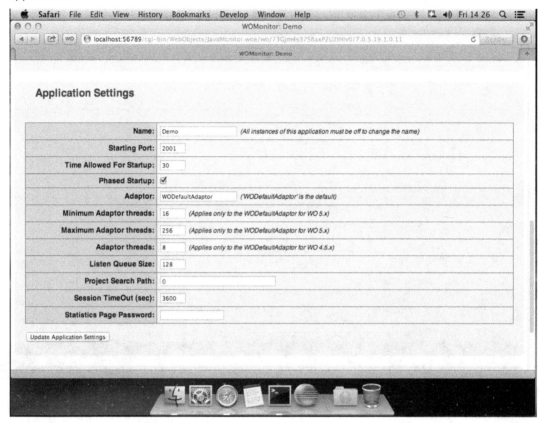

Picture 26-13 Application Settings

Each instance of an application is assigned a dedicated network port. The default for the first instance is port 2001. *JavaMonitor* will assign subsequent port numbers to additional instances.

TIME ALLOWED FOR STARTUP tells *wotaskd* how long to wait until to try again. Depending on what an application does during startup you might need to adapt this time value. The default is 30 seconds.

Setting *PHASED STARTUP* is probably a good thing. You do not want all applications started at the same time when your server reboots.

One important setting in this section is *SESSION TIMEOUT*. The default is 3600 seconds, one hour. This value might be too high for a deployed application. Remember: a session terminates automatically after that many seconds of inactivity. When a session terminates lots of resources will be freed. Thus for performance reasons you do not want to have sessions hanging around that are not active anymore. A reasonable value might me 10 minutes (600 seconds).

Again the *JavaMonitor HELP* section explains all the values in detail.

The last section of interest is the *SCHEDULING* section.

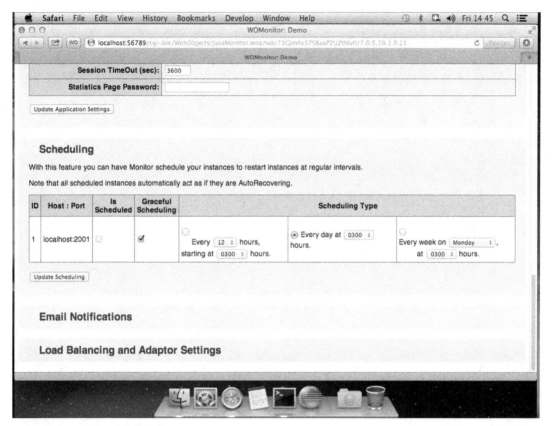

Picture 26-14 Scheduling Settings

You may want to have more than one instance of an application set up and running. This has several advantages. Should one instance crash or get stuck, there is still another instance available. Another advantage is that the operating system has more options for load balancing. Each instance in itself is multiprocessing, means that one instance can satisfy multiple requests at the same time. Having the possibility of multiprocessing and multitasking at the same time allows the operating system to better optimize resource usage. Also sometimes an application develops bad habits over time like not releasing unused memory or other resources. *wotaskd* can restart application instances at regular intervals. It is here where you specify when and how often instances should be restarted.

Again consult the *JavaMonitor HELP* section for more details.

Appendix

Table of Pictures and Graphics

Index

Index

www.ingramcontent.com/pod-product-compliance
Lightning Source LLC
LaVergne TN
LVHW062308060326
832902LV00013B/2113